The optimal personality

The optimal personality
An empirical and theoretical analysis

Richard W. Coan

Department of Psychology, University of Arizona, Tucson, Arizona

Routledge & Kegan Paul

London

First published in 1974
by Routledge & Kegan Paul Ltd
Broadway House, 68–74 Carter Lane,
London EC4V 5EL
Set in Monotype Imprint
and printed in Great Britain by
Cox & Wyman Ltd, London, Fakenham and Reading
ISBN 0 7100 7917 6

Contents

Preface

Human personality in its myriad forms has been a topic for discussion for thousands of years. Probably for as long as individual variation has been recognized, people have formed judgments about which qualities are good and which are not. Though terminology has changed, the concern with virtue and vice in human personality has continued unabated into the era of systematic personality theory construction.

Most psychologists who construct personality theories have some accompanying notions about what forms of adjustment are most desirable and about the courses of development that lead to these. These notions have been cast in a host of terms, such as maturity, mental health, integration, self-actualization, etc. In recent years, the realm of the optimal personality has received an increasing amount of focal attention among psychologists. The work of Abraham Maslow in particular has served to stimulate considerable thinking and research.

At present, the interest in the optimal personality is even more clearly evidenced in the practical realm than in the production of theories and research. Many psychologists have become active in what has been called the human potential movement. Their aim is to develop techniques for enhancing the psychological growth of normal adults. Advances in our understanding and research have not begun to keep pace with the proliferation and application of such techniques. I am broadly sympathetic to the aims of the human potential movement, but I believe it is important to gain a clearer idea of the variables affected by growth-enhancing procedures and to develop measuring instruments and research techniques with which we can assess the effects of these procedures. Although the work reported in this book was not concerned directly with growth-enhancing procedures, I hope it will provide a few of the insights and tools that are needed.

This book reports an attempt to analyze the domain of personality variables represented by concepts of the optimal or ideal personality. Chapter 2 provides a review of the extant concepts that underlie this work. The chapters that follow report attempts to construct instruments to measure various sets of concepts, and they summarize the major findings obtained with these instruments. Altogether a six-hour battery of tests—most of them novel instruments—was devised. Some components of the battery were individually factored to determine what meaningful components could be isolated and quantified within them. The battery as a whole was subjected to a factor analysis, which is reported in Chapter 9. The final two chapters provide a synthesis and interpretation of the findings reported throughout the book. Chapter 10 deals specifically with the many sex differences found and with the issue of masculine and feminine modes of functioning. Chapter 11 is concerned with the implications of the work for the entire issue of the ideal personality or optimal mode of functioning.

The basic purpose of this book, then, is to report a major attempt to apply techniques of multivariate analysis to the domain of the optimal personality and to examine the theoretical implications of the findings obtained. The basic issues are of fundamental significance for the personality and clinical fields of psychology. I hope that psychologists in these areas will read this book and see uses in their own work for both the findings and the instruments reported here.

The book was written more for the consumption of the specialist than for the general reader. It was not designed to fit the textbook needs of any standard psychology course, but it could be used as supplementary reading in various courses in the clinical, personality, and measurement areas. I have used it myself as a text in a course in personality assessment.

I am grateful to the many people who contributed to the research reported in this book. The work could obviously not have been done without the cooperation of the several hundred students who agreed to submit to my battery or to some part of it. Of the people who contributed labor to various stages of the research, I wish to extend particular thanks to Dr Jay Mann, Dr Zipporah Dobyns, Dr Kathleen Durning, and Miss Victoria Mills.

Richard W. Coan

Chapter 1

Approaches to psychological theory

The field of personality theory differs from other fields of psychology primarily in its perspective. It deals to some extent with nearly all the processes and phenomena that concern other branches of this science, but it treats them in the context of the total functioning person. Inevitably a field of such broad content mirrors most of the basic controversies that characterize the science as a whole. The history of psychology itself is a record of highly varied effects wrought by men of differing temperament in response to diverse needs and influences. As the author has previously shown (Coan, 1968), most of the variation in theory can be described in terms of the combined operation of six underlying dimensions. The dimension of greatest consequence is *subjectivism* v. *objectivism*, for this lies at the core of our basic decisions about subject matter. The subjectivist is concerned with experience and with the differences between processes that are conscious and those that are unconscious. He tends to employ methods, notably introspection, designed to fit his chosen content, and he is inclined to use concepts—of self, will, purpose, etc.—that reflect the perspective of the self-reflective observer. The objectivist prefers to avoid strictly psychological subject matter altogether and study only behavior or to deal with the subjective realm indirectly. In the latter case, he may treat it as a region of hypothetical links between observed stimuli and responses or attempt some sort of translation of it into S-R terms. Since he approaches his subject matter as an external scientific observer of physical events, his theorizing is likely to reflect a deterministic and mechanistic outlook.

A second dimension, *holism* v. *elementarism*, is concerned with the level of organization on which the theorist focuses his attention. Both in observing and in conceptualizing, the holist works at a high level. He tends to deal with the total person or with complex processes. The elementarist prefers the greater certainty afforded by a concentration on relatively specific variables.

The third dimension is *qualitative* v. *quantitative orientation* and is more clearly marked at the latter pole. The quantitative theorist strives for quantitative formulations of principles, quantitative description and conceptualization of individuals, or normative generalizations. He tends to prefer research methods that permit more or less precise measurement. The qualitative theorist displays less need to employ numbers for any purpose and is, therefore, freer to delve into areas of content that do not lend themselves readily to quantification.

Next we may distinguish a *personal* from a *transpersonal orientation*. (The term *transpersonal* seems an appropriate construction. Unfortunately since the author first began using this word, it has come into increasingly wide usage with a different meaning. The term *apersonal* might obviate confusion.) In the former case, there is a concern for the characteristics of individual people. In the latter case, there is an interest in understanding the process—the course of learning, the perceptual phenomenon, the sensory event, etc.—apart from the particular individuals in whom it is found. A dimension of *dynamic* v. *static orientation* contrasts a concern with ongoing processes and change with a concentration on more invariant features. Dynamic theorists are more likely to manifest an interest in problems of motivation, learning, and emotion. The aspect of experience studied by the structuralists, on the other hand, reflects a more static orientation.

A final dimension of *endogenism* v. *exogenism* relates mainly to the sources of behavior and experience to which the theorist attends. The endogenist outlook is directed toward characteristics that are biologically inherent either in human organisms in general or in the individual constitution. The exogenist orientation is toward the external influence and its effects on behavior and experience. As conceived here, this is basically a dimension pertaining to the theorist's interests, but obviously certain biases— particularly those regarding the 'true' source and the inherent modifiability of various traits—covary with these interests.

These six dimensions are largely independent of one another. Thus, it is possible for a theorist to stand at either extreme on a given dimension and, at the same time, be in any position with respect to the others. Since the dimensions are intercorrelated to some extent, however, some combinations are more likely than others. In the study in which the six dimensions were first identified as a group (Coan, 1968), it was found that they yielded two broad second-order factors. These were called *synthetic* v. *analytic orientation* and *functional* v. *structural orientation*.

The first second-order factor subsumes the first three dimensions discussed above. Thus, the synthetic orientation is subjectivistic, holistic, and qualitative. The analytic orientation is objectivistic, elementaristic, and quantitative. The synthetic theorist shows a tendency to deal with human experience as he finds it, hoping somehow to grasp it in its entirety. The analytic theorist seeks instead to find understanding through a departure from this uninterrupted totality. He tends to deny the importance of experience as such, to deal with actions without reference to conscious processes, to narrow his attention to small components, and to superimpose the number system on his observations.

The factor of *functional* v. *structural orientation* relates mainly to the fourth and fifth dimensions and, to some extent, the sixth. What we are calling the functional theorist is both personal and dynamic and tends to be endogenist. The structural theorist is apersonal and static and is more likely to be exogenist. The structural outlook is like the analytic outlook in involving a greater departure from what is initially observed. The functional theorist is more directly interested in the people he sees and in the events manifested in them. The structural theorist seeks insight through some sort of abstraction from these.

As we might expect, there is some positive relationship between these second-order factors, so that the synthetic and functional orientations tend to go together, while the analytic and structural orientations accompany each other. We may call the former combination *fluid* and the latter combination *restrictive*. Thus, it is possible to recognize a very broad general dimension running through the whole realm of psychological theory. At one extreme of it we find theorists who are subjectivistic, holistic, qualitative, personal, dynamic, and endogenist. At the other extreme are the restrictive theorists, who are objectivistic, elementaristic, quantitative, transpersonal, static, and exogenist. Apparently the underlying disposition of the former is to experience people and life in their wholeness. Theorists of the latter type, however, seek the order that can only be obtained through deliberate control, analysis, or selective attention to more specific components or aspects of the phenomena they study. The characteristic relationships of the fluid and restrictive orientations to the more specific ones we have discussed are shown in Figure 1 in the form of a bipolar hierarchy.

The fluid and restrictive orientations correspond fairly closely to a number of polarities that have been recognized before and described in other terms. This is one of the dimensions that tends to

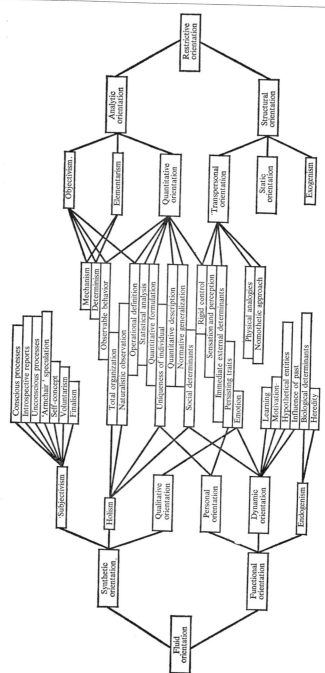

Figure 1. A bipolar hierarchy of theoretical variables. (The variables shown in the middle are relatively specific, while those on the left and right sides represent more general and mutually opposing trends.)

distinguish the humanist (*Geisteswissenschaftler*) from the natural scientist (*Naturwissenschaftler*). The tenderminded philosopher depicted by James (1907) would tend to be fluid, while the tough-minded philosopher wold tend to be restrictive. In psychological theory, it is possible to distinguish two main streams of influence which Allport (1955) characterizes as Leibnizean and Lockean, that also align clearly with the fluid-restrictive dimension.

Such a broad sweeping dichotomization of traditions in any field of human thought is bound to do much violence to the specific facts of history. At the same time, of course, it fits a fair number of facts and has the obvious virtue of simplicity. For a very simple reason, however, a scheme like the Leibnizean–Lockean dichotomy *appears* to fit theoretical trends in psychology somewhat better than it actually does: extreme positions are usually more conspicuous than subtle intermediate combinations. On the contemporary scene, we have no difficulty recognizing the radical behaviorist or the radical humanistic psychologist, for we immediately sense the coherence of their respective positions. Yet, relatively few psychologists would espouse either position in its entirety, and each has shortcomings that are easy to discern.

The radical behaviorist is the clearest modern specimen of the restrictive genus—the best contemporary representative of the Lockean tradition. Whatever his specific position, the behaviorist stresses observable behavior and, in one way or another, denies conscious experience—either as a proper object of scientific study, as a focus of research, as something to be represented directly in scientific language, or even as something that 'really exists'. With its emphasis on objectivity, the behaviorist movement has fostered refinements in research methodology, encouraged greater clarity and precision in theoretical work, and fostered a tremendous amount of research in the area of learning.

With all these benefits, however, behaviorism has led to the neglect of many important traditional problems of human experience. To the behaviorist, these problems have tended to appear either meaningless or unresearchable. With the restrictions that behaviorists have sometimes imposed on language and observational methods, of course, they inevitably cannot do anything significant with some of these problems. Surely, we can learn little about the aesthetic experience by recording the time a man spends looking at a particular painting. We learn nothing about the religious experience by studying genuflexion and church attendance, and we reduce romantic love to an absurdity by trying to translate it into such terms as genital reflex and positive reinforcement.

The humanistic movement in psychology is somewhat more diversified than the behavioristic movement, but in so far as it embraces a number of reactions against behaviorism, it too contains its share of excesses. To study experience without reference to behavior would be as empty an enterprise as the opposite course, but some humanistic psychologists seem to move in this direction. In others, we find an anti-theoretical gnostic bias stemming from an overemphasis on the importance of the understanding achieved from raw, unanalyzed personal experience. Surely we lose something as we proceed from the raw experience to intellectual analysis and theoretical construction, but we gain the insights provided by another kind of perspective. Science can stagnate as much through the avoidance of abstraction as by an overindulgence in it.

An excess in the humanistic camp that may be of more serious consequence because of its frequency is an over-reaction to systematic research procedures, particularly to those entailing a use of mathematics. Some humanistic psychologists seem to spurn any use of statistics. The writer once heard a convention speaker report with pride that he was daring to do 'non-quantitative' research. Surely a scientific investigator should be free to study important questions without being bound to some particular use of numbers, but the virtue of a deliberate abstention from quantification is not at all clear. Merely to note the presence or absence of a certain experiential effect is to engage in a rudimentary bit of quantification. We may gain nothing further by proceeding from our observation to a statistical operation, but we surely have nothing to lose in the process. The statistical procedure does not erase our data. It does not automatically generate profound revelations, but it may point to an order we would otherwise have overlooked.

Perhaps the essence of the present argument is that one achieves the sacrosanctity of the pure type at considerable cost. The behaviorist who is overly intent on being a 'true' scientist ends up confining his attention to a sterile subject matter. The overreactive humanist often fails to deal with important experiential problems in a way that permits scientific progress. Either kind of extreme tends to some extent to draw people with deficiencies, in the one case people with a limited talent for intellectual analysis, in the other case people who lack psychological sensitivity.

In the view of the writer the behaviorist movement—while it has assumed many forms and undergone numerous modifications —continues to offer the greater threat to progress in psychology, because it has had an increasing influence on the composition of that population known as psychologists. In an effort to be 'objective' scientists, we have urged students to take courses in mathematics and the natural sciences while discouraging them from minoring in the humanities. In this manner, we have tended to draw into our ranks many keen observers of the physical world, while shunting from our graduate student population young people who are more aware of the nuances of their own feelings and attitudes. In addition, our training is often better designed to enhance the former talent than the latter one. Yet psychology can hardly thrive without an ample supply of psychologically sensitive observers.

Now that the author has successively alienated several sets of readers, however, we can consider the common argument that unites his diverse insults. Scientific progress requires a certain flexibility. Psychology profits from an infusion of ideas from various external sources. We benefit from the influences of the physical and biological sciences on the one hand and art and literature on the other. We benefit even more from the interaction of such influences, for each provides certain correctives for the other. Psychology gains much more as well from the joint presence of the restrictive researcher and the speculative gnostic than it would if either of these men succeeded in casting the whole science in his own mold.

The principal labor of forging a science, of course, is performed by those who are not stuck on the narrow track of purity and methodological virtue, who instead address themselves persistently to the basic questions psychology needs to answer, and who do not fear the insights that may come from any quarter. They recognize that common combinations need not be inevitable combinations. A subjectivist does not have to be holistic and non-quantitative. An objectivist need not be elementaristic and quantitative. Psychological issues that demand an apersonal perspective do not necessarily require an accompanying analytic orientation.

With respect to specific pairings, this point has doubtless been made many times before. In advocating a 'molar' behaviorism, Tolman was voicing a plea for an objectivist holism. Objectivism itself serves a purpose as long as we stand to learn anything by concentrating on the relationship between overt behavior and observable environmental influences. If all objectivists focus too narrowly on specific S-R connections, however, they must fail to do justice to the complex organization of the total behavioral system, and the need for a bit of holistic seasoning will persist.

A trend toward quantitative holism can be seen in the multivariate research movement. Multivariate researchers display a great variety of positions on theoretical issues, but they share a common interest in the information that cannot be obtained through a segmental examination of one-to-one relationships. They may study the total personality, psychopathology, thought processes, the physiology of emotion, or learning, but in any area of investigation they tend to be concerned with complex issues and to stress the importance of an understanding of overall organization. The multivariate researcher is likely to start out with the same questions as the strictly speculative holist, but he employs a more systematic procedure and arrives at an answer that rests on a larger fund of information.

Most of the present book is based on multivariate research employing factor analysis as a statistical tool. In most respects, however, the viewpoint expressed in this work is that of a fluid, rather than a restrictive, psychologist. In the author's opinion, the most important problems of psychology are problems of human experience. The most fruitful approaches to an analysis and conceptualization of experience, however, are likely to entail treating it in the context of a total network that includes behavior, biological processes, and past and present environmental stimulation. The author makes no pretense of doing full justice to this total package in the work reported herein, but the present research does constitute an effort to cope with some of the intricacies of an exceedingly complex issue.

Chapter 2

Concepts of the optimal personality

Personality theorists are not uniformly fluid in their basic orientation, but their field of study at least requires an holistic outlook. This is particularly true when we are concerned with such broad issues as the ideal course of personality development and the ideal structure of the adult personality. While it is possible for a personality researcher to devote his attention to fairly segmental problems, these issues demand a consideration of the total organization of the individual person.

As with many broad issues in personality theory, the matter of ideal structure and development has been the object of considerable speculation and little systematic research. The profusion of relevant thought is reflected in the multitude of terms we employ to represent the optimal personality. The terms used most frequently over the years are *adjustment, normality*, and *maturity*. Yet each of these would probably be rejected by most theorists as an ideal label for the ideal condition. The term *mental health*, or *positive mental health*, has come into vogue fairly recently, but its demise is foreseeable. However one chooses explicitly to define it, this term inevitably connotes an absence of symptoms and is linked to a medical model that personality theory is destined to outgrow.

Personality integration is a less tainted term, but it has the possible drawback of implying—though vaguely—a particular mode of development and organization. Such terms as *self-actualization* and *self-realization*, which have come into wider use recently, are also tied to a particular outlook—in this case, one that stresses the unfolding of constitutionally based potentials. There are other terms that more clearly bear the stamp of individual theorists and thus remain somewhat bound to specific theoretical systems—e.g. Fromm's *productive character*, Rank's *creative artist*, Jung's *individuation*, and Freud's *ego strength* and *genital character*.

Given such an assortment of terms, we may wonder whether the many theorists who speak of an optimal personality are all talking about the same thing. In a sense, they are not, for the number of specific definitions exceeds the number of terms. The words subjected to frequent use—adjustment, normality, maturity, self-actualization, integration, mental health—have all acquired a variety of meanings. Nevertheless, there is a prevalent impression that these diverse meanings are merely different protuberances of the same underlying substance. Thus, when we study a group of people who are functioning well by almost any broad criterion, we are not surprised to discover that, as a group, they manifest many of the qualities we have previously designated by a variety of the terms listed above. In recent years, psychologists have shown a strong interest in creativity, and they have found that in many ways creative people tend to be 'good' people.

There is a common tendency then, to think of desirable personal characteristics, however labeled, as forming a single dimension. It simplifies our thinking considerably to believe that all good things go together, and it is understandable that we might wish to regard personality in this way. Some of our practical concerns, further-more, have led us to study extreme groups that tend to bolster this viewpoint. Chronic patients in psychiatric hospitals tend to be lacking in many ways, and people who make notable contributions to society tend to function well in many ways. It is not at all certain, however, that all good things go together in the general population. The fact of the matter is that we really do not know how many different things we are talking about when we speak of mental health, maturity, and personality integration, because few of us have made any effort to conduct a systematic analysis of the total realm represented by such terms.

To understand more clearly what is involved here, we must first get a clearer picture of what specific characteristics have been incorporated into concepts of the optimal personality. This is not the place for an exhaustive review of all such concepts, for such a review could fill a rather large volume. The greater part of a small book by Jahoda (1958) is devoted to a review of concepts. Although that book is now over a decade old, it remains a fair overview of the territory, and the author has benefited from ref-erence to Jahoda's work in his own efforts to identify the salient elements in current speculation about the optimal personality.

Popular concepts

One need make only a casual survey of extant definitions of optimal personality to discover that they constitute a heterogeneous array of variably overlapping concepts. There are many alternative ways in which we might classify them. As a matter of convenience, we may turn our attention first to the most common types of concepts, those that enjoy a certain popular status both inside and outside scientific circles. Most conspicuous is the adjustment concept. In terms of such a concept, the optimal person is one who achieves a smooth existence. He gets along well in his work, in social interactions, and in private experience, and in all situations he experiences a state of well-being. Negative emotional states— anxiety, anger, depression, etc.—occur very infrequently, and the individual both appears to be and regards himself as being happy or contented. Probably few social scientists would regard such a state as ideal, for there are too many things happening in this twentieth-century world that really ought to engender a bit of distress. Fundamental contradictions seem to be built into the very fabric of our society. Perennial tranquility requires limited awareness. One might achieve it by living within a small sphere of activities and experiences and having little to do with books and the news media. The only other route to perpetual adjustment is a kind of chameleon conformity. One bends with the pressures that prevail at the moment and avoids experiencing any need for overall consistency by limiting reflection. Thus, one can speak of Christian principles and even feel them and act upon them during certain periods but put them aside when attention is turned to business and political matters. It is easy to see the virtue of the perpetual adjuster if one values comfort, but we would probably have a greater respect for an individual who occasionally encountered conditions that he found intolerable and tried to change.

The common notion of normality in a statistical sense is a related concept. According to this concept, the desired state is maximal similarity to the mass of humanity. This requires conformity to group standards of behavior, and it is conducive to adjustment in a broad social context. Yet to the extent that the standards of most people in a given society are internally contradictory, one must accept contradictory standards to be normal. Behavioral standards are culturally relative also, so that what is normal in one group or society may be abnormal in another. The clearest ground for objection to normality as a basis for an optimal personality concept, however, is that we can find abundant reasons for wanting to modify certain common modes of behavior. The other side of this coin is the fact that the most valuable contributions to human progress are wrought by exceptional, or statistically abnormal, individuals. As a basis for conceptualizing the optimal personality, statistical normality seems to offer a very weak theoretical foundation.

The concept of mental health, construed in terms of an absence of psychopathological symptoms, poses similar problems. In fact, it poses the same problems as the normality concept to the extent that the definitions of health and pathology are culturally relative. By virtue of the same behavior, one may be viewed as a prophet in one society and a psychotic in another. A more subtle shortcoming of the mental health concept is the underlying assumption that what we are dealing with is strictly analogous to the phenomena of medical health and sickness. However much we may underline the idea that mental 'health' is a positive thing, the term most clearly connotes a well-regulated organism that is free of various well-known disorders that would interfere with its functioning. Unfortunately, much of our theorizing about personality has its roots in a clinical setting, and it has become only too easy for us to think of almost any personal characteristic as a pathological symptom or as a 'defense' against pathology. The medical theoretical model (at least in the specific form of the disease model) seems a rather inadequate basis for conceptualizing the optimal personality, just as it is for conceptualizing personality in general.

Intra-individual consistency

Many of the attempts to find a theoretically sounder basis for an optimal personality concept involve some notion of intra-individual consistency. Most common perhaps is some idea of motivational consistency. The ideal individual is thus internally adjusted in the sense that he is free of internal conflict. If the personality is viewed in terms of levels of awareness, the emphasis may be upon a consistency of conscious and unconscious forces. Essentially the same idea may be stated in terms of consistency among forms of expression. The ideal person then is one who verbally acknowledges the same needs that are apparent in his dreams, his waking fantasies, and his overt acts. Alternatively, we may think of motivational consistency as manifested over time in the convergence of actions upon well-defined long-term goals. Such a concept implies a high level of organization in the individual's behavior, but not necessarily persistent recurrence of the same actions.

Some theoretical systems focus less on motives and more on

attitudes, beliefs, concepts, and modes of perception. Consistency in this case is likely to be seen in the form of a unifying outlook. Thus, Allport (1937) spoke of a unifying philosophy of life as a criterion of maturity. The self-regarding sentiment had earlier served in an integrative role in McDougall's system. The basic notion of cognitive consistency is receiving increasing attention at present and will probably underlie a great deal of thinking in the personality realm in the near future.

In more specific forms, cognitive consistency has often been noted as a feature of well functioning people. Sometimes the concern is with the value system and with the emergence of central values that lend greater coherence to one's life. The vocational counselor frequently detects a relationship between the clarity of the interest pattern and other aspects of the individual's organization. Since the introduction of the Q-sort, various forms of self-concept consistency have received much attention—in particular, the agreement of the phenomenal self with the ideal self. Logically, this kind of agreement would seem to be essentially a matter of self-esteem, but it has sometimes been viewed as representing a more basic kind of integration.

Adequacy of coping

Sometimes the ideal personality is conceptualized in terms of success in coping with life problems or in terms of the kinds of intellectual functions that make successful coping possible. This is true of Freudian theory to the extent that it stresses a well-developed ego. Freud conceptualizes the ego primarily in terms of the cognitive processes that underlie reality contact. Thus, every form of psychopathology is regarded as involving a disturbance—pervasive or circumscribed—in intellectual functioning.

Some theorists stress the realization of intellectual potentials in general, with particular concern perhaps with the productive utilization of these potentials. Others shift the specific emphasis from reality contact to efficient problem solving or some other manifestation of sound functioning. Some adjustment concepts emphasize the importance of being able to resolve life problems and thus cope successfully in general with situations that entail emotional conflict and stress. When attention is paid to a variety of different forms of intellectual functioning, the ideal condition is likely to be viewed in terms of evenness. Lopsided functioning—i.e. a sharp contrast between relatively high and low abilities—is usually seen as an indication that some capacity is not operating properly.

Creativity has received considerable attention in recent years both as an object of research and as an object of theory. Many optimal-personality concepts feature personal characteristics conducive to creative experience and work, and there is some overlap between characteristics found in highly creative people and characteristics attributed to people regarded as optimal in other respects. Creative *ability* as such is not often cited as an ingredient of the optimal personality, but it tends to serve as an implicit selection criterion in biographical approaches to research on the optimal personality. In Maslow's study of 'self-actualizers', for example, it is difficult to avoid the impression that overall intellectual capacity and creative ability in particular were part of the basis on which historical cases were chosen.

Actualization of potentials

The term *self-actualization* has come into use only in recent years. Yet the basic notion implied by this term is apparent in the earlier work of Jung, whose treatment of it remains more sophisticated than those of most of the theorists who have since used the term. The idea that development in general or ideal development in particular involves an actualization of inborn potentials is also evident in the writings of such philosophers of the past as Spinoza and Kierkegaard. In a broad sense, for that matter, it has roots that extend far into ancient times in both Western and Eastern thought.

In recent treatments of the optimal personality, one can find many views regarding the nature of the potentials that an individual can realize or actualize. The emphasis may be upon intellectual potentials. Thus, within the limits of his inborn capacities, the self-actualized person would display a wide range of manifest abilities. *Actualization* here may refer simply to the availability for use of any ability or it may denote the productive utilization of the ability.

In most self-actualization theories, intellectual functioning is accorded a secondary role or is treated only in an implicit way. The focus is on the other kinds of potentials, and these are of many kinds. In many theories, the potential is essentially motivational. A man is thought to be at a low level of development to the extent that he is preoccupied with his own personal comfort or physical needs. If a part of human nature consists of a potential for investing interests in things beyond one's own personal being, then the self-actualized person will be one who finds greater importance in science, art, religion, or in mankind as a whole. He tends to identify, or ally himself, with groups or causes that extend far beyond the boundaries of his own skin. Acting accordingly, he will freely do things designed to benefit mankind or the specific causes and principles with which he associates himself.

In other treatments, the emphasis is rather on the unfolding of all the possible modes of experience possessed by people. The self-actualized individual would be able to think, feel, and sense in a variety of ways and would thus enjoy a richer existence than others. Since no theorist wishes to equate self-actualization with a mere carefree indulgence in sensations, however, there is usually an accompanying stress on aspects of experience that are not available in early stages of development. Thus, the theorist may distinguish different forms of experience that must be successively unfolded, or he may underline the capacity for flexibly shifting from one mode to another as circumstances demand.

Awareness

Man differs most essentially from other animals in his awareness and his use of symbols. These two qualities are closely intertwined, since all of our experiences are affected by our use of symbols. By virtue of his symbols, man's thought processes and awareness are much less bound by the immediate stimulus context than those of any other creature. In mythology, human consciousness is subject to manifold representation, but it seems to be recognized universally as the prerequisite of human status. Man's origin or his elevation above other creatures is marked by the advent of light, the acquisition of fire (whereby he can introduce his own light into regions of darkness), or by eating of the fruit of the tree of knowledge.

Attaching great importance to the thin edge that accords them supremacy over the other beasts of this planet, people have always tended to accord special status to the man who displays awareness beyond the ordinary. The status is ambiguous, however, for the man venerated as a sage, seer, or prophet at one time and place may be feared as an agent of the devil at another. In any case, the equation of the optimal personality with a special awareness is a very old idea. Thus, the Buddha is literally 'he who awoke' and who thus cast off the dream with which the rest of us are still deluded. In any conception of the ideal condition of awareness, the stress may be on either a symbolic, analytical comprehension that can be verbalized, or a non-analytical, non-symbolically-mediated immediate awareness that is not subject to direct expression in words. Almost all Eastern traditions emphasize the latter, but the former is characteristic of many Western traditions.

In much of personality theory, awareness has been treated in a negative form. Thus, psychopathology is found to involve a loss or lack of awareness by virtue of repression, selective inattention, or perceptual defense. It follows that cure will entail an overcoming of the loss. In the humanistic tradition, however, we find to varying degrees a concern with the positive value of enhanced awareness. Increasingly we encounter discussion of various means for achieving this enhancement—meditation, permitting fantasies to unfold without deliberate efforts to direct them, attending to the contents of each of the senses, etc.

There are differing views as to the character of the awareness to be sought (the extent to which it is symbolically mediated and structured), and there are differing views regarding the specific contents of the important awarenesses. Thus, some theorists stress access to all perception and ideas that pertain to oneself. Others stress access to all the contents of immediate sensory experience. If maximal scope of awareness is desirable, all possible contents of experience ought to be available for conscious recognition and differentiation—both the symbolized idea and the unsymbolized impression, whether pertaining to the external environment or to a more private realm, etc.

In many theoretical systems that focus on symbolic understanding, or verbalized insight, there is a concern with the veridicality of ideas. Thus, Freudian theory stresses reality contact as a basic property of the ideal state. Where realistic thought is valued, particular importance is usually attached to realistic self-appraisal. In fact, the presence or absence of reality contact in general is often seen to depend on self-insight—misperception implies defensive projection which, in turn, presupposes inadequate self-awareness.

The quality of experience

Many of the qualities we have considered under other headings above presuppose an openness to various kinds of experience. Thus, a full realization of diverse intellectual potentials requires a willingness to experience different kinds of thought processes, so that one is able to approach problems both analytically and intuitively, both on a general level and on a particular level, etc. Similarly, breadth of awareness is possible only to the extent that one is willing to admit experiences of varying content. In specific forms, such as sensitization and tolerance of ambiguity, a certain openness has been recognized as working in opposition to mechanisms that reduce awareness. Lately, there has been a growing interest in openness to experience in general as a core quality of the optimal personality.

Sometimes the quality is identified more as a kind of honesty or genuineness, for it is recognized that one can experience many sensations and entertain a vast assortment of thoughts about oneself and the world while maintaining a good deal of self-deception. There are many levels on which we can experience the fact that we are vain, selfish, and stupid. The individual who is really most open does not play the game of using a verbalized insight to ward off full realization of the fact to which it refers. Honesty in the realm of experience, of course, is allied to honesty, or spontaneity, of expression. The latter quality has itself sometimes been viewed as the goal of optimal development. For years, its cultivation has been sought through such avenues as psychodrama. More recently, various group-encounter techniques have been similarly employed.

There are many other specific qualities of experience that have received the primary attention of theorists. We have already noted self-esteem, or self-acceptance, as a quality that has been emphasized at least in a great deal of relevant research. The sense of identity has been stressed by some. The experience of power, adequacy, or control has also received theoretical attention. It is obviously intertwined with variables we have considered in terms of adequacy of coping. It is not a strict function of any of these, but whether a sense of control is realistic depends on the success of actual coping. The experience of one's relatedness to the world has also been accorded focal treatment in many ways. Sometimes the important variable is seen as a willingness to form commitments—which can be viewed as yet another form of openness—and thus to be personally involved in something beyond one's own realm of comfort. The social realm may be viewed as the most vital locus of involvement. A specific aspect of social relatedness—such as Buber's I–thou orientation—may be stressed. Several of the qualities of experience we have noted here are regarded together by Eriksen as ingredients of the optimal course of development.

Social relationships

We have just noted certain aspects of social orientation. The focus may instead be on social relationships without special attention to how they are experienced. Freud's genital-character concept points to the capacity for a mature form of love (the true object-cathexis). Other theorists deal with interpersonal relationships in general, stressing the ability to accept other people, to relate to them, to be sensitive to their needs, to interact successfully with them, etc. For still other theorists, the focus is shifted from immediate interaction altogether to variables in a larger sphere of human relatedness—an identification with mankind as a whole, a devotion to the cause of human betterment, etc.

A contrasting variable that has sometimes been regarded as lying at the core of the ideal condition is autonomy or independence. In theoretical treatments that stress creative experience and production, this tends to be viewed as a correlative variable. A high degree of self-directedness and a high degree of loving concern for others are not necessarily incompatible, but it should be noted that in some situations they will come into conflict. One cannot be fully autonomous while responding to the needs of another. Among highly creative people in the arts and sciences too, one can find some who either withdraw from social contact or treat other people callously, if not brutally. In applying theory to specific cases then, it makes a great deal of difference whether we regard autonomy or positive social relatedness as a key element in the optimal personality.

Some overall implications

The point just noted illustrates a fact of much more general significance. If we examine various pairs of qualities that have been attributed to the optimal personality, we find some that are interdependent, while others seem unrelated. In still other cases, we find qualities that tend toward mutual exclusiveness or whose expressions are at least incompatible in some situations. Thus, we must sometimes choose between autonomy and positive social relatedness. Similarly, the orderly states implied by concepts of stability and internal consistency cannot be maintained consistently if one is very spontaneous and open to new experience. Perpetual tranquility is also incompatible with openness and social concern. A high level of self-awareness and self-insight may preclude a high level of self-esteem unless personal expectations are very modest, and if one is really concerned with the welfare of others, he must share some of their distress. The man who can witness violence and suffering and feel no involvement can maintain a kind of successful 'adjustment' that his neighbor forsakes, but he seems a more limited man for doing so.

It is important to recognize these contrasts because many of the things that have been written and said about the ideal condition— whether stated in terms of mental health, maturity, self-actualization, or some other term—appear to assume a grand single continuum extending from the lowest to the highest level of attainment. Development is then viewed in terms of a sequence in which each stage presupposes successful passage through previous ones. There is an accompanying tendency in theoretical treatments to use illustrative cases that reinforce this assumption. Thus, many of the good features of creativity and self-actualization seem to go together when we examine the lives of Johann Sebastian Bach and Leonardo da Vinci. To avoid complications, we ignore Richard Wagner and Vincent Van Gogh.

The implication of the present argument is that the optimal state probably involves a number of fairly distinct dimensions. It would be possible, then, to reach an exceptional level in one respect while progressing no further than the average man in another. Some desirable qualities might even prove to be negatively interrelated. To resolve this matter, it is essential to examine many traits in combination within a common population. In the pages that follow we shall examine some pertinent research findings and then consider their implications for a theory of the optimal personality.

Chapter 3

Research strategy for the study of the optimal personality

We have seen that the optimal personality has been described in many ways. It is generally agreed, however, that no trait that we might single out as the chief defining characteristic can be regarded as operating independently of the total system. When we speak of the ideal goal and of stages leading to it, we are concerned with variables and events that affect almost everything the individual does or feels. In dealing with the optimal personality, we must deal with the total personality. Our understanding of the former is limited by our understanding of the latter.

The total system of behavior and experience that constitutes any single person is obviously very complex. If we could abstract from a large number of persons only those features that they have in common, we would still be confronted by a common organization containing an extremely elaborate pattern of interdependencies. The few personality theorists who venture to formulate 'comprehensive' theories do so by focusing on only a few aspects of the total organization—cognitive processes, modes of perception, patterns of social orientation, etc.—and trying to describe and explain as much as possible in terms of these.

Understandably, there has been much more speculation about the nature of the total personality system than there has been research designed to illuminate it. This kind of research is a formidable undertaking, and most investigators prefer to confine their efforts to more restricted problems that yield more clear-cut results. The one researcher who has made an exhaustive attempt to define the total personality through systematic examination of the interrelationships within comprehensive sets of variables is Raymond Cattell (1957, 1965). Whatever the future fate of Cattell's theoretical formulations, all psychologists who undertake a similar task must either ignore his work deliberately or acknowledge a debt to the findings netted by his pioneering efforts.

In a long succession of studies with various types of measurement applied to subjects of various age levels, Cattell has tried to assess his subjects on large sets of variables designed to represent the whole 'personality sphere'. Practically speaking, the personality sphere is the entire range of gross behavioral characteristics in terms of which we can describe individuals and distinguish them from one another. In effect, it was defined operationally in Cattell's earliest studies in terms of the domain covered by all personality trait terms in our common vocabulary.

How well Cattell has succeeded in actually exploring all regions within the personality sphere is debatable. Perhaps he has largely covered the territory assessable by extant personality tests, but as in many other fields of science the extent of the unknown is pretty much a matter of conjecture. It is reasonable to assume that the total realm composed of readily discernible features of overt behavior is essentially the same as the total realm symbolized by our common personality trait vocabulary. We usually talk about people and differentiate between them in terms of things that would be easily perceived by any observer in the course of time. We less often try to describe them in terms of modes of experience that are not mirrored directly in behavior, and it would be more difficult to do so with our present vocabulary. Thus, our language is rich in words to describe the ways in which people express emotions, but it is deficient in words to describe feelings that are not expressed. Not only is there a shortage of terms to describe the contents of experience; there is a still greater shortage of words to describe the structural features of thought and experience, i.e. the characteristic modes or styles of experiencing that persist over many contents. Available words provide a rather faulty guide to the important ways in which people differ from one another.

Cattell has probably dealt with a far greater assortment of variables than any other personality theorist or researcher. In the view of the present author, however, no one has yet done full justice to the total behavioral-phenomenal system—either with respect to its major ingredients or with respect to their overall pattern of interrelationships. It is the experiential or phenomenal variables that have been most seriously slighted. At this point, no doubt some readers will insist—in their true objective, scientific spirit—that all we can ever know of another person is what is expressed overtly in some form of behavior. Thus, for all practical purposes, anything in the phenomenal realm that is not expressed in behavior does not exist, while anything of real importance there will eventually be identified behaviorally. Hence, it is redundant to speak of a special class of variables that might be called phenomenal.

This line of reasoning contains some subtle metaphysical and epistemological premises that are certainly questionable, but granting them for the sake of argument, we may still reject this position for many reasons. First of all, if there is any point in trying to understand people, there is an obvious merit in trying to understand the total package, and experience is part of it. If the purpose of science is to make orderly sense of all the contents of human observation, and if we wish to make sense of ourselves and other people, there is no good justification for ignoring anything in the realm of experience. As the author has previously argued (Coan, 1964b), the behaviorist is in a rather unique position in permitting a methodological bias to dictate his subject matter. But it is rather pointless to worry about which position is the more 'scientific'. The behaviorist may pre-empt that label if he wishes.

Whatever intellectual arguments we may choose to introduce, of course, what we ultimately admit as fit subject matter for description and conceptualization is basically a matter of personal preference. If we attach any importance to experience itself, there are good practical reasons for rejecting the position of our hypothetical behavior-centered antagonist. Each of us who is given to periods of introspection encounters some phenomena that seem rather fundamental and important but which are very difficult to describe. We can see that these experiential effects are not mirrored in our behavior in any direct and simple way. We think we can find some of these same things in other people, but again not expressed in any direct and simple way, and conversation may provide a bit of confirmation. We would not detect these features in the experience of another person if we had not found them in ourselves. The most complex systematic analysis of responses and stimulus-response contingencies would probably not reveal them either, for in the absence of 'direct and simple' expression one must look for expression in a complicated and variable pattern of response relationships. Though the phenomenal variable may seem fairly simple, its behavioral counterpart can be so intricate that we will never find it unless we are deliberately looking for it—and we will not do this unless we have the phenomenal variable itself in mind at the outset. Conversely, of course, a simple behavioral effect may have very complicated counterparts in the phenomenal realm.

An adequate personality theory, then, must deal with both behavioral and phenomenal features of the person. Both of these can be best understood when brought together in a common overall network of relationships. Perhaps the limitations of a one-sided approach are most apparent in the efforts of some psychologists in mid-twentieth-century America to reduce the whole realm of psychopathology to faulty habits. Thus, the behavioral symptoms of the psychotic are said to *be* his psychosis (not just a part of his psychosis), and one can effect a cure by systematic de-conditioning and re-conditioning. No one can doubt that all these symptoms are subject to alteration through conditioning techniques, of course, but if one sits down with the schizophrenic, establishes sufficient trust to permit effective communication, and begins to gain an understanding of the world that this patient experiences, one starts to suspect that his bizarre, dramatic actions are a rather trivial part of what is going on.

It is likely that the psychology of the future will attempt to establish order within a far more comprehensive set of variables than those with which we now deal. Behavioral, phenomenal, stimulus-history, and situational variables will be brought into a common framework with neurological, bio-chemical, and anthropometric variables. A clear recognition of the ultimate value of this grandly comprehensive scheme might serve as a spur to progress, but the present state of our biological knowledge does not permit us to move far in this direction as yet. The primary concerns of this book lie in the behavioral-phenomenal realm, which at present poses an ample challenge by itself. It is to be hoped that physiological research in years to come will establish the relationships we need in order to do more than merely pay lip service to the biological underpinnings of personality.

The need for constructive analysis

Up to this point, the main thesis of this chapter has been that in research on any problem that involves the total personality we must be prepared to deal with comprehensive sets of variables—and ideally with sets that sample some aspects of the personality more adequately than anyone has to date. It does not serve our needs, however, merely to collect a vast hodge-podge of scores. For any kind of useful understanding of people, we must be able to find some order in these scores that we are capable of grasping. This means essentially that we need to find within our grand system of variables a relatively small number of components that are of major importance and we need to discern the nature of their interrelationships.

The most common way of accomplishing this aim is to proceed

by some mixture of guesswork, intuition, and reasoning from theories one has already adopted. This procedure is sometimes highly productive. Even in the hands of a very gifted observer, however, it tends to be inefficient. The most brilliant personality theorist will overlook some important distinctions and attach significance to some variables out of all proportion to their actual role in the total personality.

The obvious alternative to such a casual speculative approach is a relatively systematic method of quantitative analysis. Factor analysis is the technique most often employed. Factor analysis is essentially a procedure for analyzing the intercorrelations among a set of variables to determine how they might best be accounted for in terms of a relatively small number of underlying influences. Thus, it points to a set of components (or factors) which, as a group, account for more of the variation in our vast array of scores than will any comparable set of components that we might derive through speculation. At the same time, each of the components that it yields possesses an internal coherence that the products of the armchair often lack. We may view the original variables as representing elements or specific forms of expression of the factor, and these must display substantial intercorrelation for a factor to emerge.

Factor analysis, then, can be a very valuable tool in our quest for an underlying order in the total personality. All the same, however, it would be foolish to regard it as a magic lamp that will surely guide our steps to the truth. In application, factor analysis remains something of an art. There are several stages in its use at which crucial decisions are variously made by different investigators. The most vital of these decisions will determine how many factors will be employed to account for the intercorrelations of the variables and whether the factors will themselves be permitted to intercorrelate. Even the growing number of unsophisticated users who are willing to accept whatever decision somone else has arbitrarily incorporated into a computer program will never ensure uniform application of factor analysis.

There are some who will ask why we should bother to employ such a precarious tool, but this question simply reveals a misunderstanding of its purpose. The tool is designed to aid us in a task that is basically one of theoretical analysis and construction. We are confronted with a system of enormous complexity, and we want to reduce it to a conceptual schema that we can manage inside our heads. The schema will necessarily be simpler than the monumental system of variables and observations on which it is based and to which it refers, but we would like it to 'fit' the observations as well as possible within the limits imposed by our very human desire for simplicity. At best, what we end up with is a compromise between our demand for simplicity and our demand for precisely fitting all observations. As in all matters of scientific theory, others will attach different weights to such considerations as simplicity and precision and arrive at somewhat different schemata. In any case, we are seeking something that is not rigidly determined by our data. For any set of observations, there is no one schema that can properly be regarded as the true one, for the schema is not intended to be a statement of truth. It is a set of constructs which we have created within whatever broad limits we allow our observations to impose and which we then superimpose on our observations to help us make sense of them. Factor analysis serves a very valuable function in the process of theoretical construction by re-arranging the information contained in our observations, but it cannot supplant the theorist himself. Anyone who either assumes it will automatically generate profound insights or dismisses it as an insufficiently rigorous technique fails to understand the purpose it normally serves.

In its most important application, then, factor analysis functions as an aid in theory construction. If we wish to understand the organization of the personality, this is essentially the kind of tool we need, for it must be understood that this task is not a purely empirical enterprise. Whatever the state of our factual knowledge of personality at any time, the picture we possess of its overall organization will always be as much a product of theoretical construction as of discovery. This state of affairs is not just dictated by the sheer complexity of our immediate subject matter, for it is actually inherent in all scientific understanding. In merely proceeding from direct observation to verbal concepts, we are introducing a novel structure.

Furthermore, we almost always start with some sort of implicit structuring before we even begin to formulate specific concepts for a given realm of study. Every theorist carries with him certain abstract models, or patterns of interpretation, that govern the kinds of concepts he will devise. Some of these models are obviously based on physical systems, such as the hydraulic or the electrical, but others are more subtle because they are yet more abstract. Thus, one theorist tends to think in terms of layers or levels and always introduces concepts that are interrelated in terms of a series or sequence. Another will think in topological terms and devise concepts subject to any kind of ordering that can be visualized in two-dimensional space. Some theorists seem to like well-defined boxes or compartments and are prone to find qualitatively distinct classes, while others are prone to find underlying continua with differences expressed in terms of quantitative gradations. The tendency to conceptualize progressive change in terms of a succession of triads (thesis and antithesis revolved by synthesis) is so widespread, from ancient oriental mythology to modern history and developmental theory, that we easily overlook the underlying model. As a rule, we are least likely to recognize those features of our models that approach universal application because they stem from basic properties of the human nervous and sensory systems. It is interesting to speculate on the character of the conceptual schemes we might concoct if the sense on which we relied most heavily for information about the world were attuned to odors or magnetic fields instead of that narrow band of radiant energy that normally stimulates our retinas.

The implicit models that guide our understanding and theorizing can be very helpful, but they can also restrict the scope of our comprehension if we fail to recognize their operation. Because we use them, our theories always have a certain arbitrary character. If we are aware of this and of the models that produce it, we can better appreciate alternative conceptual schemes and have a deeper understanding of the domain to which our theories pertain. It is undoubtedly futile, however, to suppose that we can ever devise theories free from the influence of man-made models. Merely to assign a verbal label to something presupposes a dichotomous structuring of the universe that separates the recipients of the label from everything to which it is not applied. And all those elaborate formulations that we call scientific theories are inevitably created by human beings, they are designed to serve human purposes, and they are stamped with the many peculiarities of the human perceiver. Is there really a point in wishing it were otherwise?

The ordinary applications of factor analysis presuppose a descriptive model that underlies nearly all common psychometric procedures. The basic assumption is that attributes in general can be conceived in terms of continua and that with respect to any given attribute any individual can be adequately described in terms of a position on a continuum. For the factor analyst, as for most psychologists concerned with multi-trait description, the model expands to a dimensional one. In this model, a domain of traits is construed in terms of a set of independent or semi-independent dimensions, and the individual is regarded as subject to full description in terms of a set of coordinates that reveal his position in relation to a system of intersecting axes.

The dimensional model has proved to be extremely versatile. Its popularity stems from the fact that it is conducive to efficient description. If the dimensions are derived through a procedure like factor analysis that ensures mutual independence, this model provides a basis for description that is maximally economical for any desired degree of precision. Perhaps no other model could serve the same purposes any better on a grand scale. There will be situations, however, where other models may fit our needs better. Wherever we decide to forgo the assumption of quantitative continuity, for example, we are likely to find other models—such as the topological one—more useful.

Where the dimensional model seems suitable, we must still recognize certain limitations inherent in it, for it will not fill all our needs. As it is customarily applied, for example, it is addressed to statistical interdependence but not directly to functional interdependence. Thus, factors X and Y will be represented by mutually orthogonal axes if they correspond to trends that are uncorrelated in the population we have studied. The variables underlying these two factors, however, may still interact in all sorts of ways. Certain effects may depend on the conjoint elevation or depression of both factors. Furthermore, one factor may operate in interaction with other influences as a cause with respect to the other factor and still be essentially uncorrelated with it. Thus, the fact that anxiety and neuroticism appear as independent factors in some data does not mean that they are functionally unrelated. Some, but not all, of the interactions among factors are evident in the numerical patterns within factor matrices and in the equations we would write to predict selected variables from combinations of factors.

Functional interrelationships, then, entail a complex ordering that the dimensional model is not really designed to handle. The model is designed to deal with patterns of correlation and from these we can infer functional dependence to a limited extent. If we are going to view the shortcomings of the model in proper per-spective, however, we must note that not all the restrictions in our common use of it are inherent in the model itself. It is applicable to any set of relationships that can be expressed in terms of inter-correlations. Ordinarily we quantify the covariation of variables measured on a single occasion over a sample of persons, but there are many other forms of covariation that we might study instead— that of differences between scores obtained on different occasions, that of response fluctuation in a single person over time, that between persons over a sample of test variables, etc. Each of these may reflect some functional dependencies that the others will not (see Coan, 1961, 1966).

It should be noted that even when we are not concerned with the nature of the interactions that produce our correlations, we are still interested usually in inferring a kind of relationship not directly expressed in our data. The usual application of factor analysis and the dimensional model is to the experimental design known as R-technique, where variables are correlated over a sample of persons. To be a little more precise, we correlate stimulus variables with respect to covariation in responses observed over a sample of persons on a given occasion. A factor extracted from such correlations is necessarily a dimension of individual differences, or in other terms, a component of transpersonal variance. We usually interpret it, however, as a component of the system of intellectual or personality variables found within individuals. In doing this, we assume that, in certain ways, people are similarly organized and that those variables that operate in a unitary fashion in the production of individual differences will operate in a unitary way within the personality of a single individual. These are very useful assumptions, but we should be wise to realize when we are making them.

In recognition of these assumptions, some researchers have advocated supplementing R-technique analyses with P-technique. In P-technique, we observe correlation over a series of occasions within a single subject. This can provide valuable information about the intra-individual coherence of factors. Its value is limited, however, since it can only be applied to variables which display appreciable temporal fluctuation and which are free of unmanageable practice effects. In any case, here as elsewhere, it is best not to become overly addicted to a particular method. Valuable as R-technique factor analysis is, we are in a better position to interpret its products if we gather additional information by other means. The other means would include the application of factor analysis to other forms of covariation, P-technique being one such possibility. In addition, we would want the knowledge that we could obtain from intensive study of individual cases without statistical analysis and from controlled experiments in which we deliberately manipulate certain independent variables. If we are seeking a comprehensive picture of intra-individual organization and of the functional relationships among component variables, a varied methodology is probably essential.

It was suggested above that for some purposes we might prefer an alternative to the dimensional model. Some of the deficiencies of this model may be surmounted, however, simply by supplementing it with others. The supplemental use of a hierarchical model enables us to handle some patterns of relationship for which the dimensional model alone is inadequate. We see increasing use of a four-level pyramidal hierarchy first applied to factors by Burt (1941, 1949). In a pyramidal hierarchy, variables are represented by a two-dimensional array of compartments. The importance or generality of influence of a variable is indicated by the elevation of the compartment in the hierarchy, and patterns of influence or subordination are shown by lines that connect compartments on different levels. The common organization chart is basically a pyramidal hierarchy, and the figure presented in Chapter 1 represents an adaptation of the model. When the model is used in conjunction with factor analysis, the compartments usually correspond to factors or trait dimensions. Ordinarily, factors of coordinate status in a set of data or realm of observation—e.g. those factors derived from a common correlation matrix through a single set of extractions—are regarded as lying at a common level.

Burt arrived at the notion of four basic levels through a logical analysis of trait distributions, and he equated the four levels with the four types of factors known as general, group, specific, and error. In application to oblique factor systems, it is customary to equate levels with orders of analysis. Thus, the original scored variables would constitute one level, the first-order factors a higher level, the second-order factors a still higher level, etc. In Eysenck's use of the hierarchy, on the other hand, the levels are distinguished in more strictly psychological terms and conceptualized in terms of types, traits, habitual responses, and specific responses. Eysenck regards the factors which he derives as lying at the type level.

The need for dealing with dimensions in terms of a hierarchical system or something comparable is obvious when we realize that the same characteristics will be represented by a single factor in the context of one study and by several factors in another, depending on the mode of sampling variables and subjects, and on the manner in which the analysis is conducted. From the same set of correlations, one factor analyst may derive a small number of broad factors, while another will derive a larger number of more specific factors that correspond to components of the broader ones. It is possible to treat any given domain in terms of either a small number or a large number of dimensions depending on the relative importance we attach to broad, economical description on the one hand, and to precision of detail on the other. We gain a more comprehensive picture of relationships if we bring the alternative sets of dimensions into a common hierarchy.

What we need for theoretical purposes, however, is a hierarchy in which elevation corresponds to generality of expression within the total system of behavior and experience that we call personality. The author has previously spoken of this as *referent* generality (Coan, 1964a). It must be distinguished from the level of generality which is manifested statistically in a given study in terms of order of analysis or observed variance magnitude, though it is obviously related to this. It is clear that in a given set of factors, some will have higher referent generality—i.e. they will represent broader influences—than others. The observed variance magnitude of a factor (the sum of squared variable-factor correlations), however, is an imperfect indicator, since it is affected by variations in variable sampling over different areas of content. Within a given study, second-order factors will tend to be of higher referent generality than all first-order factors, but the situation is more complex when we compare factors from different studies or different researchers. Eysenck's first-order factors are comparable to the second-order factors that Cattell derives from questionnaires. One thing that becomes abundantly clear from such considerations is that the notion of four fixed levels is a pointlessly arbitrary restriction in the hierarchical model. For theoretical purposes, it would be more fruitful to treat elevation in the hierarchy as a genuine continuum of psychological reference. (For a more extended treatment of this matter, see Coan, 1964a.) For any given purpose, of course, it may be convenient to regard a system of variables and factors as occupying a limited number of levels, but the number should be determined by our data and our theoretical needs.

The problem of measurement

The sort of personality research we envisage calls for the use of comprehensive sets of test variables that will be subjected to multivariate analyses guided by models suited to the complexity of the relationships with which we hope to deal. We have said little, however, about deciding more specifically what to measure and how to measure it. The task of determining which psychological variables should be assessed is one for which no rigid or detailed prescription can be written. In a sense, we are conducting our research in order to find out which variables merit assessment. We must make some preliminary decisions about this, however, on the basis of a logical analysis of the realm of assessment. To do this systematically, we should begin by defining the realm as clearly as possible, setting forth its components as specifically but inclusively as we can on the basis of our present understanding. We can then proceed to subdivide the realm into assessable component areas.

In such a procedure it is inevitable that our choice of variables will be guided by our preconceptions, but we can at least hope to avoid too narrow coverage. If we wish to ensure breadth and avoid the biased selection of variables that might stem from any one theoretical orientation, it behoves us to be fairly eclectic at this point. In defining the realm and selecting variables, we can be guided by many theories and by all pertinent information—whether from personal experience or previous studies—that comes to our attention. If we then aim at measuring variables that are fairly specific and study interrelationships among large numbers of them, we can expect our data analyses to reveal some structures that we have not wholly anticipated.

The choice of an appropriate measurement operation for any given variable poses further problems. In fact, unless the variable is defined as some fairly simple behavioral characteristic, it is not likely that any obvious measurement operation can be relied upon to provide a good measure of it. Most of the variables with which we are likely to concern ourselves in the personality field are of such a character that unambiguous direct measures are simply unavailable. It often happens, of course, that a researcher chooses what he considers an obvious measure of some construct—rigidity, let us say—only to find ultimately that it fails to correlate with other supposed measures of the construct and does not relate to other variables in the way he would expect from his understanding of the construct.

In seeking to measure any single construct, we could best proceed by employing a variety of measures and determining their interrelationships. These interrelationships might help us to identify some single operation or set of operationships by which we could best measure the construct. On the other hand, they might yield information that would lead us to abandon or revise the construct itself. If our aim is to assess a broad realm of variables, not too clearly structured by past research, we are confronted with a double selection problem. We must identify, at least tentatively, the psychological variables we wish to assess and we must choose a set of measurement operations that can reasonably be considered relevant to them. If possible, we should employ several measurement operations that we expect to yield information pertaining to each psychological variable, but a generally loose relationship between operations and variables is unavoidable.

Perhaps we can deal more efficiently with the matter of choosing measurement operations if we turn our attention more directly to the measurement theory that is implicit in the foregoing statements. It is assumed here that psychological measurement is of an indirect character. In general, magnitudes in the variable we want to assess will relate only imperfectly to obtained scale magnitudes, but the variable is measured only to the extent that some relationship exists. This view obviously runs counter to an operationist conception of measurement, which would simply equate the measured variable with those aspects of behavior quantified in the testing situation. In terms of such a viewpoint, carried to its logical conclusions, adequate assessment of personality would require an indefinitely large, if not an infinite, number of measurements. The present view assumes that the total personality can be adequately represented by a reasonably small number of properly selected test behaviors.

The behavior elicited in a testing situation is usually of slight interest in itself. It is of value in so far as some feature of it covaries with a variable of more general importance, the variable usually being a construct in terms of which we would like to characterize a wide range of behaviors. If we equate *measurement* with *covariation*, it is obvious that a given test response characteristic can serve potentially as a measure of a wide range of personal traits. For some it will be a relatively good measure, for others a very poor one.

If our aim is global personality assessment, we must select a set of test behaviors and a set of quantifiable test response-characteristics that, as a group, will share variance with a great variety of personality features manifested outside the test situation. How can we best ensure this? Commonsense considerations suggest that a given test result is likely to be most revealing of characteristics that closely resemble the responses elicited by the test or which are directly related functionally to those responses. There is no clear rule for deciding in advance where the essential quality will be found, but on *a priori* grounds it seems unreasonable to expect to learn much about a man's philosophy of life if we only observe the way he walks, or to learn much about his motoric style by securing word associations. To generalize a bit further, it is unlikely that any single kind of test behavior—whether it consists of conceptual associations to inkblots, figure drawings, copying designs, telling stories in response to pictures, or responding to questionnaire items—is likely to furnish all the information needed for comprehensive assessment. We should be prepared to make varied use of varied test behaviors.

Even when psychologists have accepted this bit of advice, they often proceed to make rather naïve assumptions about the connections between constructs and test behaviors. One such assumption is that the theoretical free associations of the tester offer some guarantee of profound insight into the character of his subject. In such a fashion, sloppy thinking of a fairly predictable sort often assumes the guise of intuition. Thus, if a subject reports that he sees ears a in Rorschach blot, someone is bound to suspect paranoid trends, while if he sees bottles, babies, or mouths, we can expect the diagnostic write-up to take note of his oral eroticism. Similar reasoning appears to underlie the occasional assumption that a grand magical parallel exists between features of the test behavior and broad features of the total personality where only the most tenuous grounds can be adduced for positing a functional connection. Thus, if the subject is asked to draw a tree, every feature of the resulting production is regarded as indicating, by analogy, some major aspect of his conception of his own life. If he is asked to mark a path in a pencil maze, he draws a line that is supposed to reveal his behavior at all the important choice points of life. Thus, the subject who takes avoidably long detours in the maze is said to have a strong superego.

Probably the most frequent locus for naïve assumptions is the most common type of test operation, the questionnaire item. Questionnaires have frequently been criticized because of their transparency, and the layman is inclined to believe that he can create any picture of himself that he wants on a questionnaire. The layman is correct to the extent that any item that works well for a given purpose is bound to possess some face validity, at least in the eyes of people with reasonable insight. For this reason, a truly 'subtle' questionnaire scale is probably unattainable. If we select items on the basis of demonstrated workability (i.e. appropriate covariation) rather than on the basis of face validity, however, we end up with scales that are somewhat more subtle than most that have been used in the past. We also discover in the process of constructing scales this way that some face valid items do not work the way one might expect.

An occasional questionnaire scale constructor still proceeds, as many psychologists did in past decades, on the assumption that subjects will give literally valid responses to almost any item we may decide to present. If the subject endorses the statement, 'I am not afraid to be myself,' this is regarded as a sign that he has the courage to experience and express his full nature. If we studied the correlates of the response, however, we might discover that the individual who endorses this statement tends merely to be less self-aware than the individual who rejects it and that he is more careful to avoid situations that might seriously challenge his defenses.

None of this, however, should be construed as a rejection of the questionnaire method of measurement. The questionnaire method undoubtedly deserves its widespread use, because it is the most versatile technique—it is applicable to a wider range of variables than any other technique—and because for some information it is the method of choice. The author agrees with Allport, Rogers, and others who have long stressed the importance of the information that only subjective self-report can provide, but it is essential that we understand what kind of information questionnaires actually yield.

Like any other test response, a questionnaire-item response can be considered a valid measure only for those features of the total behavioral-phenomenal system that covary with it. In the case of a badly worded item, it may measure only a transitory impulse to mark an (a) or a (b) when confronted with an incomprehensible series of words. In a more fortunate case, it may relate to a complex of stable characteristics. The range of characteristics potentially assessable by means of questionnaire items can only be determined by large-scale studies of the future in which they are employed in combination with many other forms of measurement. It seems likely, however, that they will prove more useful on the whole for measuring experiential variables than for measuring behavioral variables. Suppose, for example, that a subject marks the (a) answer to the question, 'Would you rather (a) go to a party or (b) read a book?' Assuming that the response is a function of the verbal content of the item (he has read and understood it before marking it) and that it possesses a certain stability, we now know that the subject indicates a preference for going to parties when filling our questionnaire forms. There are two obvious low-level inferences that might be drawn from this: first, he thinks of himself as a person who prefers going to parties; and second, he actually does ordinarily go to parties when confronted with such a choice. Both inferences may be correct, but the former is probably the safer bet. Naturally if we are going to make much use of the item, we shall expect it to covary with many additional characteristics. It would not be surprising if the characteristics with which it correlated most highly were other features of the self-concept rather than overt behaviors. If this is the way questionnaires usually work, they have a vital role to play, but they will obviously need to be supplemented by other forms of measurement in comprehensive personality research.

In the research on the optimal personality reported in this book, there is a heavy reliance on questionnaire materials, although some of these were used in rather novel ways. The non-questionnaire techniques were those that lent themselves to group administration. Altogether a fair variety of approaches was utilized, but it must be understood that any information that could have been obtained only through individual testing or through observation outside a classroom setting was not gathered. We may hope, then, to illuminate some facets of the optimal personality, but it would be a vain pretense to claim that this research can offer as comprehensive a picture as we should like.

Chapter 4

Development of a research battery: measures of personal consistency

Most of the research findings reported in this book are based on the analysis of a six-hour battery that was group-administered to several hundred university students at the University of Arizona during the spring and fall of 1967. The great majority of the subjects were volunteers drawn from classes in elementary psychology. Some additional volunteers were drawn from advanced classes, and one class in experimental psychology was tested *in toto*. Since most liberal arts students take the elementary course, the total sample represents a fairly diverse college population, but of course, it is not strictly representative of the local university population as a whole.

There were 361 subjects altogether—170 men and 191 women—for whom essentially complete sets of battery scores were available. All findings that involve relationships between tests are based on the responses of this group. For three of the questionnaires that we shall discuss, however, many additional cases were obtained by classroom testing. Each of these questionnaires was subjected to a separate preliminary analysis involving all available cases before the battery as a whole was analyzed.

The battery was assembled with a view toward illuminating the realm of variables that enter into various concepts of the optimal personality. In cases where a pertinent variable was sufficiently well defined, it was possible to utilize two or more specific measures that could be expected to bear on it. In areas where the components have been less clearly articulated in theory, it was necessary either to assume that relevant information would be yielded by some combination of loosely related measures, or to employ lengthy inventories that could be individually analyzed. No doubt some important aspects of the optimal personality cannot be adequately assessed with this battery. Some have not been well tapped by any psychometric device to date. The mere decision to seek the kind of information that can be obtained by applying many measures to a large sample imposes practical limitations on the kinds of measures that can be used. Of necessity, this research is confined to tests that are susceptible to economical group administration. Varied as it may be, the sample also affects the character of assessable variables. Its relatively high intellectual level permits the use of a wide assortment of verbal measures, but some variables that one might study in a psychiatric hospital population cannot be effectively studied in a college population because their variance is too restricted. In this realm of investigation, however, we must be content to cast light in a few small corners. The truly definitive study is a task for the very remote future.

Phenomenal organization

We may use the term *phenomenal organization* to refer to the systematization or 'crystallization' of modes of experiencing oneself and the world into stable and individually characteristic patterns. Elsewhere (Coan, 1966), the author has suggested that increasing organization of this sort is likely to occur as an accompaniment of normal development within any one area of experience, but that the influx of new ideas and experiences in some periods of life may result in decreased organization within the total personality. It seems likely that as organization occurs with respect to a given set of ideas or objects, these elements in our experience will tend to arrange themselves in hierarchies (of goodness, desirability, relevancy, etc., depending on the way in which we experience them). To the extent that a set of elements has been organized into a well-defined hierarchy, the individual will display internally consistent patterns of choice among these elements over time. To judge the phenomenal organization of any individual properly, we should have to begin by defining the ingredients of his world of experience and then determine the consistency of his choice patterns. The instruments that have been devised thus far, however, assume that we can do a reasonable job of assessing individual differences in phenomenal organization by examining responses to common elements of experience that we can consider familiar to all subjects.

The first instrument designed for such a purpose by the author involved the value choices of children in the primary grades (Cattell and Coan, 1959). This test was too short for adequate reliability, but it was later expanded by Burkholder (1963), who used it in a study of behavior problems. She compared children in three problem areas—aggression, withdrawal, and anxiety—with a control group with respect to both value choice consistency and the scales of a factored personality questionnaire. It was found that children in each of the problem areas showed less consistency on the average than did the controls and that value consistency discriminated better between the total problem group and the control group than did any single questionnaire factor.

A test entitled Value Choices, employing the same basic design as the child instrument, has since been constructed for adults. In effect, in taking this test, a subject is asked to rank a set of four elements by the method of pair comparisons. Each scoring unit consists of a preferential question stem for which there are four available alternatives. With the alternatives presented in all possible pairs, we have a total of six questions for each scoring unit. These are distributed over three testing sessions to prevent a direct comparison of questions containing the same elements, and the elements are ordered within questions in such a way that a consistent response is not likely to result from a positional response bias. The following is a representative question stem with the four available alternatives:

Which of these ideals do you consider more important: —— or ——?
a. devotion to God
b. love of humanity
c. search for scientific truth
d. creation of artistic beauty

For the set of six items formed from such a set of elements, there are 2^6, or 64 possible response patterns. Of these, 24 are internally consistent patterns, since there are 24 possible ordinal arrangements for four elements. The 40 remaining response patterns are inconsistent. It is not possible to score for multiple inconsistency within a given scoring unit, because any inconsistent pattern may be converted to a consistent one by the alteration of a single response. A given set of six items, then, functions as a binary item for scoring purposes—it can contribute only one point to the raw score scale of value consistency. An obvious shortcoming of the Value Choices test, when compared with other questionnaire devices, is the amount of testing time required to secure any given range of scores and a desired level of reliability. The value consistency test included in the research battery contains 24 scoring units, and it has been found to have a corrected split-half reliability of 0.86. Perhaps this is less than would be wished, but it seems fairly respectable when one considers that the units were deliberately composed of highly varied content.

The value system of the subject obviously provides only one possible source of content for a test of phenomenal organization. Two other tests were constructed with the same basic design for inclusion in the battery. One of these was called Interest Inventory. This test contains lists of activities presented in pairs, and the subject is asked to indicate the activity he prefers in each pair. As in Value Choices, the lists contain spaced systematic rearrangements of the same elements. One of the 24 scoring units in this test involves these four elements:

a. help someone who feels upset
b. take part in a debate
c. decorate a store window
d. solve a mathematical puzzle

This test was designed primarily to provide a measure of consistency of interests, but the elements were selected in such a way that it could also be scored for each of the following eight broad interest areas:

1. artistic
2. musical
3. linguistic–literary
4. scientific
5. mechanical
6. social welfare
7. social ascendance
8. outdoor

In addition, a score was obtained for differentiation of interest pattern. This is a measure of the extent to which the interest pattern as a whole is characterized by well-defined high and low interests—i.e., the variability of the overall interest score pattern. A maximally differentiated pattern would contain four interest scores at the high extreme and four at the low extreme, while an undifferentiated pattern would contain a flat profile of medium scores. As conceived for scoring purposes, both differentiation and the individual interest scores are independent of the overall investment of the individual subject in areas of interest. Since every response contributes a point to one of two alternative interest scores, the interest variables constitute an ipsative system and may best be viewed as measures of relative interest. In the light of common clinical experience, however, we may assume that an undifferentiated pattern is most likely to occur in an individual who has difficulty in becoming very involved personally in any area of interest. With an ability and a willingness to become involved, a clearer, more differentiated pattern is likely to emerge.

The other test of phenomenal organization was called Self-Rating Pairs. Here the subject was given a list of paired adjectives and asked to indicate which member of each pair was more descriptive of him. An illustrative scoring unit contains the four adjectives *artistic, forgetful, kind,* and *determined,* which are presented in all possible pairs. Only twelve scoring units were used in this test, but in view of the importance of the self-concept in the total sphere of experience, the test probably merits further development and expansion for future applications. In principle, it could be scored not only for consistency but for a number of trait dimensions as well. The battery test of self-rating consistency, however, was designed to yield only one additional score—for independence *v.* yielding. For this purpose, in some items we used adjectives which Barron (1963) found to be preferred by subjects who acted independently in an Asch-type situation.

Since all three consistency measures of phenomenal organization rest on the same rationale and entail the logical compatibility of sets of responses given over time, one might expect them to measure similar things, including contaminants as well as variables pertinent to our theoretical interests. It might be argued that each is likely to be affected by response stability; it is obvious in any case that instability is conducive to inconsistency. To the extent that a response given by a subject on one occasion is incompatible with the response he would give to the same question on a second occasion, it is likely to be incompatible with responses to related questions on the second occasion as well. It would make no sense to partial out the effect of 'mere stability' from our consistency measures, however, since both response stability and response consistency may best be viewed as depending on the same underlying organization.

We might also ask whether our consistency measures are governed by general intelligence, especially in view of the fact that they involve the logical coherence of responses. So far as our college sample is concerned, the answer is *no.* The best indicators of intelligence used in research with the battery are essentially uncorrelated with the consistency measures. The child test of value consistency used by Burkholder did prove to be related moderately to an intelligence scale, probably because both were affected markedly by the capacity of the child for maintaining attention and responding meaningfully in a group-testing situation.

Within a college population then, the consistency measures apparently tap aspects of phenomenal organization that are independent of general intelligence. It is interesting to note, however, that they are not tapping a common general dimension of organization. In a factor analysis of the battery, they show only a slight tendency to be loaded by the same factors. Their intercorrelations are low, the highest being 0·19 between interest consistency and self-rating consistency. It seems plausible that the self-concept, the interest pattern, and the value system might show many different degrees of internal consistency in a given individual, but it is really a bit premature to speculate very much on what each of the consistency measures taps in general. In the context of the present research battery, they all prove to be of low communality—they fail to correlate sizeably with other variables.

Perhaps one reason for the failure of these measures to correlate highly with other variables is the inability of each of them to discriminate adequately throughout the entire range of phenomenal organization. The score distribution for each is negatively skewed. Individual differences among subjects of high consistency are not effectively assessed. To correct this, we should either have to demand more subtle discriminations of our subjects or simply add many more items of the present type.

On the other hand, we might take the low communalities and the low intercorrelations among the three tests to mean that none of them is satisfactorily tapping a variable of general importance. One may suspect that each of these tests is overly sensitive to immediate situational influences that enter into individual testing sessions. Obviously it takes carelessness or inattentiveness on just one occasion to disrupt the consistency of the responses in a given scoring unit. There is one bit of evidence, however, that runs counter to this view of the three tests. Since the interest, self-rating, and value tests were always presented contiguously in our testing sessions, any situational determinant that affected one test should have affected all three alike. Nevertheless, the respective split-half reliability coefficients of the three tests are considerably higher than the intercorrelations among them. This would seem to indicate that each of the tests is reliably measuring something that the other two are not.

For the present, it seems reasonable to assume that in adults different parts or aspects of the total behavioral–phenomenal system are subject to widely varying degrees of organization. Perhaps our three measures reflect very different parts of the system. To clarify the picture further, we must use them in combination with other instruments designed to yield more closely-related information. At the same time, there is undoubtedly room for much improvement in the present instruments.

Logical consistency of the attitude–belief system

It is a commonplace idea that troubled people tend to act and think irrationally. Perhaps our reasoning more often follows the converse pathway. Encountering someone who does not think the way we do, we immediately conclude that he is proceeding illogically and suspect, therefore, that he is neurotic. Given more information, we might find that he has started with premises much different from ours and that we have not been fully aware either of his or of our own. There are so many bits of evidence that seem to relate soundness of functioning to the logical coherence of attitude and beliefs, particularly in emotion-laden areas of content, however, that it seems quite worthwhile to pursue the matter further.

Cattell was probably the first to design an instrument that was intended to measure attitudinal consistency. His approach was to employ three-item units. Each item is an attitude statement with a Likert-type response scale. The three items together constitute the two premises and conclusion of a syllogism, but they are presented widely spaced in a lengthy attitude battery. The unit can be scored only if the subject agrees with both premises. If he does, the conclusion is scored in accordance with a key. This test is subject to several *a priori* objections. For one thing, it is highly uneconomical, since the score for any subject may be based on only a fraction of the items employed. In any case, the subjects will not all be judged on the same items. A more serious problem is that, to offset the foregoing difficulties, the items themselves are deliberately designed to ensure reasonable likelihood of scorability and discrimination. This means that the items designated as premises are statements that most subjects will endorse, while the conclusions are less likely to be endorsed. (Ideally, each would be accepted by half the subjects and rejected by the other half.) Unfortunately, these conditions can only be met if the logic is not very tight. Examining Cattell's syllogisms, one is left with the impression that the premises and conclusion often have a loose fit and that either response to the conclusion can really be rationalized satisfactorily if both premises are accepted. Perhaps we should not dismiss the test too readily on these grounds alone, for it may still measure something useful. There is no clear evidence, however, that Cattell's syllogisms tap anything in the realm of emotional integration or soundness of functioning. The principal association appears to be with factors that Cattell identifies as reactive dismay (or pessimism) and hypmanic smartness (Cattell and Warburton, 1967).

In research with children, the author devised a modified syllogism unit that avoids some of the obvious difficulties of the Cattell test (see Cattell and Coan, 1959). The revised unit contains four binary items, which form a syllogism in mood Barbara with the first premise doubled. Viewed schematically, the four items are as follows:

First premises: All M is P/Q.
              All N is P/Q.
Second premise: All S is M/N.
Conclusion: All S is P/Q.

In each item, the child chooses one of two given alternatives. His choice in the case of the second premise defines the middle term of the syllogism and thereby determines which first premise will be heeded for scoring purposes. If he chooses M, we look only at the initial first premise, since the other one is irrelevant.

With such a syllogistic form, every unit can be scored, but the scoring is always based on just three of the four items. Consistent patterns of response would be P-MP, Q-MQ, -PNP, -QNQ, the hyphen indicating in each case the premise that is ignored for scoring purposes. With such a scheme, the probability of responding consistently by chance is 0·5. A typical unit in the child test contains these four items:

1. Do you think things that are easy to do are (a) fun or (b) a little tiring and boring?
2. Do you think things that are hard to do are (a) fun or (b) a little tiring and boring?
3. Do you think (a) school is easy or (b) school is hard?
4. Do you think school is (a) fun or (b) a little tiring and boring?

To eliminate the possibility of direct comparison of answers, the items are distributed over four different testing sessions. Consistency is thereby more likely to depend on a stable system of attitudes. One may ask, however, how likely we are to deal with the attitudes that the subject actually possesses. In constructing units entailing tight deductive relationships, we have had to force the subject to choose in each item between two categorical statements, even if neither one represents his own viewpoint. It is hard to see how we can circumvent such problems so long as we employ the syllogism as a model in constructing items. The tests of phenomenal organization also entail logical consistency, of course, but they are based on a scheme that utilizes irreflexive transitive relationships and which, therefore, requires items that demand only relative judgments of the subject. The result is items that are far more palatable from the subject's standpoint. The demand for categorical judgments in the four-item syllogism probably poses fewer difficulties in child testing than it would in adult testing. We are not in a position to say what value it really has, however, because it has never been tried out with a sufficient number of items to ensure minimal reliability.

The obvious problems inherent in the syllogism unit led the author to try a slightly different tactic in constructing a test for use in the optimal–personality research battery. The new departure does not involve a very fundamental innovation, since the concern is still with the sort of consistency that is manifested in compatible or incompatible categorical judgments. The syllogism was abandoned as model, however, and a pair of items (presented in two separate testing sessions) was employed as the basic unit. Some of the two-item units can be construed as truncated syllogisms in which one of the premises is merely implicit, so that the innovation is still more trivial than it appears to be. Perhaps this is so, but the mere introduction of a more economical unit affords the major advantage of permitting more efficient discrimination based on a larger number of units.

A four-point Likert response scale with no middle category was presented with each item, but for the purpose of scoring for consistency only the direction of the subject's answer was considered. For any item pair, there are four possible patterns of agreement and disagreement. In general, the items can be designed so that one of these combinations will be logically inconsistent or will, at least, tend strongly toward incompatibility, while the responses in each of the other combinations can be reconciled. This means in a sense, that it is easier to identify inconsistency than consistency in the attitude–belief system. In any case, it is simpler for scoring purposes to look for inconsistent patterns and score for inconsistency.

It is easiest by far to devise item pairs for which the agree-agree (A-A) combination is inconsistent, but some pairs that could be keyed A-D and D-A were included in the battery scale to reduce the possible contamination of an acquiescence response bias. A representative item pair, keyed A-A, would be:

1. Things would be better if we always expressed our thoughts and feelings frankly and openly.
2. There are some feelings and reactions that we should keep to ourselves, in order to avoid hurting or offending other people.

These two statements are of approximately equal generality of content. In some cases, one statement refers to a special instance of the generalization contained in the other. The following pair, also keyed A-A, would be an example:

1. Public execution (by hanging, electric chair, or gas chamber) is a proper punishment for very serious crimes, such as murder.
2. Nothing on earth is more precious than human life, and there is no justification for the deliberate destruction of it.

The correlational evidence obtained for the present scale of logical inconsistency of attitudes and beliefs shows that it is negatively related to realism of thought. There is nothing to suggest that the high scorer is less well adjusted than the low scorer, but his development appears more limited because he tends to adjust by conformity. The overall picture presented by the correlates of this scale is one of conservatism. The inconsistent subject tends to accept conventional ideas of various kinds without question. He is likely to prefer a fairly simple, orderly, well planned life and tends to avoid exposure to new thoughts and experiences.

It is possible, of course, that conservatives are really no more prone to inconsistent attitudes than people who are more liberal and independent in their thinking and that an ideological bias of the author is bound up in the items. In the absence of a well-defined item universe from which to sample, perhaps the best way to test this would be to secure the services of a psychologist of different outlook for a bit of additional test construction. For item pairs that will discriminate within a test of the present design, however, we need incompatible statements that will be fairly widely accepted. Of necessity, these will be rather conventional in content. If we could find a satisfactory way of assessing incompatible attitudes and beliefs of a more idiosyncratic character (the elements of a paranoid delusional system being an extreme case in point), we might find that we were dealing with a somewhat different variable.

The present scale also correlates highly with an overall tendency to agree with attitude statements, as assessed in a different questionnaire. This suggests that the inconsistency score is partly governed by an acquiescence response bias as a result of the preponderance of *agree* answers in the key. It is a mistake, however, to regard the tendency to agree as 'just a response bias', with no significance beyond test-taking behavior, for it is known to reflect certain personality variables itself. Within this battery it proves to be related to a number of measures involving conventionality or conformity, though not as markedly as the inconsistency measure is. At any rate, we could argue that any confounding of the inconsistency score with acquiescence merely enhances the capacity of this test for measuring what it measures anyway. To allay any doubts about contamination from irrelevant response bias, however, it would be useful to construct more items for which *disagree* answers could be keyed and re-examine the correlates of inconsistency.

Consistency of self-description

We have already considered the logical consistency of self-description in the case of the test called Self-Rating Pairs. Our concern now is with consistency of different forms of self-description or between self-descriptions obtained under different instructions. The best known measures of this sort are based on Q-sorts. Q-sorting is a procedure in which the subject sorts out a set of statements or phrases into a limited number of categories of pre-defined frequency according to how well they describe how he is, how he would like to be, how some other person is (e.g. his father or his therapist), etc. The most widely used measure is the correlation between the phenomenal-self sort (how the subject thinks he is) and the ideal-self sort (how he would like to be). The agreement between these would seem to be essentially a matter of self-esteem or self-satisfaction (more precisely, verbally expressed self-satisfaction). It evidently tends to be low in neurotics and to increase as a function of psychotherapy, but it can also be unrealistically high in the presence of severe psychopathology. With respect to the overall adequacy of functioning of the personality, it has an ambiguous meaning, but it nonetheless furnishes relevant information.

An obvious drawback to the Q-sort measure is the amount of time for testing and scoring to secure a single value. Basically equivalent information can be obtained much more economically by other procedures. For the purposes of the present research, the test of Trait Ranking was constructed. In this, the subject is asked to write numbers beside a list of 10 to 15 adjectives to indicate their order of relevance to a given concept. For a measure of self-ideal discrepancy for personality traits, two lists of 15 adjectives each were used. The subject was first asked to rank the items in each list according to how well they described him. Later he was asked to rank them according to how he would like to be. The discrepancy variable was scored in terms of overall difference between ranks secured under the two sets of instructions. The items used in these lists were chosen in such a way that they would not vary markedly in social desirability (which would have reduced their discriminatory power) and so that they would cover a wide range of characteristics. Cattell's factor studies of rating variables proved a valuable guide in the selection of adjectives that met the latter requisite. The two lists were as follows:

List 1	*List 2*
easygoing	frank
reflective	persevering
calm	carefree
overactive	deliberate
confident	modest
cheerful	talkative
conscientious	relaxed
adventurous	sociable
artistic	practical-minded
decisive	assertive
poised	idealistic
self-sufficient	trustful
unconventional	imaginative
company-seeking	sentimental
sensitive	tough-minded

The above adjectives all refer to personality characteristics. Since an important part of any individual's experience is that pertaining to his own body, it is of interest to know whether his experience of his body is comparable to his experience of himself as a behaving person. In the present context, it seemed worthwhile to find out whether self-satisfaction with respect to physical characteristics is distinguishable from self-satisfaction in general. To secure pertinent information, the author constructed an additional list containing the following ten items:

well-proportioned body
good complexion
attractive facial features
energetic
tall
slender
well-coordinated
strength
excellent health
attractive hair

This list was presented under the same two sets of instructions employed with the preceding lists, and it provided the basis for a measure of self-ideal discrepancy for physical traits. The items in this list are all stated in presumably favorable terms to increase the likelihood of securing wide individual differences in response, but the list is undoubtedly too brief to provide a highly reliable measure. The correlational evidence obtained for it, however, seems to indicate that its meaningful variance is essentially a function of overall self-esteem. The correlation between the two discrepancy measures is 0·390, which is the highest correlation obtained for either of them. Evidently a favorable body image goes with a favorable personality image in most people. The correlations of these measures with other battery variables serve mainly to document an interpretation of self-ideal discrepancy in terms of self-esteem (high discrepancy going, of course, with low self-esteem).

There are many other rank comparisons that might provide information bearing on important aspects of overall functioning. For example, we might compare a subject's self-ranking with his ranking for 'people in general' or 'my friends'. Discrepancy in this case might reflect wilful independence or a sense of alienation. There are many such possibilities that warrant experimentation, but they have not been explored with the present trait lists.

Undoubtedly the comparison that would be most valuable of all would be that between self-ranking and the 'true' ranking of the subject. This would provide a measure of realism of self-description, or self-insight. Unfortunately, there is no good way of securing the true ranks. If we turn to other psychological tests that might furnish the true picture, we find that those most likely to yield information on any traits we are likely to employ for self-ranking are questionnaires—i.e. other tests which also utilize self-description as the measurement operation. An alternative to which some investigators have resorted is to use rankings by acquaintances as the true ranking. People vary, however, in the extent to which they are visible, or knowable, as well as in the extent to which they are apt to be systematically misperceived by others. For these and other reasons, this method will tend to accord greatest self-insight to the individual who is well liked, conspicuous, and outgoing.

The direct measurement of self-insight still seems a goal beyond easy reach, but it is possible to obtain pertinent information indirectly from self-description alone. The overuse of highly improbable descriptions (as in the L scale of the MMPI), for example, would be presumptive evidence of low insight. In the present battery, the author introduced a measure of unrealism of self-description that, in principle, should be capable of discriminating over a wider range of levels of self-insight. It makes use of pairs of adjectives which have very similar behavioral referents but differ greatly in connotative meaning. One word in each pair is rather negative or derogatory in tone, while the other is more favorable or neutral. Fifteen such pairs were devised. For testing purposes, they were placed in two lists in such a way that each list received one member of each pair and included altogether about half the negative words. The two lists contained the following words (arranged so that the members of each pair are side by side):

List 1	List 2
conceited	self-confident
gullible	trusting
reserved	unapproachable
amusing	silly
determined	stubborn
reckless	bold
practical-minded	unimaginative
insensitive	rugged
fearful	cautious
dominant	bossy
spontaneous	impulsive
thin-skinned	sensitive

List 1	*List 2*
compulsive	orderly
idealistic	impractical
eccentric	non-conformist

These two lists were incorporated into the Trait Ranking test and administered in two separate sessions. In each case, the subject was asked to rank the words in the list according to how well they described him. Like the self-ideal discrepancy measures, unrealism of self-description was scored in terms of a sum of rank differences between the two lists. A subject secured a low score by according the two members of each word pair similar rank positions in their respective lists. Since this would seem to require disregarding the emotional tone of the word in the interest of accuracy of description, we might best characterize this subject as displaying self-objectification. A high score may result simply from lack of self-awareness or self-reflection, so that both rankings entail a good deal of random response. More often, however, the high score probably reflects a defensive attitude manifested in a preference for the favorable terms and rejection of the more negative ones.

Unrealism of self-description proves to be essentially uncorrelated with self-ideal discrepancy, but interestingly enough, it displays similar patterns of covariation with certain other measures that are similar to those found for self-ideal discrepancy. The subject who is high on self-ideal discrepancy tends to report subjective distress, particularly anxiety symptoms, on other tests, as well as a lack of experienced control, especially in the context of social interaction. This proves to be true also for the subject who is *low* on unrealism—i.e. the subject we have characterized as self-objective. His distress, however, appears to be part of a more general pattern of independence, openness, and sensitivity. This suggests that he tends to accept discomfort as an inevitable consequence of a basic willingness to experience things. The questionnaire measures of distress, of course, in common with the low unrealism score, depend on a willingness to report shortcomings or 'symptoms'. The control correlates of unrealism refer primarily to the subjective realm. The high, or unrealistic, subject reports a possession of emotional control. The self-objective subject tends to report a lack of control over emotions, thoughts, and other internal processes.

Consistency with a socially defined standard

The optimal-personality concept that most obviously entails consistency with a socially defined standard is that of statistical normality. Closely related to this are adjustment concepts that stress conformity or compatibility with the group. We noted the shortcomings of such concepts in Chapter 2. At least one psychologist who conceptualizes the optimal condition in much different terms, however, has proposed a measure that seems directly to reflect conformity. Lecky (1945) was theoretically preoccupied with what he regarded as a basic integrative process tending toward ideational consistency. He considered the striving for internal consistency to be a universal tendency but recognized that people varied widely in the extent to which they achieved it.

He viewed the ideal individual as one who best succeeded in achieving consistency, but his proposal for assessing consistency rests strictly upon the questionable assumption that the most typical members of any group are those most likely to approximate the ideal. If we assume that the urge toward the adjustive state of consistency is strong in all of us, it may seem plausible that the mass of any group will be drawn toward the optimal condition, while a smaller number of less adjusted deviants will fail and thus differ in various ways from the mode. We immediately face a logical difficulty, however, when we recognize that any individual is subject to multiple classification in our society because he is a member of many groups. By Lecky's criterion, he could be a typical college student, Catholic, or basketball player, while failing to be a typical Midwesterner, philosophy major, or part-time sales clerk. He may voluntarily join certain groups because he finds them compatible with his own thinking and temperament and thus tend to become a typical member of them—but by Lecky's criterion, it would seem to make no difference in his assessed consistency whether the group happens to be the Unitarian Church, the Chicago police force, or the Ku Klux Klan. We can learn a great deal about an individual by knowing to what group his ideas, attitudes, and behavior conform, but this information can hardly have quite the meaning that Lecky assumed.

Lecky properly objected to a prevalent measurement orientation which equated neurosis with a preponderance of 'negative' behaviors or reactions and which sought to measure it through inventories of symptoms. The optimal state, in terms of such an approach, would be simply an absence of symptoms, but the alternative that Lecky offered seems even less defensible. He constructed a 200-item questionnaire which inventoried symptomatic behaviors in eight different areas. He then defined the integrated pattern as the set of mean scores for any given group. Departures from central tendency in either direction on any scale would be regarded as indicative of less consistency. Even if we ignore the emphasis on conformity and the problem of defining the group appropriate for any subject, we can find fundamental weaknesses in this proposal. It is actually a defective index of group conformity, since with items of low homogeneity and extreme response cut, there is a considerable difference between test score agreement and item-response agreement. In terms of item responses, the maximally conforming individual may be one who reports no symptomatic behaviors, no matter how many the average member of the group reports. Conformity to a test score mean is not the same thing as conformity to item score means.

If we wish to assess behavioral conformity or non-conformity, it would seem best for most purposes to do this in terms of specific test responses. It seems unwise to view such conformity in general as desirable or undesirable. That would surely depend on the particular response, on the relationship of this response to the rest of the individual's behavior, and on the group with which we compare him. In so far as deviance represents an independence requisite for constructive growth, it can obviously be preferable to conformity.

One pertinent measure employed in the research reported in this book was called *response idiosyncrasy*. This was simply a tally of responses that were relatively infrequent in three long questionnaires. With respect to its mode of derivation, the measure is similar to the F scale of the MMPI. For two reasons, however, it is likely to yield somewhat different information. For one thing, items of very extreme response cut were excluded from the present questionnaires. Therefore, the response idiosyncrasy score necessarily depends on responses that are less deviant than many used in the F scale. Second, the overall content of the present questionnaires covers a broader realm than does the MMPI and is focused less on psychopathological symptoms. The subject who scores high on response idiosyncrasy is essentially reporting feelings and attitudes that are relatively unpopular or unconventional in the context of a college population.

From present indications, this measure does not provide much important information about the optimal personality. It showed little marked correlation with variables outside the questionnaires from which it was scored. It should be noted, however, that this measure was treated as an incidental product of the present battery. No items were deliberately constructed with a view toward exploiting response idiosyncrasy. Indeed, item selections were made in such a way as to preclude a very satisfactory measure of this. There is a need for research designed systematically to explore the meaning of deviant responses in the context of many kinds of item content.

Granted that response popularity or conformity does not in general reflect characteristics we could consider optimal, there is still reason to think that consistency with *some* group-defined standard may reveal such information. The Strong Vocational Interest Blank provides a good illustration of the point. This test yields scores on a variety of occupational scales. For each scale, the items are keyed according to the difference between the responses of people in general and people in a specific occupation. If a subject responds consistently like people in general, he earns a flat profile of scores. Such an individual is likely to appear either apathetic or unsettled much of the time. The subject with sharply defined peaks in his occupational profile is likely to seem more free of conflict and capable of approaching life with a clear sense of direction. In short, a pattern that reflects response conformity to some specific group—whether it is engineers, artists, salesmen, or some other—is more indicative of the achievement of internal integration. This is true, of course, because any high score in this test represents a cohesive pattern of emotional investment. With a different set of items or a different selection of criterion groups for keying responses, this might not be the case. In the present battery, the sort of information conveyed by a peaked Strong profile is assumed to be reflected in the measure we have called differentiation of interest pattern.

Consistency with group-defined trends

A still different approach to the assessment of personality integration or optimal adjustment is one in which consistency within an individual's pattern of responses is measured but the nature of consistency itself is defined by trends within a social group. McQuitty (1952, 1953, 1954) has offered several proposals of this sort that are applicable to sets of multiple-choice items for which we have general population data. His chief proposals involve the calculation of a concomitance index for every pair of response alternatives that can be jointly chosen by any subject (e.g. alternative (a) for item 1 and alternative (a) for item 2; alternative (a) for item 1 and alternative (b) for item 2, etc.). The concomitance index is essentially an expression of the degree to which subjects giving one of the responses tend also to give the other one.

There are several things that can be done with the concomitance indices for a set of items. One procedure that McQuitty recommends is to form a matrix of all the indices that correspond to the set of item alternatives endorsed by the individual subject, and subject this matrix to factor analysis. There are some indications that the matrices obtained for normal subjects yield fewer factors than those obtained for psychotics. Performing a separate factor analysis for every individual one might wish to test, however, would be quite laborious. One of the simpler alternative procedures suggested by McQuitty is to calculate the mean of all the values in each individual's concomitance matrix. This mean will tend to be inversely related to the number of extractable factors.

A basic assumption underlying McQuitty's method is that if two responses have a marked tendency to appear jointly in the same individuals relative to their overall incidence in the general population, it is because they have a natural tendency to go together in consistent or organized patterns of behavior. A response combination that is infrequent is most likely to be found in an individual who is poorly organized and whose behavior at one moment shows little systematic relationship to his behavior at another moment. Two measures that rest on the same rationale—consistency with correlation and intra-factor consistency—were employed by the author in a study of child personality structure (see Cattell and Coan, 1959). The first of these seemed the more promising of the two and was applied as well in the present research battery.

Consistency with correlation is a somewhat cruder measure than some of McQuitty's proposals, but it is easier to apply and should yield basically the same kind of information. For the purpose of this measure, we select within any given questionnaire a number of pairs of items that display relatively high correlations. For each pair, we credit the subject one point if his responses are consistent with the direction of the correlation observed in the total sample. In the case of two binary items that correlate positively, for example, the subject earns one point for either an a-a or a b-b response combination. If the items are negatively correlated, he receives a point for an a-b pattern or a b-a pattern. Item pairs in three different questionnaires were utilized in the present research to obtain a score for consistency with correlation. It is unlikely that the measure, in its present application, is very dependent on any one type of item content.

In the earlier child research, consistency with correlation appeared to reflect an overall trend characterized by good organization, perseverance, and dynamic integration, but no more than a fraction of its total variance could be attributed to any one personality factor. It presents a similar picture in the present research. It does not correlate very highly with any other single variable studied, but it displays a consistent overall pattern of correlations which we can describe in terms of a positive relationship to variables involving control and organization and a negative relationship to variables involving distress or loss of control.

Chapter 5

The scope of awareness

Psychologists have long recognized the importance of individual differences in the range and contents of experience. They have often been concerned with variations attributable to inborn capacities, to the accidents of the life situation, and to the structure imposed by the school curriculum. They have realized, at the same time, that a major source of variation resides in the disposition of the individual to confront certain experiences, on the one hand, and his tendency to avoid situations in which he senses danger, on the other.

Because of the strong influence of Freud, this aspect of experience has been treated primarily in a negative form in the mainstream of personality theory. The main tools which psychoanalysis supplies for the description of individual behavior patterns and personality structures are the defense mechanisms, or anticathexes. The most basic of these, of course, is repression. According to Freud, the fundamental defensive maneuver for overcoming anxiety is a loss of awareness. This loss and the conflicts that precipitate it lie at the heart of all neuroses. By the same token, of course, retention of awareness would imply either the endurance of anxiety or the absence of neurotic conflict.

Freud obviously saw value in the broadening of awareness, for most of his therapeutic endeavors were directed toward an undoing or circumventing of repression. For several reasons, however, a positive concept of openness to experience never assumed a central place in his theoretical system. For one thing, his efforts to construct a personality theory began with an interest in explaining psychopathology, and while he moved gradually away from this focus in his later work, he retained a system of concepts better suited for the description and explanation of disturbance than for the elucidation of successful functioning. Second, Freud clung to a set of premises that prevented an adequate analysis, let alone a recognition of the importance, of conscious experience. By basic presupposition, he was an irrationalist and antivoluntarist. He felt that, in principle, conscious phenomena could not operate as causes of behavior and that, in fact, most behavior was governed by forces of which people are unaware. Thus, experience *per se* enjoys a somewhat questionable status in Freudian theory. The concept of repression has remained influential over the years, however. It has been widely borrowed by psychologists who reject most other Freudian concepts, and it echoes in a host of related ideas like selective inattention and perceptual defense.

A further shortcoming of Freudian theory that bears on the present subject matter is an overemphasis on a strong ego as a goal of normal development and of psychoanalytic therapy. In the context of Freud's use of the term *ego*, this means that supreme value is attached to contact with 'reality'. Both the growing child and the neurotic are expected to move toward a conception of themselves and the world that accords with the view of a detached scientific observer. We achieve health, then, not by becoming more aware in general, but by becoming more aware of 'what is' in the eyes of the analyst. The result is not a richer world of experience but the selection of a particular mode of experience, one characterized by thought systematically attuned to 'reality'.

From the standpoint of many other theorists, the Freudian outlook is decidedly lopsided. Realistic thinking is valued without adequate consideration as to whether it is the most natural mode of functioning in all situations or whether it is equally appropriate for everyone. Particularly disturbing to some is the fact that the Freudian view seems to attach much greater value to scientific thought than to artistic thought. Indeed, creative thinking itself poses an awkward problem for Freudian theory, because so many of the people who have analyzed it have pointed to the vital role of a stage of unsystematic, unregulated thought. The products that one achieves through continued exercise of the 'higher' processes of the ego alone seem almost destined to be of inferior quality. At best, they will not be especially innovative.

Some of the defects of the Freudian ego concept have been repaired over the years by an elaboration of the functions assigned to it, but the need for a more suitable treatment of creativity has remained a rather embarrassing challenge. A possible remedy is offered by Kris (1952), who accounts for creativity and various related phenomena in terms of 'regression in the service of the ego'. Such a concept implies, of course, that the ego on occasion can relax its hold on mental processes or refrain temporarily from operating for the sake of subsequent utilization of the enriched contents gained by regression. This may be the most satisfactory way of accounting for creativity and for the imaginal breadth of some well functioning people in a psychoanalytical framework. In the long run, however, it might be preferable to try a more fundamental modification of the Freudian ego concept or to abandon it altogether.

In the main, personality theorists who adhere more closely to the humanistic tradition in psychology tend to display a higher regard for openness to experience as such. They usually conceive of personal growth in terms of a progressive unfolding of the individual's potentialities for various kinds of experience and expression and his encounters with ever new situations in the world around him. They see a failure of growth in a clinging to rudimentary modes of experiencing or in an escape from individual expression through adjustive conformity. Creativity poses no special problem within such a framework, for richness and naturalness of experience are stressed in place of realism. Creativity, spontaneity, and independence are seen as closely interdependent facets of maturity.

This view is characteristic of most theorists who have been strongly influenced by phenomenology and existentialism and of those who have moved from the mainstream of psychoanalytic thought in a more humanistic direction. Among those who have deviated from a Freudian position, Jung in particular was concerned with elucidating the various modes of experience that one is destined to encounter on the road to full personal development. His theoretical system is by far the most comprehensive experientially based treatment of human personality that has been presented to date. As a scientific theory, the Jungian system stands in need of further refinement. For those who wish to extend our explorations to a broader range of human experience, it is a fund of insights that we cannot afford to overlook.

The research of Fitzgerald

Over the past two or three decades, psychologists have performed a host of studies inspired by concepts bearing in some way on the openness or restriction of experience—e.g. perceptual defense, complexity, and tolerance of ambiguity. Perhaps the first major effort to measure openness to experience *per se*, was the Experience Inquiry devised by Fitzgerald (1966a, 1966b). Fitzgerald set out to assess empirically Schachtel's concept of world-openness, which he regarded as a modification of Kris's concept of regression in the service of the ego. He constructed a 56-item questionnaire. This contained some items borrowed from Ås, O'Hara, and Munger (1962), that appeared to tap five principal things: tolerance for regressive experiences, tolerance for logical inconsistencies, constructive use of regression, altered states, and peak experiences. To these, a number of additional items designed to tap capacity for regressive experiences and tolerance for the irrational were added.

On the whole, we might expect Fitzgerald's items to reflect an openness to experiences that entail disorder or a lack of deliberate control. Correlating Inquiry scores with those from other scales, Fitzgerald found evidence that his scale reflected a looseness of repression and that in men openness was associated with anxiety. On word association and object sorting tests, the high scorers proved better able to shift to less regulated modes of thinking. This would seem to indicate that they possess a certain flexibility that low scorers lack and that they have some control over the occurrence of regressive experience. Important sex differences appeared on an adjective checklist. High-scoring males tended to describe themselves as inwardly sensitive, artistic, and irritable, while high-scoring females tended to describe themselves as more outgoing and aggressive.

The items of the Experience Inquiry were assembled on a rational basis and were designed to cover several aspects of openness. It is interesting, therefore, to find that they proved to have fairly high internal consistency. The Kuder–Richardson reliability estimate for the Inquiry as a whole was 0·81. A cluster analysis revealed three major cluster domains that are evidently interdependent to some degree (Fitzgerald, 1966a, p. 657):

(I) openness to inner experience and altered states of consciousness, with both a tolerance and a capacity for regressive experiences, (II) a desire for a closed, orderly, predictable, explainable environment and an intolerance for uncontrolled states of consciousness, and (III) intolerance for unusual personal and interpersonal experiences.

The Experience Inventory

Fitzgerald's work constitutes a sound beginning in the study of openness to experience, but it is important to recognize that his questionnaire is limited by its heavy (and, of course, deliberate) emphasis on phenomena of a 'regressive' nature. It would be valuable to know whether the individual who has a capacity for this kind of experience is likely to be more open to various kinds of experience that do not contain a distinctly regressive element. Ideally, we should assess the individual's capacity for all basic kinds of experience. Such a goal is not within immediate reach, however, because an adequate analysis of this total realm has never been made.

There are various logical classifications of the total realm of experience, of course, that can provide useful guidelines and help to ensure that in any broad exploration of openness we do not neglect any facet of major importance. With respect to the contents of experience, we might start with the three broad categories suggested by Mason (1961)—the external environment, cognitive activity, and noncognitive inner experience. With respect to modes of experience, Jung's attitudes (introversion and extroversion) and psychic functions (thinking, feeling, sensation, and intuition) surely represent possible dimensions of basic significance.

If we are going to consider the diverse phenomena represented by all such categories, it should be evident that we are likely to encounter some forms of experience that will be mutually independent, if not mutually exclusive. According to Jung, the two basic attitudes tend to be mutually exclusive, as do the two rational functions and the two irrational functions. Thus, an emphasis on extroversion would tend to preclude introversion, an emphasis on thinking would tend to preclude feeling, etc. Jung insists, however, that actual people always display more complexity than do the ideal pure types of his system. Furthermore, he believes that a highly developed individual tends to transcend the polarities of the attitude–function system, and that he should possess a greater capacity for all types of experience than should an individual who has failed to develop.

On the basis of extant theory and evidence, it is difficult to know what patterns one might find in people in general. It is conceivable that much of the variance in the general population is governed by a general factor of openness to experience. On the other hand, there can be little doubt that some people are selectively open. They may welcome one type of experience while avoiding or suppressing another. The first type may even serve as a defense against the second type. Thus, one may welcome experiences of a masculine nature while avoiding those of a feminine nature. One may deal in a detached, analytical, or rational way with a wide range of events and phenomena while denying that questions of worth or value are applicable or meaningful. One may seek an endless series of sensual experiences while avoiding any consideration of their personal meaning or broader implications. One may stay in noisy crowded places to avoid experiences that arise in a solitary setting, or one may indulge in fantasy rather than face the threat of real social interaction.

The problem is actually a bit more complicated than it might seem at first glance, since there are various levels on which any given stimulus or situation might be experienced. This is recognized in the well-known clinical distinction between facing and working through things on an intellectual level and facing them on an emotional level, but there is more involved than just alternative modes of apprehension. There seem to be vast individual differences in sensitivity. One individual may seek large amounts of stimulation of any kind that occurs to him and appear unable to obtain enough. On closer examination, we may find that much of the stimulation has little effect on him. He is relatively unreactive to stimuli that others find quite disturbing, basically perhaps because of the way his nervous system is constructed. Another individual, who is constitutionally more prone to autonomic upsets, may have to ration his stimulation to avoid an excess. We might be tempted to regard the former individual as more open to experience were it not for the fact that the more sensitive person readily experiences very intense sensations that his insensitive counterpart may never encounter.

The contrast is still sharper when we note that sensitivity may mean additional qualities of experience as well as greater intensity. Thus, a highly sensitive person may readily experience strong empathic reactions to people, intense aesthetic reactions, vivid images, and affective responses of various kinds. Another person who is capable of a much more limited range of effects may relish bright lights, loud noises, and social interaction in a quantity that the more sensitive man would find exhausting or intolerable. In a thorough investigation of openness to experience, it would seem essential to consider not only the range and intensity of the stimuli an individual seeks but his basic capacity for experience as well.

A further complication that any large-scale investigation must take into account is that a given situation may have basically different meanings for different people and thus provide an occasion for different kinds of experience. Thus, the sexual relationship may be viewed primarily as an occasion for sensory pleasure or an occasion for emotional intimacy, and it may be sought or avoided for either reason. Social interaction in general may mean many different things. The person who is relatively insensitive to the effects of other people or who views people in a dehumanized way may interact freely on a superficial level. He may seek or avoid social interaction depending on whether it subserves needs that are essentially non-social in character. A second individual may tend to experience a loss of personal identity in any social encounter. He may either relish or fear the loss and act accordingly. A third individual, whose sense of personal identity and individuality is far more firmly fixed, may seek in interaction an intimacy of contact that he never achieves.

In view of all the above considerations, we cannot realistically regard the thorough assessment of openness as an easy task. It would be essential to consider not just the experiences the individual has or the objects with which he interacts, but to determine what experiences he has in relation to what objects. The problem is worthy of large-scale research in its own right. It would be presumptuous to think we could do the matter full justice within the context of a research project focused on a somewhat different issue. Nevertheless, openness to experience is clearly relevant to the concerns of the optimal personality in general, and it seemed important to give as much attention to this domain of variables as the demands for economical testing would permit.

Fitzgerald's questionnaire served as a starting point, but it seemed desirable to broaden the scope of item content to embrace experiences not particularly regressive in nature. A number of items were designed to tap modes of experience suggested by the Jungian attitude–function system. Collectively the new items might be said to tap an assortment of associations, memories, ideas, impulses, feeling states, and fantasy and dream phenomena. Altogether, a set of 114 true–false items, which was entitled the Experience Inventory, was compiled. This included 37 items borrowed essentially intact from Fitzgerald's questionnaire, as well as a few items inspired by portions of the Fitzgerald list that were not used directly. Items found in preliminary trials to have extreme response cuts (or difficulty levels) were excluded. It was found easiest to construct items for which the *true* answer represented greater openness, but an effort was made to construct 'negative' items too. A few items with no clearly open answer were also included for the sake of whatever clarification they might afford in later interpretations. Such items were utilized where there was reason to suspect that the most natural dimensions might entail a choice between alternative types of experience.

The Experience Inventory, in the form finally incorporated into the research battery, contained the following items:

1. Sometimes I get so absorbed in my thoughts that I fail to notice a lot of things going on around me.
2. I think any painting or sculpture should represent something recognizable.
3. Sometimes I enjoy thinking through problems in a very logical, systematic way.
4. I often invent formulae or schemes to organize my ideas or help me remember something.
5. I often feel a need to gather a lot of clear-cut facts before I come to a conclusion about something.
6. I often enjoy playing with theories or abstract ideas.
7. To be worth reading, a poem should say something that makes fairly clear sense to any intelligent person.
8. I often try to formulate general principles to account for things that I read about and think about.
9. I often enjoy learning some clear-cut concrete facts about people, historical events, or scientific matters.
10. I often feel a need to think things out very carefully before deciding what to do or how to react to something.
11. I often enjoy taking apart clocks and other mechanical things to see how they work.
12. I prefer not to spend much time dwelling on the past.
13. I have sometimes enjoyed taking apart plants or parts of plants to see how they were composed inside.
14. Often when I have to choose between doing two different things, I try very hard to decide which is really more important in the overall scheme of things.
15. I often try to understand the moods and feelings of other people I am with.
16. It is very important to me to feel that what I am doing is very worthwhile or meaningful.
17. I dislike having to spend much time planning things out in advance.
18. I like to play with ideas that other people consider strange or improper.
19. I have sometimes had vivid visual images that have held

c*

my fascination for some time as I sat or lay still with my eyes closed.

20. Right now, if I try, I can imagine the aroma of a broiled steak and experience it so intensely that it seems almost real.

21. I have often enjoyed simply sitting still and imagining the sound of music when there was actually no music being played.

22. I sometimes get annoyed by people who like to talk about very abstract theoretical matters.

23. I have sometimes had a very strong impression that a certain thing has happened even though there seems to be no way I could really know.

24. Sometimes I seem to be able to receive thoughts from certain people I know well when they are not with me.

25. I have been so madly in love with another person that I have found it difficult to think of anything else for days at a time.

26. Occasionally I have experienced a state in which it seemed hard to tell just where the boundary line was between me and my surroundings.

27. I try to keep all my thoughts directed along realistic lines and avoid flights of fancy.

28. At times in my life I have spent a lot of time wondering why I experience myself as this person in this body and not as someone else.

29. I often feel an intense excitement when I see certain colors or color combinations.

30. I sometimes get a great deal of enjoyment from listening to recordings of unusual sound or sound effects.

31. I often have a strong feeling, which I cannot explain, that the situation I am in is one I have been in before.

32. I find some kinds of puzzles—mechanical, mathematical, etc.—very boring.

33. When reading a story or watching a play or movie, I sometimes get so wrapped up in the actions or problems of a character that I almost forget where I am.

34. Sometimes when watching the movements of an athlete or a dancer, I feel a certain straining or movement, as if I were performing the action myself.

35. Sometimes when I am listening to music, I feel a strong wave of excitement that seems to affect my whole body.

36. Sometimes when I am reading poetry or looking at a work of art, I feel a strong wave of excitement that seems to affect my whole body.

37. I sometimes feel annoyed by people who get very emotional about different things.

38. I have sometimes experienced a very powerful feeling of movement when looking at certain paintings or pieces of sculpture.

39. I have sometimes had the feeling that my own life and the world around me were completely meaningless.

40. When I come to a conclusion, I always have a good idea of how I have arrived at it and what facts it is based on.

41. For a period of time when I was a child, I pretended to play and do things with an imaginary companion.

42. I often have dreams about people I have never seen before.

43. I sometimes daydream about being in strange and distant places.

44. I prefer not to waste my time daydreaming.

45. I have sometimes imagined myself as some kind of animal.

46. I have sometimes imagined myself as a member of the opposite sex.

47. In my daydreams I imagine myself performing all sorts of actions that I would never really carry out.

48. Fairly often I dream in color.

49. Fairly often when I am dreaming, I know I'm dreaming and feel that I have some control over my dream.

50. I sometimes daydream about having some special power or about being able to do remarkable things that I cannot really do.

51. At times I have solved problems or created something (such as music or poetry) in my dreams.

52. I seldom have dreams at night.

53. Most of my dreams seem to be meaningless.

54. I often think of various people I know as resembling certain animals.

55. I often see things—like faces, animals, etc.—in cloud formations.

56. I sometimes think of trees as expressing certain feelings, attitudes, or movements.

57. Certain sounds seem to give impressions like those of colors, so that I can almost see colors when I hear these sounds.

58. In some kinds of sounds—such as the wind, the noise of machinery, etc.—I often imagine I hear voices.

59. I can directly recall things that happened before I was five years old (not just from what people have told me since then).

60. I often start thinking silly or comical thoughts in situations where I am supposed to be serious.

61. At times the solution to a problem has occurred to me in a dream.

62. It is possible that there are species on other planets which are far more highly evolved than human beings.

63. It is possible that the mind can leave the body and experience things at a great distance from the body.

64. It is definitely impossible for one person to read another person's mind.

65. I prefer people who are constant and predictable to those who are very changeable.

66. The idea that any of the flying saucers people have sighted come from outer space is pretty silly. They can all be explained in other ways.

67. Children should read stories about real things, not stories about fantastic things like fairies, dragons, and giants.

68. At times I have felt a strong urge to do something shocking in a public gathering.

69. At times I have felt a momentary pleasure at seeing someone else get hurt or embarrassed.

70. Sometimes I have felt a strange thrill at the thought of being forcibly controlled or even hurt by someone else.

71. At times when I have been sick or needed help, I have enjoyed having someone else take care of me.

72. I often feel a strong need to be completely alone.

73. At times I feel a painful sense of loneliness and want very much to share an experience with someone else.

74. At least once in my life I have thought about committing suicide.

75. Although I wouldn't actually do it, I can imagine myself killing another human being.

76. I have sometimes imagined performing sexual acts that many people consider unnatural.

77. I have sometimes felt a strong physical attraction to certain other members of my own sex.

78. People are intolerable who take 'sacred' things in a light and humorous way.
79. I would like to get beyond the world of logic and reason and experience something new and different.
80. I like to indulge in emotions and sensations with the feeling of just 'letting go'.
81. I would enjoy a contest in a carnival in which I had to break a pile of dishes.
82. I enjoy 'wild' parties.
83. I find myself uncomfortable in the presence of unconventional or 'peculiar' people.
84. Sometimes I have had the impression that the walls or the ceiling were moving and changing size or shape, even though I knew that this was impossible.
85. I think that our most intense experiences can be communicated in words to others.
86. Eventually everything will be explained by the laws of science.
87. It is often better to act upon one's feelings than upon a logically reasoned plan.
88. I usually prefer to do things in tried ways rather than new and different ways.
89. I have had experiences which inspired me to write a poem or a story, or make up a humorous tale, or paint a picture.
90. I am often bored when left alone.
91. I avoid 'putting people on' or doing things just to see the reactions of others.
92. Sometimes I imagine what it would be like if the world were different, e.g. if there were no laws, if we could read each other's minds, etc.
93. While lying in bed or reclining in a chair I sometimes find myself perceiving faces, objects, etc. in the shadows of the light or the design of the ceiling, etc.
94. At times I see unusual relations between things.
95. Poetry has little effect on me.
96. I am quick to see 'double meanings' in things people are saying or in what I am reading.
97. I usually try to understand my dreams.
98. Solutions to problems or ideas for new projects come to me 'out of the blue.'
99. When solving a problem I am inclined to consider all possibilities even though some are unrealistic or absurd.

100. Sometimes I wander off into my own thoughts while doing a routine task so that I actually forget that I am doing the task, and then find, a few minutes later, that I have completed it without even being aware of what I was doing.

101. At times I have carried on real conversations with another person while I was asleep (e.g. with someone who walked into my room).

102. At times I have focused on something so hard that I went into a kind of benumbed state of consciousness, or at other times into a state of extraordinary calm and serenity.

103. I can look at an object—a leaf, a stone, a flower—for a long time, continuing to discover different things about it.

104. At times I have actively stared at something familiar and had it become very strange before my eyes.

105. I have had the experience of doing some task in the middle of the night (e.g. jotting down a note, answering a phone call) with no memory the next morning of having done it.

106. I have never had a strange or weird experience.

107. I have had the experience of being caught up by music or dancing, becoming so enraptured by it, and having it live and express itself through me so that I seemed to cease to be.

108. There have been times when I have been completely immersed in nature or in art and had a feeling of awe sweep over me so that I felt as if my whole state of consciousness were somehow temporarily altered.

109. I have experienced moments of inspiration and creativity, when artistic expression, ideas, or the solutions to problems I had struggled with came to me with a special intensity and clarity.

110. I would like to try parachute jumping.

111. At amusement parks I usually avoid roller-coasters, ferris wheels and similar 'thrill' rides.

112. I have been so strongly in love with someone that I somehow felt that my own self was fading and I was at one with the beloved person.

113. It is possible that we had a previous existence of which we have no memory.

114. It is possible that our sense organs (i.e. eyes, ears, etc.) do not bring us our most important information.

An analysis of the Experience Inventory

Since most of the items in the Experience Inventory were deliberately designed to tap openness, it was possible to assign them an *a priori* keying for this variable. On the basis of this keying, a total openness score was obtained for all subjects who took the complete battery so that its relationship to other measures could be studied. There remained doubt, however, as to the propriety of regarding openness as a single dimension. For this reason, a factor analysis of the 114 items was undertaken.

The items were intercorrelated on the basis of the responses of 383 subjects, who were drawn from various psychology classes. When squared multiple correlations were used as communality estimates, the first principal axis accounted for about one-quarter of the total variance. This is a relatively large amount for a problem of 114 variables, but it still leaves a good deal to be explained by other factors. All succeeding principal axes were considerably smaller, however, and sixteen were extracted altogether and rotated to a position of oblique simple structure.

The rotated factors were arranged in order of decreasing variance. As one might expect, the ones near the beginning of the series prove to be far more clearly interpretable than those later in the series. There is necessarily a better basis for interpreting them, since they load more items and are well represented in the items they load most highly. In all, the first nine factors appear to be rather clearly interpretable. It is reasonably certain that each of these would prove replicable if the items were re-factored on the basis of the responses of another sample of comparable size. Factors 10 through 16 must be considered of more doubtful identity. As for the specific nature of the factors, we may make the following observations on the basis of the content of the items loaded by each of them:

Factor 1
The items loaded negatively by this factor report a variety of aesthetic experiences. Those at the positive pole reflect a more prosaic orientation. We may call this *aesthetic insensitivity* v. *aesthetic sensitivity*. The items that best represent the unique content of this factor include 2, 7, 90, and 95 at the positive pole and 36, 38, 89, and 108 at the negative pole.

Factor 2

The positive items indicate an inclination to perceive things in various odd and novel ways and to entertain unusual associations to all objects of perception. Negatively loaded items suggest fact-mindedness and adherence to logical and systematic thought. Actually the factor is poorly marked at the negative pole. Among the many items of substantial positive loading are 54, 55, 56, 84, and 93. An appropriate title for this factor would be *unusual perceptions and associations*.

Factor 3

If factor 2 involves a certain freedom in the perceptual realm, factor 3 involves freedom in the realm of abstraction and thought. Here we see the sort of willingness to entertain novel and unusual ideas that is likely to be high in avid readers of fantasy and science fiction. Items 6, 8, 18, and 99 illustrate this quality rather well. A reasonable title would be *openness to theoretical or hypothetical ideas*.

Factor 4

A number of items loaded by factor 4 suggest an access to unconscious processes that favors their utilization for creative or constructive purposes. The subject reports creation and problem solving in dreams, reception of telepathic communications, and the experience of 'inspiration'. The best loaded items include 24, 49, 51, 61, and 98. We might call this *constructive utilization of fantasy and dreams*.

Factor 5

This factor loads such items as 31, 63, 113, and 114 on the positive side and 64, 66, and 67 on the negative side. It appears to involve *openness to unconventional views of reality* v. *adherence to mundane material reality*. We might expect this factor to be closely related to factor 3. In comparing the two factors with respect to item content, we find that the high scorer on factor 3 describes himself as open while the high scorer on factor 5 directly indicates an interest in a specific class of unconventional ideas (which the low scorer explicitly rejects).

Factor 6

The high scorer dreams in color, daydreams, experiences painful loneliness, tends to be absentminded, and reports some experiences like those of the high scorer on factor 2. The low scorer reports an absence of night dreams and says he avoids both fantasy and rumination about the past. Items 48 and 100 have high positive loadings, while items 12, 27, 44, and 52 have high negative loadings. If we go by the most prevalent theme of the salient items, this is *indulgence in fantasy* v. *avoidance of fantasy*.

Factor 7

This is clearly a factor of *deliberate and systematic thought*. The high scorer frequently experiences a need for this and may find it pleasurable, as we see in items 5, 9, 10, and 14. On the other hand, there is little in the item content to suggest a rigid avoidance of unsystematic or capricious thought. Such a defensive pattern seems more likely in the low scorer on factor 2.

Factor 8

The high scorer reports fantasies of possessing special powers, of performing actions he would never really carry out, and of being in strange places. The remaining item content is consistent with an interpretation of this factor in terms of *unrealistic fantasy content*. The items that best represent the factor are 43, 47, and 50.

Factor 9

The low scorer indicates a desire for exciting activities and stimulation, as in items 82 and 110. The high scorer is best characterized by the things he dislikes or avoids—'thrill' rides, people who talk about abstract theory, doing things in new and different ways, changeable people, and unconventional people (see items 22, 65, 88, and 111). We might call this *preference for predictable constancy* v. *excitement*.

Factor 10

The most highly loaded items (25, 73, and 112) entail a need for interpersonal relationships. They refer to absorbing experiences of romantic love, a painful sense of loneliness, and boredom in solitary circumstances. This interpretation, however, is a bit too narrow to fit the content of the other loaded items (such as 46, 79, 80, and 102). The common core of this factor is actually hard to identify, but a tentative general label that affords a reasonable fit would be *need for involvement*.

Factor 11

The item content loaded by this factor seems superficially to be very heterogeneous. Thus, we find from the four most salient items (33, 34, 71, 81) that the high scorer responds empathically to athletes, dancers, and story characters, that he would enjoy breaking a pile of dishes, and that he has enjoyed being cared for when ill. Perhaps the common element is a flexible 'ego-boundary' or a willingness to abandon one's customary or expected role. A tentative title would be *ability to relax personal identity and control*.

Factor 12

The high scorer reports thoughts of suicide, the experience of anomie, masochistic pleasure, a need for solitude, and impulses to do shocking things in public (items 39, 68, 70, 72, and 74). Several items suggest a sort of Hamlet syndrome. Perhaps a core ingredient is actually self-destructive fantasy. A broad tentative label which, in several of its senses, fits much of the item content is *experience of alienation*.

Still greater difficulties are encountered in the interpretation of the remaining factors. They are all of small variance and are effectively represented by very few items. None of them is free of ambiguity, but for the sake of initial approximation, they may be labeled as follows:

Factor 13. Experience of unconventional impulses v. *motivational restraint*.

Factor 14. Relaxation of conscious control of thought and action.

Factor 15. Passive enjoyment of imagery.

Factor 16. Scientific analysis and speculation.

It is obvious that many of these factors involve some sort of openness to experience or involve individual differences in the scope of experience or awareness, but the open end of a given factor may be either at the positive or the negative pole. Each factor was rotated in such a way that the loadings would be predominantly positive, and in some cases the loaded items were mainly of a non-open type. In some factors, the two poles seem merely to involve contrasting forms of experience, each of which might tend to preclude the other. More often than not, however, one end can be reasonably viewed as more open than the other. Thus, for the first five factors, the open poles would be negative, positive, positive,

positive, and positive (or low, high, high, high, high with respect to scales of factor scores).

Since the solution was an oblique one, the factors are moderately intercorrelated. The intercorrelations range from zero to 0·51, and there is an overall tendency for the later, smaller-variance factors to be more independent than the larger factors. It is illuminating to study these correlations, for wherever they are substantial in size, they follow a simple rule quite consistently: factors in which the open end is high intercorrelate positively, as do those in which the open end is low, while the correlations between the two sets are negative. In short, the factors intercorrelate in a manner that is quite consistent with the notion of a general openness factor. It is obvious that if we did a second-order analysis, the first second-order factor would be a factor of general openness. Thus, our dissection of the Experience Inventory leaves us with the impression that a number of semi-independent components of openness can be distinguished but that they are subject to the influence of a weak but pervasive general factor.

Much more work needs to be done with measures of the present type, and further research has been done with the components of the Experience Inventory. In this more recent work, it was deemed most fruitful to concentrate on the realm represented by the relatively clear factors near the beginning of the above series. Efforts to date have provided evidence for the replicability of the first seven factors and have resulted in the construction of a shorter, revised Experience Inventory which contains refined scales for those seven factors (see Coan, 1972).

The scope of early memory

People vary enormously in the extent to which they can recall childhood events. There are some who retain impressions that they trace to the first or second year of life. There are others who can remember nothing that happened before age six or seven. There is reason to suspect that access in conscious experience to the events of the early years is related to openness in general. Those who are able readily to enter the world of children and understand their feelings and perceptions seem, as a rule, to maintain this access. They are able to preserve a certain freshness of outlook that most people lose with advancing age to the extent that they remain in touch with their own past. Freud supports this overall impression by explaining childhood amnesia in terms of repression. On the basis of Freudian theory, we should expect the loss of recall of the early years to be a direct function of the individual's tendency in general to employ repression—a mechanism that restricts the range of content available to conscious experience.

The situation is probably a bit more complicated than this, however. Freud undoubtedly exaggerates the role of repression as a determinant of childhood amnesia. The child's basic capacity for storing and retaining impressions is probably a far more important source of individual differences in later recall. This capacity will obviously depend partly on the child's basic intelligence, and it may depend even more on how his life is organized. He is more likely to recall events that fit into a meaningful pattern or structure than events that he views as a disconnected series of chance happenings. It is conceivable, of course, that a certain kind of spontaneity or openness will make for poor retention.

Perhaps a still more important source of variation in early recall is the individual's predisposition to dwell or to avoid dwelling on past events. Some people who eagerly seek new experiences have a habit of always 'facing forward' and display a limited concern with things that have already occurred. Such an orientation, of course, would preclude some of the experiences available to a person who remains more closely tied to his past. In any case, the individual most likely to display a rich recollection of his childhood is the one who makes a practice of reviewing early events frequently. He may do this in a persistent effort to find an overall meaning in the total pattern of his life. The effect may be highly constructive, and the practice may even be indispensable if he happens to be a child therapist or a skilled writer of children's literature. On the other hand, it may be a means of escaping from present experience or an obsessive habit with limited adjustive value.

By itself, the ability to recall early events in one's life would seem to represent an openness to one realm of experience, but in view of all the above considerations, its relationship to other sorts of openness is not altogether obvious. One may have many motives for recalling or trying to recall childhood events. In addition, there are important variations in the mode of recalling. Behaviorists in theory, and psychoanalysts in practice, have stressed verbal mediation. There is no doubt that words lend a certain form to thought and to the ongoing events in one's life. Verbal structuring may facilitate the storing of a childhood event and provide a handle by which one can retrieve it years later. Yet psychological theorists (perhaps because they are usually such verbal people themselves) often seem to attach undue importance to the role of words in thinking and remembering. The writer finds that many of his own lasting childhood impressions—particularly for events that occurred before he was three years of age—center around salient feeling states for which he has not yet found suitable descriptive terms. Undoubtedly, the extent to which events are and can be subjected to verbal structuring varies with the age at which they occur, and it varies from one individual to another. As tools of thinking and recalling, the value of words is really somewhat equivocal. They enable us to perform some mental feats of a logical character that would not otherwise be possible, and since they serve as devices for abstracting, they permit a certain overview of wide spans of events. On the other hand, they tend to impose an artificial structure of their own, and they operate as filtering devices. They rivet our attention on those features that are repeatedly selected as objects of social communication, and they help us to ignore those features that people in our culture have not learned to talk about. Thus, words enable us to function a bit like the filing systems and mechanical contrivances that we employ to store large quantities of information in standard skeletal form.

A heavy reliance on verbal mediation is likely to ensure that certain kinds of early experiences will not be retained or later recalled. Sometimes an early event stands forth in clear relief and leaves a lasting impression because we sense in it a basic or prototypic mode of experiencing ourselves or some part of the world. In such a case, there is no ready verbal label that we can apply because we have not encountered the experience before and have thus had no opportunity to acquire a label. If, in addition, the experience is of the sort that adults have learned to ignore, we may find that no simple verbal designation is available. In the course of repeated subsequent recall of the event, we may impose an orderly verbal structure upon it, while losing touch with its most vital affective content.

In the recall of some events, one may be able to re-experience many of the impressions that he encountered at the time of occurrence. In other cases, little is left but an abstract verbal structure. We see the extreme instance of the latter in an event that we do not remember directly but know about because we have heard it reported by others. Our present concern, of course, is with events for which there is some sort of direct recall. It would seem important in studying these events to know what kinds of impressions are retained, but it would obviously be difficult to distinguish between impressions that are based directly on a memory trace and those that are manufactured in one's efforts to reconstruct the event.

The recall of childhood events is definitely a very complex matter. In view of its possible bearing on openness to experience and other variables under investigation, it seemed worthwhile to secure whatever information a very brief questionnaire might yield. For this purpose, a test called Early Memories was constructed. It contains the following items:

1. Very *briefly* describe the earliest event in your life that you can directly recall (not an event that you know about just because someone else has told you it happened).
2. How old were you at that time? (Estimate if necessary, but be as precise as you can.)
3. Can you remember the name of your first-grade teacher (the earliest one if you had more than one)? If so, what was her (his) name?
4. Can you remember in what part of the room you sat in the first grade? If so, where did you sit?
5. Right now, what specific things can you remember that happened BEFORE YOU WERE EIGHT YEARS OLD? (Indicate by checking the appropriate spaces.)
   Can you remember:
   a. listening to a story before you were 8?   Yes____No____
   b. playing a game before you were 8?   Yes____No____
   c. a dream you had before you were 8?   Yes____No____
   d. a toy or other possession to which you
      felt strongly attached before you were 8?   Yes____No____
   e. a time when you got hurt (physically or
      emotionally) before you were 8?   Yes____No____
   f. a time when you were afraid before you
      were 8?   Yes____No____
   g. a time when you were embarrassed or
      ashamed before you were 8?   Yes____No____
   h. a time when you were very angry before
      you were 8?   Yes____No____
   i. a time when you were very pleasantly
      excited before you were 8?   Yes____No____
   j. a particular place where you liked to
      spend a lot of time before you were 8?   Yes____No____

6. In some of our memories of early events, there is some
   particular impression, sensation, or image that seems to linger
   in our minds. The impression appears to be very close to
   what we actually experienced at the time of the event, so that
   we seem to feel, see, or hear something just as we did long
   ago. Of course, this is only true for some people and not for
   others. As you think about things that happened in the first
   seven or eight years of your life, what kinds of impressions
   do you experience (if any)? (Please check where appropriate.)

   _____ visual images (of people, places, etc.)
   _____ sounds
   _____ odors
   _____ skin sensations (heat, cold, textures, etc.)
   _____ pain
   _____ tastes
   _____ feelings of movement or muscular effort
   _____ moods or emotions
   _____ no particular impression

The instrument was designed with a view to economy of
administration. It might be worthwhile to attempt a more extensive inventory of remembered early events, but this would be time
consuming. The present test—particularly the last question—is
obviously subject to response biases, but there is no easy remedy for
this. Three scores were derived from this test for use with other
battery measures: age of earliest memory (based on question
2), number of specific early memories (based on questions 3, 4,
and 5), and variety of revived impressions (based on question
6).

Miscellaneous activities

One further test was added to the battery to provide information
pertaining to the scope of experience. It occurred to the writer
that the Experience Inventory, with its heavy concentration on
feelings, thoughts, fantasies, sensations, and images, might tend
to favor the solitary, introverted experiencer. It is conceivable that
some subjects who will manifest little openness on such a questionnaire will be people who seek new experience through physical
and social activity. They might report a limited range of subjective
phenomena, since their attention would be focused more on the
environment. To test this possibility, battery subjects were given

the following list and asked to indicate the activities in which they had participated:

1. Running for student-body office in high school or college.
2. Running for office in a fraternity, sorority, or other campus organization (including high school organizations).
3. Being a member of an athletic team or recreational club in high school or college. (Subjects were asked to specify the activities involved.)
4. Being a cheerleader.
5. Being a pompon girl.
6. Being a baton twirler.
7. Taking part in a speech contest.
8. Taking part in a rodeo.
9. Speaking before a group of at least 200 people.
10. Performing before a large group (singing, playing a musical instrument, acting, etc.).
11. Participating in a civil rights protest.
12. Participating in a public protest action for any other purpose.
13. Dancing any step currently or recently in vogue (e.g. watusi, frug, jerk, monkey, swim, twist, surf, Madison).
14. Roller skating.
15. Skate boarding.
16. Ice skating.
17. Skiing.
18. Riding on a toboggan or bobsled.
19. Swimming.
20. Diving from a high board.
21. Swimming with a face mask or snorkel.
22. Swimming underwater with scuba or other equipment.
23. Surfboard riding.
24. Water skiing.
25. Fishing.
26. Deep-sea fishing.
27. Sailboating.
28. Speedboat racing.
29. Rowing or paddling a boat (rowboat, canoe, kayak, etc.).
30. Riding the rapids in a boat.
31. Backpacking.
32. Mountain climbing with mountain climbing equipment.
33. Hunting with a rifle.

34. Horseback riding.
35. Riding a motorcycle.
36. Riding in a motorcycle race.
37. Riding in an auto race.
38. Flying in an airplane.
39. Flying in a helicopter.
40. Parachute jumping.
41. Jumping on a trampoline.
42. Jumping from the roof of a house or garage.
43. Jumping on a pogo stick.
44. Riding a bicycle.
45. Riding a unicycle.
46. Walking on stilts.

This test, known as the Activity Checklist, yields one overall score for miscellaneous activity. The items cover several kinds of social, athletic, and recreational pursuits, and it would be worthwhile in future research to examine these more systematically and determine whether they have differing implications for the total personality. Two or three items in the checklist are essentially feminine in character, but it is apparent that a great number of items refer to activities more often chosen by men than women. It may thus appear that item selection is strongly biased in favor of higher scores for men. A strong case can be made, however, for the view that the expected sex difference is inherent in the variable we are trying to measure. A checklist that would realistically reflect in its scores the true magnitude of the population sex difference would have to be based on a fairly exhaustive survey of human activities.

Correlates of the experience measures

Relationships among the three tests we have considered in this chapter—the Experience Inventory, Early Memories, and the Activity Checklist—and their relationships to other measures were examined for the 361 subjects who took the entire battery. For the 16 factors of the Experience Inventory, factor scores were derived by multiple-regression procedures. Correlations among the three tests are not particularly high, but in direction they are consistent with the notion of a general openness dimension. The variables represented by the Activity Checklist and the Experience Inventory may represent alternative ways of seeking new experience, but they are not mutually exclusive. The correlation between miscellaneous activity and total openness (the *a priori* score variable of the Experience Inventory) is 0·17.

The variables of Early Memories prove to be related to one another and to certain Experience Inventory variables, but they show little relationship to anything else in the battery. Age of earliest memory correlates −0·39 with number of specific early memories and −0·18 with variety of revived impressions, while the latter two variables correlate 0·42 with each other. Age of earliest memory correlates no more than 0·23 with any of the other scores derived from the battery. For the other two memory measures, the meaningful relationships seem to be confined to the Experience Inventory. Number of specific early memories and variety of revived impressions correlate 0·34 and 0·32 respectively with total openness. With respect to specific factors, these variables prove to have greatest affinity for factor 2 (unusual perceptions and associations), for which their correlations are 0·34 and 0·35 respectively. Thus, the extent of early memory appears to be related to openness in general; if it has profound implications beyond this for the total personality, the present research fails to reveal it.

A number of the variables under consideration manifest sex differences. On the average, men score appreciably higher on miscellaneous activity, while women tend to show more openness on the Experience Inventory. More specifically, significant sex differences are evident on factors 1 (aesthetic insensitivity), 2 (unusual perceptions and associations), 4 (constructive utilization of fantasy and dreams), 6 (indulgence in fantasy), 9 (preference for predictable constancy), 13 (experience of unconventional impulses), 14 (relaxation of conscious control of thought and action), and 15 (passive enjoyment of imagery). Men tend to show greater openness on factors 9, 13, and 14, while women tend to show greater openness on all the others. Broadly speaking, men tend to be more open than women in the realm of action, while women tend to be more open than men in the realm of feeling and thought.

It is hardly surprising that miscellaneous activity, which proved only slightly related to the Experience Inventory measures, has a much different pattern of correlations with other battery variables. As we might expect, miscellaneous activity relates most highly to other measures that reflect a confident, outgoing, extraverted trend. Understandably, the Experience Inventory variables tend to be related to other measures that suggest emotional sensitivity, aesthetic interests, liberalism, and independence. Further evidence that the openness scores tend to go with a certain intellectual and emotional flexibility is provided by data presented by Wyrick (1969). She asked subjects to indicate their present views on a number of attitude items and also to indicate which attitudes they had ever held, regardless of whether they still maintained them. The tendency to acknowledge many attitudes under the second set of instructions, relative to the number presently held, was found to correlate significantly with the total openness score and with eight of the factors.

A more surprising finding within the present battery is a pervasive tendency for the openness variables to go with measures that suggest emotional distress—anxiety, lack of control over internal processes, tension, psychosomatic symptoms. This trend is most pronounced for the *a priori* total openness score, but the effect is mirrored in most of the specific factors—in particular, factors 2 (unusual perceptions and associations), 8 (unrealistic fantasy content), and 10 (need for involvement). To some extent, the Experience Inventory shares a response bias with the measures of distress. The subject earns scores that indicate openness or distress to the extent that he is willing to report qualities that people are likely to view as abnormal or undesirable. It is doubtful, however, that the apparent relationship between openness and distress can be entirely dismissed as an artifact of our measurement techniques. There is reason to believe that a willingness to face new experience carries with it a willingness to experience some unpleasant consequences. To some degree, anxiety is an inevitable price that one must pay for the growth afforded by openness. We shall consider this matter again later in the light of further analysis of the battery.

Chapter 6

The experience of control

The experience of control—the sense that one actively chooses, successfully wills, or achieves mastery over himself and the circumstances in which he finds himself—is obviously one of the most fundamental features of human experience. People vary considerably in the extent to which they have this experience, and each of us finds in his own life that it differs from one time or situation to another. Clinical evidence clearly attests to the importance of this variable. People who function in ways we regard as successful and productive seem usually to maintain a strong sense of mastery and appear to approach new situations with a confidence that they will succeed in coping. An experienced loss of control, on the other hand, is perhaps a universal concomitant of psychopathology. The loss may be fairly circumscribed in mild disorders. In severe psychoses, it tends to be generalized and is linked to an experienced loss of identity. In some psychotics, we may find evidence at the same time of a paradoxical sense of great power. In this case, the individual feels there are tremendous forces operating within him, but since they are not perceived as fully aligned with a clearly distinguishable conscious identity, he may be terrified at the prospect of their getting out of hand. In other cases, we may find a defensive identification with an image that embodies mastery—God, in the extreme instance—with the result that the individual reports an unusual degree of control. The verbal report is misleading, of course, because we will inevitably discover, if we get to know this psychotic well enough, that the loss of control which his delusion is designed to alleviate, remains a more pervasive feature of his total realm of experience.

There is little doubt then, that the experience of control is relevant to our present interests. There is reason to wonder, however, whether it is really a central ingredient of the optimally functioning personality. Adjustment seems to imply a sense of control, but one can have this sense without being creative or productive. Anxiety seems always to involve a sense of loss of control, but a total absence of anxiety is surely not the ideal state of affairs. The picture is complicated further by the fact that a loss of control is not necessarily disturbing and is, in fact, a requisite for creative work and for what have been called 'peak' experiences. So long as we insist on maintaining conscious control over everything that goes on in our lives, we prevent the occurrence of intense aesthetic or inspirational experiences and we preclude the emergence of novel ideas and insights. Thus, a pronounced need to maintain control at all times would seem an undesirable state of affairs, for it would serve to restrict the range of experience within rather pedestrian bounds.

Alfred Adler was probably the first major personality theorist to focus special attention on the experience of control and to assign a central place in his system to the striving for mastery or control, but such a variable could hardly have gone unnoticed in earlier times. There is reason to believe that Adler was influenced by Nietzsche's notion of the will to power. In turn, Nietzsche's ideas may be viewed as an outgrowth of earlier treatments of will by such philosophers as Hume, Kant, and Schopenhauer. Broadly speaking, a philosophical concern with will, personal choice, personal control, etc. may be viewed as inherent in an orientation that leads one to understand and explain objects and persons from their own viewpoint rather than from that of an outside observer. This internal or introspective orientation is characteristic of thinkers in those traditions that have been called tenderminded or Leibnizean. In so far as these traditions have dominated in continental European philosophy, continental philosophers have been concerned with the matter of personal control.

The experience of active control is commonly viewed as prime evidence for the existence of a free will—i.e. as evidence that personal choice is a cause or determinant of events. An interest in the experience, however, presupposes no particular position with respect to related philosophical issues. To be sure, there is an historical tie between the psychologist's interest in the experience and the philosopher's concern with such problems as the will. Both presuppose an introspective orientation, and by and large an interest in the experience is and has been most evident among psychologists active in humanistic movements that have been influenced strongly by phenomenology, existentialism, and related movements in philosophy.

The psychologist who has drawn most attention to the issue of control in the last few years, however, is Julian Rotter, whose thinking reflects a blend of humanistic and behavioristic traditions.

Rotter's work is of particular interest to us because it has provided
the foundation for much of the research pertaining to the experience of control and most of the efforts to measure this variable as a
personality dimension. Rotter (1966) defines the *locus of control* in
terms of the person's expectancy regarding the effects of his own
behavior. A person is said to display internal control if he perceives events as being a consequence of his own actions and
therefore under his own personal control. He is said to manifest
external control if he regards events as being unrelated to his
own efforts.

The measurement of control

Much of the research pertaining to control as a dimension of
experience or expectancy has been reviewed by Lefcourt (1966)
and by Rotter (1966). The first attempt to construct a measure of
this dimension was reported by Phares (1957), who devised a 13-
item Likert-type scale. This was revised and expanded to a 26-
item scale by James (1957). In later work, Shephard Liverant
further expanded the James–Phares instrument and devised subscales on an *a priori* basis for six areas of content—academic
recognition, social recognition, love and affection, dominance,
social-political events, and general philosophy. It was found, however, that the subscales did not yield very different kinds of
information and further work by Liverant, Crowne, Rotter, and
Seeman was again concentrated on a single general dimension of
control. This work led to construction of the I-E Control Scale
(Rotter, Seeman, and Liverant, 1962), a test composed of 29
forced-choice items.

Apparently the first instruments designed to measure experienced control in children were two tests constructed by the writer
in 1955. Unaware at the time of the work of Rotter and his associates
but responding perhaps to the same *Zeitgeist*, the writer devised a
Picture Interpretation Test and a Story Completion Test for
research on personality structure in six- and seven-year-olds (see
Cattell and Coan, 1959). In each item of the first test, the subjects
were shown a picture projected on a screen and asked to choose
between two interpretations of the circumstances in it. In each
story completion item, they were to choose between two possible
outcomes for a given story stem. All items in both tests involved a
choice between the assumption or maintenance of control on the
part of the central character and control by an external force or

agent, but an effort was made to distinguish different sorts of external influence. In addition to an overall score for internal v. external control, each test was designed to yield a subscore for what was called ego control v. benevolent external intervention and a subscore for ego control v. malevolent external intervention.

A story completion test for use with older subjects has since been reported by Adams-Webber (1963). Several additional tests have also been constructed for children. Bialer (1961) devised the Locus of Control Scale for oral administration to younger subjects. Another self-report instrument is the Intellectual Achievement Responsibility Questionnaire of Crandall, Katkovsky, and Preston (1962), and another test employing pictures is the Children's Picture Test of Internal-External Control devised by Battle and Rotter (1963). Instead of interpreting situations, however, the subject is asked to fill in a word balloon for one of the depicted figures, as in the Rosenzweig Picture-Frustration Study.

Much of the evidence on the extant questionnaire scales seems to support Rotter's notion of a generalized expectancy for internal or external control. It has been shown that the external subjects are more likely to perform on other tasks (such as those involving level of aspiration) in the way most people would if they viewed the outcomes as largely governed by chance. There are also group differences in scores that accord well with theory. Subjects drawn from disadvantaged ethnic minority populations tend to display relatively external scores, while Peace Corps volunteers and civil rights activists (people who apparently assume their individual actions can have important social consequences) tend to be relatively internal.

In addition, there is some evidence that people who score near the external end of the range tend to be more conforming than internal subjects. The internals are more inclined to try to maintain independence of judgment, and they are somewhat more motivated for individual achievement. The relationship of scale scores to adjustment is rather unclear, and one would not predict a simple relationship on theoretical grounds. Conflicting findings have been obtained for the correlation of internal–external control with anxiety. Schizophrenics on the average score toward the external end of the range.

There is further support for the idea of a generalized expectancy in the correlation between questionnaire scores and scores derived from other measurement media. Adams-Webber (1963) has shown a relationship between the I-E Control Scale and his story completion test, while Cardi (1962) has related the scale to ratings derived from a semi-structured interview. There is also some evidence that the non-questionnaire instruments devised for children yield the same kinds of predictions as the adult questionnaires. Thus, Battle and Rotter (1963) found the most external scores on the Children's Picture Test in Negro children of low socio-economic background.

The author's child tests were employed as part of a large battery that was administered to first- and second-grade children and subjected to factor analysis. Perhaps the most interesting finding was that the internal scores from both instruments converged in a common factor tentatively identified as Wary Realism. They were accompanied in this factor by a variety of measures involving restraint in preferences and self-description. This suggests that the internal choices in the Picture Interpretation and Story Completion Tests reflect a need to maintain some kind of control, more than an expectancy that control will be maintained.

The additional associations of the individual control measures were weaker but possibly more consistent with an expectancy interpretation. Malevolent external intervention in the Picture Interpretation Test went with measures pointing to low self-confidence and a low setting of aspiration levels relative to performance. Benevolent external intervention in the Story Completion Test went with measures relating to low planning and productivity. This suggests that the child who chooses story completions in which the hero's problem is resolved by help from without is accustomed to such assistance himself.

The development of the Personal Opinion Survey

The extant verbal scales have been found to have some general predictive power, and there is some evidence that they yield information that agrees with that obtained by other methods of measurement. As we have noted, these findings lend support to the idea of a generalized expectancy for internal or external control. Furthermore, Rotter (1966) reports two factor analyses of the I-E Control Scale that indicate that a large part of the variance of this instrument can be attributed to a general factor.

This evidence of a single broad dimension of experienced control, however, is not altogether convincing. There remains a good deal of casual evidence that people can experience control selectively with respect to different phases of their lives. The fact that a large part of the variance of Rotter's scale can be accounted for by a general factor could have been predicted on two grounds. First, the methods of item selection that culminated in this scale operated both directly and indirectly to enhance the internal consistency of the final composite. Second, the work that went into the development of this scale was inspired by a concept of generalized expectancy and by a theoretical system that places particular emphasis on social reinforcement. This circumstance undoubtedly imposed some limit on the scope of potential item content. Even the subscales of Liverant, which proved not to be very independent, were all inspired by social learning theory and not designed to explore fully the possibility of independent areas of expectancy. One could argue further that the demonstrations of the scale's predictive power are confined to situations for which the theory and the scale are particularly suited.

It is not the author's purpose, however, to disparage Rotter's social learning theory or the I-E Control Scale. The theory is one of admirably broad scope, and the scale appears to operate well within the framework that the theory provides. If we start out, however, with a focus on the varieties of human experience, rather than on social learning or on a particular expectancy interpretation of control, we are led to a path somewhat different from that which Rotter and his colleagues have followed. It seems clear that the experience of control embraces a wide range of phenomena that have not been covered in past attempts to construct measuring instruments. It was for this reason that the author undertook the construction of an inventory, the Personal Opinion Survey, designed to permit more general exploration of the dimensions of experienced control. (The author is indebted to Dr Zipporah Dobyns for her valuable assistance in the early stages of research with this inventory, especially for her contributions to item construction.)

The Personal Opinion Survey contains 130 true-false items deliberately varied in a number of ways. Items were designed to cover many types of content. We may think of content possibilities in terms of three broad areas: external events, personal characteristics, and the body. The first of these would include the actions of people with whom one interacts, the immediate physical world (including mechanical things, other human products, natural objects and surroundings, the weather, etc.), intellectual problems, and broadscale natural and human events. Personal characteristics would include both relatively persistent features (habits, traits, status, goals, life style, etc.) and more immediate, transitory events (emotional states, moods, thoughts, actions, etc.). Aspects of the body relevant to experienced control would include processes subject to physiological fluctuation (heart rate, respiration, gastro-intestinal processes, sensory functions, the operation of the skeletal musculature, etc.). They would also include features subject to long-term growth and development (strength, coordina-tion, weight, physical skills, attractiveness, physique, etc.).

The items of the I-E Control Scale and of its precursors appear to be concentrated primarily in the realm of external events. This seems in keeping with the theoretical framework that fostered their development, though it is not clear just what the inherent content boundaries of social learning theory are. The *experience* of control, as we speak of it here in application to such diverse phenomena as physiological processes, thoughts, and habits, can be broadly defined in terms of an *expectancy* that events will pro-ceed in accordance with personal intention or wish. To this extent, our control concept is essentially equivalent to that of social learning theory. In the terms of social learning theory, however, the object of expectancy is a *reinforcement* resulting from an action of the individual. The imposition of the reinforcement paradigm tends to fix our attention upon a sequence of organism-environ-ment relationships—preceding, entailing, and following an overt act. At any rate, the research inspired by Rotter's treatment of control has shown this content focus. In the interest of exploring a broader domain of experience, the author would prefer for the present to work with a more inclusive—perhaps looser—concept of experienced control.

Consideration in present item construction was also given to the fact that when events are perceived as not under personal control, the external force may be construed in many ways. It may be seen in terms of a clear social or physical locus, or it may be of a much more indeterminate character. Either by intention or effect, it may be beneficial or detrimental, or it may be quite indifferent so far as the welfare of the individual is concerned. A few items with no clearly 'internal' answer were included merely to permit later clarification of possible variations in perception of the external agent. Much item construction in the past has been guided by an *a priori* conception of a simple polarity involving personal control *v.* chance or fate. For each type of content noted so far it is possible to construct either 'first-person' items, which refer specifically to control or lack of control on the part of the subject himself, or 'third-person' items, which deal with the capacity for control on the part of people in general. Items of both types were employed for each major area of content.

Not all the item variations we have noted above are novel. Some have been tried by others (though not in all the present combinations) and have not yet been shown to be of great importance. Many of the items themselves that were included in the Personal Opinion Survey are borrowed from other scales. The total set of items looks less cohesive than those of earlier scales, and it represents a territory with less certain boundaries. This is inevitable, of course, for it is designed to provide more comprehensive coverage of the manifestations of experienced control and hence a more stringent basis for assessing the tenability of a general control dimension.

The 130 items are as follows:

1. People can stay healthy all the time by getting the right food, sleep, and exercise.
2. I can almost always go to sleep at night without any difficulty.
3. Falling in love usually just happens whether we seek it or try to avoid it.
4. Physical skill is mostly due to persistent practice.
5. Sometimes when I have to speak to someone important or in front of a group, I feel a tightness in my chest or throat that makes it difficult to talk.
6. I usually plan my work carefully before I start it.
7. Even with regular exercise, considerable stiffness and loss of control of the body is inevitable in old age.
8. I am almost never bothered by either constipation or diarrhoea.
9. It is impossible to stop thinking or to prevent unwanted ideas from coming into consciousness.
10. A child plays an active role in forming his own personality and character.
11. I am bothered occasionally by stomach discomfort.
12. I often have trouble organizing my work as much as I need to in order to get anything done.
13. The increasing number of divorces means that more people are not really trying to make their marriages work.
14. I wish I didn't blush so easily.
15. I have some habits that I have not been able to break.

16. If I spent enough time working at it, I could become a fairly skillful acrobat.

17. It's almost impossible for a person to change his likes and dislikes deliberately.

18. I can always hear and see things as well as most other people.

19. Once I have started something, I feel I must finish it.

20. Our increasing technology should someday allow us to control natural phenomena like the weather.

21. Sometimes I have had an itch on my skin that I could not seem to get rid of.

22. No matter how she looks to begin with, almost every woman can make herself attractive by proper attention to her hair, skin, and clothing.

23. A person can control almost all of his mental processes if he tries to.

24. My life is in the hands of a divine power who ensures that things all happen for my own good even if I don't understand them at the time.

25. Everyone is responsible for what he is as well as for what he does.

26. My individual influence may be small, but I can still have a definite influence on important political events by voting, writing letters, and participating in organizations.

27. A lot of your habits and feelings are caused by things that happened when you were small, and there isn't much you can do to change them.

28. I make my own decisions, regardless of what other people say.

29. To be a great dancer, you have to be born with exceptional muscular coordination.

30. Peace will not be easy to attain, but there are steps people could take now that would eliminate war.

31. I find it difficult to control my weight.

32. The most important historical developments in human society follow a natural course, and there is very little that people can deliberately do to alter them.

33. I can nearly always finish the projects I start.

34. A person can control all of his emotions if he tries to.

35. Physique is largely determined by heredity, and there is very little anyone can do to alter his physique.

36. In some respects, the condition of the world appears to be

getting worse, and there is not much anyone can do about it.

37. If there is a supernatural power, it is not personally interested in the needs and wishes of individual human beings.

38. When I decide I need to change any of my habits, I can make a resolution to do so and stick to it.

39. There is nothing I can do as an individual that will affect major political events.

40. I sometimes have trouble with my muscles twitching or tightening up.

41. Most school grades are an accurate indication of the student's ability and effort.

42. No matter how tense or 'keyed up' I get, I know I can relax if I decide to do so.

43. Advertising and brain washing prove the helplessness of almost all people to resist outside pressure.

44. I can always keep from laughing if someone tries to tickle me.

45. Mankind seems unable to undo its own increasing pollution of the earth's surface and atmosphere.

46. I almost always succeed in carrying out my plans.

47. I have sometimes felt faint at the sight of blood or suffering.

48. Sometimes I can't seem to get my hands or feet to move quite the way I want them to.

49. At times I have started laughing or crying and have had trouble stopping.

50. When scientists have gained enough knowledge, we shall be able to control the future biological evolution of the human species.

51. I am confident I will be able to reach my goals.

52. With practice and concentration, a person can control many processes that go on in his body.

53. Men working and thinking together can build a just society without supernatural help.

54. When someone gets mad at me, I can always do something to remedy the problem.

55. Making a lot of money is largely a matter of getting the right breaks.

56. There is plenty I can do about what is happening in the world today.

57. Sometimes I feel depressed for no apparent reason at all.
58. I have difficulty in starting to do things.
59. When I really need to concentrate on something, I can do it no matter what is happening around me.
60. People usually do as they please, no matter what I say.
61. Everyone can and should decide for himself what is right and wrong.
62. You have to be careful how much you count on people because they will often let you down.
63. Many people could be described as victims of circumstances beyond their control.
64. If one just follows his own convictions he can get people to respect and admire him.
65. Often I cannot understand why I have been so cross and grouchy.
66. If I had time, I could figure out the solution to almost any kind of puzzle.
67. I have some bad habits that are so strong that it is of little use to fight them.
68. I think I could accomplish almost anything I wanted to if I tried hard enough.
69. Most people get at least a little pleasure out of seeing someone else in trouble.
70. You need to get the right breaks to become a successful leader.
71. At times, I have been so angry that I just couldn't help doing or saying things that I wouldn't ordinarily do or say.
72. I am easily embarrassed.
73. When I am very upset or depressed, I can always find some way of overcoming my problems or my feelings about them so that I end up feeling better.
74. I can often change a person's mind by discussing things.
75. The future is too uncertain for anyone to make serious long-range plans.
76. It is difficult for people to have much control over the things politicians do in office.
77. Anyone can learn how to interact with people and have good friends.
78. Often I feel unusually cheerful without any good reason at all.
79. Teachers nearly always give students what they have earned.

80. If I really wanted to, I could learn to speak any foreign language fluently in a few months.
81. Successful people like artists, inventors, and statesmen are usually motivated by forces they are unaware of.
82. As far as international affairs are concerned, most of us are the victims of forces we cannot understand, let alone control.
83. I have had periods of several days when I couldn't do what I was supposed to because I couldn't 'get going'.
84. Sometimes I feel that I have little to do with the grades I get.
85. I am often uncertain about what is the right thing to do, and I need the advice of other people.
86. If you try hard enough, you can make anyone like you.
87. Anyone who is willing to devote enough time and effort to it can attain a position of leadership and authority.
88. Although it probably expresses something, a lot of modern art doesn't make any sense to me.
89. I tend to trust people more than I should.
90. If I had time, I could figure out the answer to almost any mathematical reasoning problem.
91. I feel increasingly helpless in the face of what is happening in the world today.
92. I find it difficult to understand mechanical things.
93. When you have a problem you cannot handle by yourself, someone else will usually notice and try to help you.
94. Anyone who is willing to work hard can be successful.
95. I almost always understand why I feel and react as I do.
96. I can look down from high places without feeling nervous.
97. I can stand more pain than most people can.
98. Sometimes I worry a lot about something that is not really important.
99. If he is sincerely concerned, any individual can have some real influence on national and world events.
100. If I had enough time and the right books to refer to, I could understand any kind of scientific theory.
101. Most people inwardly dislike putting themselves out to help other people.
102. I often have trouble remembering where I put something.
103. Sometimes an idea runs through my mind and I cannot stop thinking about it no matter how hard I try.

104. I find if I want things done right, it doesn't usually pay to rely too much on other people.
105. I do many things which I later regret.
106. I nearly always get the grades I deserve.
107. My feelings are easily hurt.
108. Wars are inevitable, in spite of efforts to prevent them.
109. When I have a problem I can't solve by myself, I can almost always count on somebody else to help me.
110. Most people don't realize the extent to which their lives are controlled by accidental happenings.
111. I often find it hard to keep my mind on something I am working on.
112. Most people can make their decisions, uninfluenced by public opinion.
113. Many times I feel that I have little control over the way people react to me.
114. Almost everyone tries to help other people when he recognizes that they need help.
115. When I am very excited or upset, I can still carry on with my work as usual and get things done.
116. If one wants to badly enough, he can overcome almost any obstacle in the path of academic success.
117. People are so unpredictable that it is hard to really get to know them.
118. Most people are pretty blind to the needs of other people. They don't usually notice the problems of other people.
119. Most of the disappointing things in my life have been the result of my own actions.
120. No one can determine all by himself the right way to live. Everyone needs to listen to the ideas of other people in deciding what is right and wrong.
121. You just can't figure out how to please some people.
122. Many of the people I have to deal with just act the way they want to without taking my needs into account.
123. I often feel I get blamed or punished when I don't deserve it.
124. When I have to make a major decision about my life, I can best do it by relying entirely on my own judgment and standards.
125. I have more trouble with numbers or mathematical problems than I do with most other things I try to figure out.
126. Most people have to rely on someone else to make their important decisions for them.

127. If I had enough time and the right tools, I could figure out how almost any machine is put together and how it works.
128. People's misfortunes usually result from the mistakes they make.
129. I can usually get people to do things the way I want them to.
130. I have sometimes felt that difficulties were piling up so high that I could not overcome them.

An analysis of the Personal Opinion Survey

Since most of the items of the Personal Opinion Survey entail the presence or absence of personal control, it is possible to key them on an *a priori* basis and thus derive a total score for experienced control. Such a score has been used in the research that has been done with this instrument, but the instrument was actually designed to determine whether we can justifiably assume the dimension that this score presupposes. Hence, the first major undertaking was a factor analysis of the items.

The items were intercorrelated on the basis of the responses of 525 subjects drawn from a variety of psychology classes. When unities were inserted in the diagonal cells of the correlation matrix, the first principal axis accounted for 7 per cent of the variance. When squared multiple correlations were used as communality estimates, the first principal axis accounted for about $16\frac{1}{2}$ per cent of the variance. Even allowing for the fact that the dice were loaded somewhat by the inevitable peculiarities of individual questionnaire items as variables to be correlated and factored, this would not augur well for the idea of an all-encompassing general factor. It would be more illuminating, however, to see whether we can find independent components within the whole test that represent distinguishable forms or aspects of experienced control.

Eighteen factors were extracted and rotated to an oblique solution of approximate simple structure. Examination of loading patterns indicated that most of the factors could be interpreted in terms of expectancies for control over particular classes of events. Experienced personal control and expectancies for people in general proved to be fairly independent for some kinds of content. It is obvious that the deliberately diversified item content 'paid off' in yielding some components that could not have been

D*

factored out of earlier scales. At the same time, to be sure, we extracted some components that were a bit tangential to the experience or expectancy of control. Arranged in order of decreasing variance, the obtained factors may be described as follows:

Factor 1
Most of the items loaded highly by this factor are stated in the third person. They generally express the view that one can accomplish many things if one tries hard enough. Success may lie in the academic, social, or physical realm. A very consistent pattern of content is seen in the best loaded items—items 22, 25, 61, 64, 68, 77, 86, 87, 94, and 116. We may call this *achievement through conscientious effort*.

Factor 2
Here the high scorer expresses the confidence that he as an individual has the capacity for accomplishment in various realms— mathematical, mechanical, scientific, athletic, linguistic. The areas of success manifested in the highly loaded items tend to be intellectual in character and tend to be deemed more appropriate for men than for women in our society. Well loaded items include 66, 90, 100, and 127 on the positive side and 92 and 125 on the negative side. A suitable title might be *personal confidence in ability to achieve mastery*.

Factor 3
This may be called *capacity of mankind to control its destiny* v. *supernatural power or fate*. The items refer to man's ability to build a just society, to control both his own evolution and natural physical phenomena, and the possibility of acting to eliminate war. Conspicuous positive loadings are seen for items 37, 50, and 53, while 24 has the highest negative loading.

Factor 4
All highly loaded items—6, 19, 33, and 46 on the positive side and 12 and 111 on the negative side—are stated in the first person and refer essentially to the planning, organization, and completion of tasks. The factor thus involves successful self-control in the realm of work. We may call it *successful planning and organization*.

Factor 5
Here again the items are personal. Those positively loaded—such as 21, 40, 48, 57, 103, and 130—report a lack of control of somatic,

affective, and cognitive processes. The subject is afflicted with unavoidable itching, depression, ideas that run through his mind, muscular incoordination, twitching or tightening up of muscles, unexplainable cheerfulness, etc. A fitting title would be *lack of self-control over internal processes* v. *self-control*.

Factor 6

This is evidently *lack of control over large-scale social and political events*. Both the subject himself and people in general are seen by the high scorer as helpless with respect to major societal processes. Items 39, 76, 82, and 91 are at the positive pole, while 26, 56, and 99 are at the negative pole.

Factor 7

The high scorer (as seen in items 62, 101, 104, and 118) expresses the view that most people cannot be relied upon either to meet his needs or those of others. The low scorer (who is more likely to endorse items 93, 109, and 114) views people as more benevolent and is possibly more intropunitive himself. A reasonable title would be *people viewed as undependable* v. *dependable*.

Factor 8

If we go by the few highly loaded items (positive: 41, 79, 106; negative: 84), this is *academic grading viewed as just* v. *capricious*. It is not clear to what extent this factor governs one's outlook on other kinds of rewards and punishments.

Factor 9

If we judge this by the two items most highly loaded (55 and 70), it could be called *dependence of success on luck*. The items of more meager loading combine a certain confidence in the possibility of self-control with uncertainty regarding environmental feedback. With respect to the areas of control covered by the items, there seems to be nothing very distinctive about this factor.

Factor 10

Here again there is a fair range of events embraced by item content, but a fairly persistent theme is self-control in the attitudinal or motivational realm. Items 17 and 71 are positively loaded, while 23 and 34 are negatively loaded. An appropriate title might be *impossibility of willed actions and decisions* v. *possibility of successful assertion of the will*.

Factor 11

The four most highly loaded items (positive: 54, 74, 129; negative: 60) are all first-person items and are concerned with whether the subject is able to secure desired reactions from other people. We may call this *control in immediate social interaction*.

Factor 12

This seems to be *dependence on others for direction* v. *self-sufficiency*. The subject's responses indicate essentially that he either tends to seek help or prefers to rely on his own judgment (items 85, 91, and 109 versus items 28 and 124). The high scoring subject apparently tends also to attach value in general to listening to the views of others on important matters.

Factor 13

Here the high scoring subject describes himself as victimized by others but capable of good control over his own actions (see items 38 and 123). At the negative pole are items (for example, 15) referring to unbreakable habits. The content at the positive pole suggests in combination a sort of paranoid self-sufficiency. A good tentative title would be *defensive self-reliance*.

Factor 14

The high scorer is easily embarrassed, blushes easily, and has feelings that are easily hurt (see items 14, 65, 72, and 107). The remaining item content, though meager, supports an interpretation of this as *emotional vulnerability*.

Factor 15

This is a *personal responsibility* factor. The few pertinent items (13, 119, and 128) indicate that the high scorer both considers himself responsible for most of his misfortunes and feels that other people should be assigned responsibility for their actions.

Factor 16

Like factors 5 and 10, this is a self-control factor. It differs from 10 in not being concerned with willed action in general. It differs from 5 in being concerned more with work and action than with internal processes. The most prominent items are 42, 56, 59, 73, and 115. Perhaps an accurate title would be *personal control over thought and action*.

Factor 17
This factor seems to be concerned with somatic manifestations of anxiety and with ability to withstand high places, pain, and social stress. Positive items include 5 and 47, while items 8 and 96 are negative. Perhaps a reasonably accurate title would be *nervous tension*.

Factor 18
With respect to intentional behavior, this factor is characterized by lack of control at the positive pole, item 67 having the highest loading. The high scorer has bad habits that are too strong to fight, has difficulty starting things, and is occasionally afflicted with uncontrollable laughing or crying. He is free from gastrointestinal disorders, however, while the low scorer suffers from them. We may tentatively identify this as *carefree acknowledgment of short-comings*.

There was some intercorrelation among factors, and it would be fair to say that all of the sizeable correlations were consistent in direction with the common element of control. That is to say, we found a positive correlation between factors when expected control was at the same pole (positive or negative) in both factors; we found a negative correlation when expected control went with the positive pole of one factor and the negative pole of the other. On the whole, however, these factors were more nearly orthogonal than those of the Experience Inventory, and the sizeable correlations were much less numerous. Thus, there may be a little justification for speaking of a general factor of control, or at least of higher-order control factors broader in scope than the dimensions revealed by our first-order analysis, but it must be emphasized that any such broad component must be viewed as comparatively weak. Some of the most important manifestations of experienced personal control—such as those represented by factors 2 and 5—proved to be essentially uncorrelated with one another.

For the sake of relating the Personal Opinion Survey to other measures in the personality battery, factor scores were estimated for all 18 factors by multiple regression procedures for those subjects who took the rest of the battery. It was obvious from the loading patterns, however, that these scores could be of little value for the later factors in the above series. The first six or seven factors were all represented by a substantial number of items and were subject to reliable measurement with the present items. Each of the remaining factors was represented by no more than a half-dozen good items.

Work that has been done since the research reported here has concentrated on the first six factors of the series described above and on factor 11. These seven factors have proven satisfactorily replicable, and the work has resulted in the development of a revised Personal Opinion Survey, which contains seven refined factor scales (see Coan, Fairchild, and Dobyns, 1973). The revised instrument is obviously more suitable for general use than its predecessor, and its use should add considerably to our understanding of the components of self-reported control.

Story Completions

Previous findings show a relationship between scores on questionnaire measures of experienced control and scores derived from other types of instruments, but it seems unlikely that the overlap in information is complete. There are undoubtedly some kinds of information that can only be obtained through questions calling for a direct self-report, but it is quite possible that other types of measures will furnish insights that questionnaires cannot readily provide. In particular, it seemed worthwhile in the present undertaking to see what additional insights into the experience of control might be provided by a thematic test.

The story completion task was deemed most suitable for the purpose. It is a test form that lends itself easily to a wide range of content, and it is susceptible to the flexible structuring required for focusing on specific classes of response variables. It was decided that the story completion test would be employed both as a projective measure of control expectancy and as a basis for assessing temporal perspective. We shall consider the latter use in the next chapter. Several dozen story stems were constructed and administered to pilot samples. On the basis of the pilot data, each story was evaluated in terms of its potential for discriminating with respect to various aspects of control. The following eight stems were finally chosen for use in the personality battery:

1. June has just been thrown from her horse in mountainous, deserted country, and she realizes that her leg is probably broken. The horse has run away.
2. Vic has just received word that he was passed over for a promotion and a newer man was given the opportunity.
3. Lester hears someone calling for help while he is walking home late at night.
4. Sue has just reported for work and found a note clipped to her

time card. It says 'You have been getting to work too late too often. Report to the front office.'

5. Helen has been recently widowed and she feels awkward at the first party with her former friends, where she is the only single person present.

6. Larry has been ordered by his boss to take action which Larry considers somewhat unethical although he knows it is often done in business.

7. One day Marian was crossing a very icy street at an intersection. A driver approaching the intersection applied his brakes, but his car would not stop. Marian turned in time to see the car sliding very fast directly toward her on the ice.

8. Charles had reached his fifties and his family was nearly grown when he was informed by the company for which he had worked most of his life that his job was being taken over by the new computers just ordered.

The stories were group-administered, and the subjects were given initial instructions to read each story carefully but to work rapidly and write a brief ending for each story in a space provided for this purpose. Each story poses a problem that seems to demand some sort of solution. Apart from this, however, the stories were selected with a view toward diversifying the situations involved in them. In future research, it would be interesting to determine whether independent response factors might be associated with different classes of situations, but obviously a test containing only eight stems does not permit this sort of analysis.

Every story completion was classified into one of four categories. It was given a coding of I (for internal control) if the story ended with the hero assuming control of the situation either through self-mastery or through mastery of the environment. It was classed as D (for detrimental external control) if the story was concluded with the hero as a victim of forces beyond his control. It was coded B (for benign external control) if the story ended with the hero being aided by an external force that acted on his behalf (with or without intention), thereby bringing about an effect that the hero could not or did not achieve by himself alone. A coding of U (unclassifiable with respect to control) was applied whenever the subject evaded the assigned task of completing the story or wrote a story that denied the problem situation or ended inconclusively. The U coding was used too infrequently to merit further considera-tion. Scores for internal control, detrimental external control, and benign external control were obtained by tallying the story completions assigned to these response classes.

Correlates of the control measures

In considering available information on correlates of the present instruments, it would be well to underline certain differences between these instruments and other devices that have been used to assess the experience of control. Dobyns (1969) employed both the Personal Opinion Survey and Rotter's I-E Control Scale in a study of college students and hippies. Using the total *a priori* score on the former, she found a correlation of 0·55 between these two tests. Thus, there is appreciable overlap between the two measures, but they cannot be considered strictly equivalent. There would appear to be two crucial differences between the tests. First, the Personal Opinion Survey items have a wider range of content. Second the I-E Scale items are controlled for social desirability, while those of the Personal Opinion Survey are not. These two facts account for certain differences which Dobyns' data show between the two tests with respect to their correlation with other measures.

In nearly all respects, it is considered desirable in our culture for an individual to be able to maintain control over his behavior, his feelings, and the events in his surroundings that are affected by his behavior. Therefore, any statement that pertains directly to such control is likely to represent a state of affairs that most people would clearly consider either desirable or undesirable. In eliminating items that correlate with social desirability, Rotter and his colleagues have apparently ended up with a scale concerned essentially with general beliefs and attitudes pertaining to the *possibility* of control. The Personal Opinion Survey items, on the other hand, are concerned to a much greater extent with the *personal experience* of control. Since an experienced lack of control tends to be distressing and since, conversely, acute subjective distress invariably entails an experienced lack, loss, or threatened loss of control, it is not surprising to find that the total score of the Personal Opinion Survey correlates highly with other measures (such as the Taylor Manifest Anxiety Scale and Barron's Ego Strength Scale) concerned with emotional problems or distress. According to Dobyns' data, the I-E Control Scale relates more highly to scales dealing with belief in free will and acceptance of responsibility.

The I-E Control Scale and the Personal Opinion Survey were

also used jointly by Blankenship (1969), who found that the former instrument correlated significantly with all but two of the factors from the latter. The correlations were essentially zero for factors 3 and 13. While the I-E Scale items tend to assume that the assumption of control is desirable and that the alternative is to be a victim of untoward forces, both factor 3 and factor 13 involve polarities that run counter to this assumption. In 3, the external force is benign, while in 13 the high scorer reports personal control in the face of victimization. Correlations for the other 16 factors range from 0·202 to 0·494. The highest correlations are for factors 6 and 9, which show an obvious content alliance with the I-E Control Scale. Perhaps it would be a fair summary of such evidence to say that the latter instrument taps the experience of control at a fairly high level of generality. Thus, it yields scores that should be slightly predictive of experience in a wide range of situations. For more adequate specific predictions, we are likely to need information about some of the component dimensions of experienced control.

In Blankenship's study, it was also found that both questionnaires were related to level of aspiration in an angle-matching task. When subjects were told beforehand that the task was so difficult that their performance would be strictly a matter of chance, subjects who reported high internal control on the I-E Scale and factors 1 and 6 of the Personal Opinion Survey tended to give high estimates of future performance. In a related study, Stone (1969) found significant correlations between performance estimates and several Personal Opinion Survey factors. In this study, however, which did not entail 'chance' instructions, internal control was found to be related not to high estimates *per se*, but to a tendency to give estimates that were *either* above or below prior performance. Both the Blankenship study and the Stone study suggest that the individual who reports a high level of personal control tends to assume that his own performance is not strictly bound by whatever limits are indicated by available evidence—whether the evidence consists of his own past scores or statements to the effect that his skill is irrelevant to his performance. It is interesting to note that in the latter study, as in the former, the trends are strongest for factors 1 and 6. It is not clear why these factors in particular should be predictive of personal performance estimates.

Most of the remaining information we have about the Personal Opinion Survey and Story Completions comes from an examination of their relationship to other variables derived from the personality battery for which they were constructed. There appears to be only a slight relationship between these two tests. The scores for internal control and detrimental external control in the story completions correlated 0·16 and −0·24 respectively with the total *a priori* score derived from the Personal Opinion Survey. They also displayed correlations of about the same magnitude with several of the factors derived from the latter instrument—notably factors 4, 5, 6, and 16. In each instance, the correlation was in the direction one would expect—internal control in one test went with internal control in the other—but the degree of relationship was hardly impressive. Benign external control in Story Completions proved to be essentially uncorrelated with the questionnaire variables. It attained its maximal correlation (−0·14) with factor 3, which points to a plausible relationship between an expectancy of assistance from external forces and a conventional religious outlook.

The Story Completions measures showed little relationship generally to other measures in the personality battery. It is possible that Story Completions is getting at variables that are largely independent not only of those yielded by the Personal Opinion Survey but of those assessed by the rest of the battery as well. Perhaps the problem is partly a matter of reliability. Eight stories are not a sufficient number to ensure highly reliable scores, particularly in the case of benign external control, the response category of least frequent use. As it happens, the Spearman–Brown-corrected split-half reliabilities for Story Completions are 0·57 for internal control, 0·55 for detrimental external control, and 0·42 for benign external control. While these values are far from ideal, they are well above the level of the correlations of these measures with other battery variables, and they lend support to the idea that Story Completions is tapping something fairly distinctive.

One pertinent bit of evidence that suggests some basic difference between the two tests at hand with respect to the variables they tap is the character of the sex differences that appear in a college sample. On the Personal Opinion Survey, men scored significantly higher than women on the total *a priori* score. Significant sex differences were also found on factors 2, 3, 5, 7, 12, 14, and 17. In every case except factor 7, which is not concerned with control *per se*, men reported greater experienced control than women. A near exception to this pattern is factor 1, where there was a marked trend in the opposite direction. The most obvious interpretation of these findings is in terms of the fact that men on the whole have a greater need to maintain a self-image of mastery. One could largely predict which factors would yield significant differences by assuming that men will tend more often than women to choose 'internal' answers on items that raise any question of the subject's personal capacity to maintain control. In factor 1, where women showed a greater tendency to endorse the potential benefits of conscientious effort, the subject is not confronted with this question.

In contrast, story completions involving internal control on the part of the central character were given with significantly greater frequency by women than by men. Men were more likely to provide completions involving detrimental external control. There was no significant difference with respect to benign external control. It would be difficult to explain this if we assumed the subject was giving us a description of himself in story form, but it is easy to reconcile the findings for the two tests if we but sense what he is trying to communicate with each type of story solution. The internal-control solution brings the depicted problem to a state of harmonious resolution. The detrimental-control solution either underscores the agony of the hero or provides a tragic climax, such as death, that the subject would presumably not want for himself. The sex difference is consistent with the fact that women ordinarily show a greater inclination to seek a harmonious relationship with the environment, while men are oriented more toward some kind of dynamic opposition. It seems more important to men to experience themselves as distinct individuals, clearly separated from the world about them. Perceiving, and at times actively seeking, opposition serves to enhance the sense of individuality. Where women seek a smooth relationship, men may look for an opportunity to control or manipulate. They are more likely to welcome situations that pose a threat or challenge, whether immediate and personal or second-hand (as in viewing fighting scenes in movies and television productions). The basic sex difference is probably most apparent in the realm of social relationships, but one can find it even in the realm of simple physical-stimulus preferences. Thus, Fehr (1963) found that men were more likely to prefer disharmonious color combinations. At the primary-grade level, the author (Cattell and Coan, 1959) found that boys were much more likely to prefer disturbing or threatening sounds and strange versions of common objects to their more neutral or commonplace counterparts.

In giving internal-control solutions to stories, the female subject is restoring the story world to a more peaceful order. The male subject who provides a detrimental-control solution, on the other hand, is underscoring the idea that the world of his experience is characterized by disharmony. At the same time, we may assume some sex difference in mode of responding to story heroes. By virtue of her basic mode of relating to the world, the female subject is more likely to identify with the story character and find security in a situation that is secure for that character. The male subject is more likely to view the story character with detachment, as something separate from himself. Thus, when he moves the story character into a still worse predicament or transforms him into a gory mess, he is saying in effect, 'This is the way the world is: this is the sort of thing that can happen to somebody else.' We can see an interesting parallel in the portrayal of mutilation and excruciating torture that one frequently sees in the drawings of male adolescents.

It is quite possible, then, to reconcile the sex differences found for the Personal Opinion Survey with those found in Story Completions. We may assume, in general, that the subject who most values a sense of separate individuality will have the greatest need to experience personal control, and we may assume that for most areas of experience this need tends to be stronger in men than in women. It is likely that individual differences in the questionnaire scores are largely a matter of differences in actual experience of control and only indirectly and secondarily a function of the need for control. The sex difference in the need, however, is probably the major determinant of the sex difference in the scores. Perhaps the questionnaire factor that reflects the need most directly is factor 12, where men indicated a greater preference for self-sufficiency. In a task requiring the production or completion of stories, on the other hand, the greater emphasis on individual distinctiveness on the part of males may lead them to depict greater opposition between the story hero and his environment—which entails the possibility that the hero will be a victim of his environment—while experiencing greater distance between themselves and the story hero. In a sense, then, the attribution of a lack of control to a story character may be quite consistent with a strong need for personal control on the part of the subject. It may be of interest to note that the oppositional outlook of men is reflected in questionnaire factor 7, where they showed a greater tendency to view people as undependable.

The scores derived from the Personal Opinion Survey proved to be related to a great variety of other measures in the personality battery. The correlated variables can be broadly described as representing both the positive and the negative aspects of maintaining control and order in one's life. Thus, in general, subjects who reported a *lack* of control in the questionnaire items showed signs of greater openness to experience and consequently richer experience, but they were more subject to emotional distress. Subjects who reported a high degree of experienced control showed evidence of a more stress-free but narrower existence. Thus, the total questionnaire control score correlated -0.33 with the total openness score derived from the Experience Inventory, and it was still more highly correlated with some of the component factors of that instrument. Its correlations were higher yet with anxiety indices such as the Taylor Manifest Anxiety Scale (-0.71) and components of the Sixteen Personality Factor Questionnaire. Similar patterns of correlation were found for various individual factors in the Personal Opinion Survey. The factor (factor 5) which showed the greater relationship to openness was at the same time the one most highly correlated with various indices of anxiety, psychosomatic problems, and other forms of subjective disturbance. Additional evidence on the interrelationships of experienced control, openness, and distress is presented and discussed in Chapters 9 and 11.

On the whole, the factors that proved most related to subjective distress were the factors concerned most focally with some kind of self-control—factors 5, 14, 16, and 17. In addition to the overall trend that we have noted, however, each factor tended to yield a pattern of correlations that made sense in the light of the interpretation that we gave it. In factor 1, high control tended to go with a sort of banal conformity that attaches particular importance to the norm of productiveness. In contrast, in factor 3 the internal-control pole went with a certain unconventionality of thought, while the opposite pole went with conventional thinking, especially in the realm of religion. In factor 2, where we found a greater sex difference, high control appeared to be related to quantitative ability and to a masculine interest pattern. The subject who reported a high degree of successful planning and organization on factor 4 showed predictable signs of self-regulation and restraint on other measures. Factor 11, which is concerned with control in immediate social interaction, proved to be related to measures that tap various aspects of social extraversion. In the correlates of the Personal Opinion Survey factors, we again see evidence of the multifaceted character of experienced control.

Chapter 7

Additional questionnaire instruments

General Beliefs

It has already been noted that the areas covered by our research battery vary considerably in degree of known structure. In some cases, it is fairly obvious what variables we need to assess and what measurement operations we might use for the purpose. In other cases, we are entering territory that is essentially uncharted. Perhaps the region in which our efforts were most strictly exploratory is that represented by the questionnaire entitled General Beliefs. This contains 130 items designed to provide an overall picture of the subject's basic outlook on life and the world, or as it is often called, the *Weltanschauung*. (The author is indebted to Dr Zipporah Dobyns for her collaboration in the early stages of research with this instrument and, in particular, for her contributions to item construction.)

Whether one thinks of them as a consequence, a concomitant, or a source of other personality variables, it is obvious that a person's most generalized beliefs and attitudes have a bearing on other aspects of the personality in which we are interested. People tend to develop more comprehensive views of life, the world, and themselves as they grow older, and a unifying outlook figures prominently in more than one conception of the optimal personality. It is much less clear, however, just what the range of specific contents of this unifying outlook might be, or whether in the best developed individual its ingredients are likely to assume one particular form or, perhaps, one of several alternative forms.

There is certainly no dearth of ideas about possible constituents of the *Weltanschauung*. There are various views one may hold regarding the worth of people in general and regarding human nature, and one may approach people with an attitude of acceptance, or wariness, or disgust. One may view them analytically, with detachment, as mere objects, or one may respond to them in a more personal, relationship-oriented manner. Comparable variables enter into our orientation toward the physical universe, toward various human institutions, toward science, toward religion, etc. One may seek truth through abstraction or through an immediate experiencing. One may affirm life or renounce it. Death may be something to fear, something to welcome, or something to which we resign ourselves. We may approach life optimistically or pessimistically, with levity or sobriety, with a sense of involvement or of aloofness. It would be easy to compose a list of dozens of such variables that have been regarded as important facets of the *Weltanschauung*, and many scales have been devised to measure such variables.

Clearly we are confronted with an overabundance of concepts pertaining to the *Weltanschauung*. Since the general attitude-belief system is such a complex manifold, we should really need to measure many things to do full justice to its total composition in any individual. In studying the composition of the optimal personality, it seemed desirable to consider some of the most basic aspects of the *Weltanschauung* and to see how these are related to other kinds of personality variables. It was not at all clear what components of the general attitude-belief system should properly be considered most basic or which ones are most relevant to optimal personality functioning. Extant theory and speculation provide a host of answers to such questions.

The best solution to this problem seemed to lie in seeking a set of components that would be few in number but would nonetheless account for a large amount of variation in general attitudes and beliefs. The obvious procedure was to factor analyze a collection of items designed broadly to represent the domain of general beliefs and attitudes. Constructing the items for this purpose posed special difficulties, for the territory as a whole is quite ill-defined. The attitudes and beliefs of people constitute a virtually boundless realm. The subdivision consisting of attitudes and beliefs of a comprehensive or general character shades off subtly in all directions into attitudes and beliefs of varying specificity. To ensure breadth and diversity, we consulted many sources and compiled lists of prospective variables which we then employed as guides to item construction. The final result was surely a heterogeneous collection, but there is no way of being certain that no important variables were ignored. All items were subjected to preliminary pilot testing and those that proved too ambiguous and which approached universal acceptance or rejection were either revised or discarded. The following 130 items survived this initial screening and were retained for further analysis:

1. Most things follow a set course, and there is little that any person can do to change them.
2. It doesn't matter too much how you live your life, since life has no purpose except the one you choose to live by.
3. There are good times and bad times, but on the whole life is neither better nor worse than it has been for thousands of years.
4. A person's life is meaningless unless he works hard to accomplish something.
5. One can avoid a lot of problems if he makes a habit of analyzing his motives and does not do anything without knowing why.
6. Since people differ in their needs, we should not expect everyone to live by the same moral code.
7. Since everyone's behavior is determined by forces beyond his control, ideas of blame and guilt have no place in a modern scientific world.
8. Life would be meaningless and not worth living without the love of at least one other person.
9. The individual life stops completely when the body dies.
10. Humans are better off without religion.
11. Present conditions are more threatening than at any time in history.
12. The existence of God cannot be proved or disproved.
13. We would have fewer problems if we stuck to the tried and proven ways of the past instead of trying out a lot of new ideas.
14. All events follow natural laws; therefore, we could predict everything that happens if we had enough information.
15. The weather would be unbearable most of the time if we did not have good means of heating and cooling buildings.
16. There seems to be a divine purpose in everything that happens, even if some things that happen to us are hard to understand at the time.
17. It is best to set high goals for the future and plan your life so you can reach them.
18. Faith enables a person to understand many things that people without faith cannot understand.
19. Anyone may appear different or think he is different from other people, but basically people are all very much alike.
20. Life is an exciting adventure most of the time.

21. Ideas are more important than concrete objects.
22. 'Good' will ultimately win.
23. Everything is really just a combination of atoms.
24. Of all the religions which have existed on earth, there is probably only one correct one.
25. Most people can know God through direct contact.
26. Religions are formed by culture just as are habits of dress or languages.
27. Many things that happen are just accidents or chance events. There does not seem to be any cause for them.
28. It makes more sense to think of God as an idea or principle than to think there is a divine Being with human characteristics.
29. We can best gain an understanding of people if we think of them as very complicated machines.
30. A person's life has no particular meaning except the meaning he gives to it by deciding to live in a certain way.
31. Most of the time, it is best to go ahead and do whatever you feel like doing, instead of spending a lot of time thinking about it first.
32. At a certain time late in life, it is natural to look forward to death as a welcome relief from the struggle of life.
33. It is better not to want anything so much that you will be unhappy if you can't have it.
34. God is an impersonal power manifesting itself through both living beings and the whole physical universe.
35. As man's capacity for destruction increases, he may wipe out life on earth.
36. Success is gained only by hard work.
37. If he has only himself to rely on, a man is a helpless and miserable creature.
38. Men working and thinking together can build a just society without supernatural help.
39. The future can cause present events.
40. Underlying everything, there is a divine order that people can never understand completely.
41. There does not seem to be enough time to do all the important things one ought to do during his life.
42. Man is not just an intelligent animal. He possesses certain qualities that set him apart from everything else in nature.
43. History is largely determined by the actions of a small

number of men who produce new ideas and make major decisions.

44. It is best not to take anything too seriously, but to try to enjoy life instead.

45. To live a complete life, one has to get emotionally involved in things and commit himself to certain people and certain ideals.

46. The future is completely determined by the past.

47. One can lead a good and constructive life without a clear understanding of his goals and values.

48. The world is ultimately governed by spiritual forces.

49. Truth is relative, and what is true for one person or time may not be true for another.

50. It is only natural for a person to be rather fearful of the future.

51. God is only a symbol of man's ideals.

52. Science provides more important insights than religion does.

53. Human beings are capable of only a very limited understanding of the universe.

54. Time is very precious, and one should spend most of it doing something constructive.

55. To make progress, men must learn to hold back and control some of their most basic tendencies.

56. A person can control most of the processes in his body if he makes the effort.

57. Life is a serious matter. Anyone who acts carefree most of the time is just not facing reality.

58. The more a person knows, the more he is bound to feel that he cannot be completely certain about anything.

59. A man can be master of his destiny.

60. All human action is an attempt to gain pleasure and avoid pain.

61. The world is wholly governed by physical forces such as those of gravitation and chemical changes.

62. Life is not worth living without faith in something bigger than ourselves.

63. Every person should feel an obligation to help and protect the rest of mankind.

64. Man is a very insignificant part of the universe.

65. Personal freedom must be limited for the sake of harmony with others.

66. Most things that happen to us are really for our own good.
67. One should spend most of his time working toward future goals.
68. A lot of things that happen in the world seem to be meaningless; they just don't make any sense.
69. A person can control all of his emotions if he tries to.
70. To achieve lasting satisfaction in life, you have to face life seriously and not spend much time on momentary pleasures.
71. Science is still producing new knowledge and changing some of our ideas about the universe, but there are some basic truths that no one should have any doubt about.
72. An individual can change himself if he decides to.
73. All that really exists is the physical universe.
74. Human behavior is almost entirely a product of social forces.
75. Eventually everyone will be rewarded for good and will suffer for wrongdoing.
76. A person can worship God better by himself than in a group with others.
77. The greatest human beings have been those who were able to stand alone and if necessary die for their convictions.
78. Man is basically rational and perfectible through the use of his reason.
79. Everything usually works out best if we just accept things as they come and do not fight too hard to change them.
80. Time usually seems to pass rather slowly. Life is rather dull much of the time.
81. There is a selfish motive behind most acts of kindness and generosity.
82. A person can control all of his mental processes if he tries to.
83. Things work out best if we just accept and trust everyone and relate to people freely.
84. The best way to live is not to get too emotionally involved or react too strongly to things.
85. We never quite see the world around us as it really is. What we perceive depends on what we believe and what we want to perceive.
86. Life is a struggle to survive in an indifferent or dangerous world.
87. The really important life is the life after death.

88. The only intelligent way to account for man is in terms of his evolution from lower animals.
89. Religion is the best source for peace of mind.
90. If any individual were given complete personal freedom, he would do many things that would hurt others.
91. Most of the beliefs that people have about important matters are the products of careful reasoning and reflection.
92. To make progress, men must struggle to control nature and rise above it.
93. It is a bad mistake to spend most of your time working for the future. You should try to find some pleasure in every present moment.
94. People tend to act naturally in a kind and helpful way if they are not subjected to too much control and regulation.
95. The only things we really know are the things we observe with our own senses.
96. You can best get along with most people if you try to analyze and understand them instead of getting too close to them.
97. Every man's basic duty is to serve God.
98. Nothing is really good or bad but thinking makes it so.
99. Despite the occasional tragedies of earthquakes and floods, most of the time natural events and forces tend to help us.
100. The leaders of the world control the masses.
101. It is impossible to account for the intricate world without a creator.
102. Man must suffer in order to accomplish anything really important.
103. Absolute truth can be known by man.
104. Every individual's life has a purpose that he must find and try to fulfil.
105. No matter what happens, in the long run most things really get better and better.
106. Things would be better if people would just act in the ways that come most naturally.
107. Reason is more important than experience as a means for arriving at truth.
108. It is natural and normal to want to go on living under all circumstances. There is something wrong with anyone who would want to die.
109. Every man's most important duty is to help other people and to avoid doing things that would harm them.

110. Nothing is really important by itself. A thing is important if we think it is.
111. Living organisms are basically just complicated machines.
112. All serious problems involving relationships between people can be solved through love.
113. Attending church helps people to lead better lives.
114. Every event has a cause or causes.
115. In many ways, our civilization seems to be deteriorating.
116. One can only really understand life through direct experience. Studying the lives of other people is not enough.
117. It is better to have loved and been deeply hurt than never to have loved at all.
118. Every man's basic duty in life is to be true to himself and to give full expression to his own nature.
119. The mind can sometimes leave the body and function outside it.
120. Each individual is ultimately responsible for all he is and does.
121. God seems closer out in the world of nature than inside a church.
122. Religion is unnecessary if one has a code of ethics.
123. Despite occasional periods of war and other troubles, life on the whole seems to get gradually better and better.
124. Everyone should accept blame for any bad effects his actions may have.
125. Mankind cannot survive without faith in God.
126. The most important questions that people raise are those that can be answered by the use of the scientific method.
127. Luck (good or bad) plays a large part in everyone's life.
128. The universe is governed by a divine Being who possesses infinite power, infinite knowledge, and infinite love.
129. No one can really understand another person.
130. People who can create beauty are more important to mankind than those who discover truth.

Each of these items was presented with a Likert response scale in which $+2$ represented strongly agree, $+1$ agree, -1 disagree, and -2 strongly disagree. For purposes of analysis, General Beliefs was administered not only to the battery sample but to many additional subjects drawn from several psychology classes. The items were intercorrelated on the basis of the responses of 556 subjects. Seventeen principal-axis factors were extracted and rotated to the best approximation to oblique simple structure.

In view of the problems of variable sampling posed by this realm of measurement, it would be possible for a dimension of major importance to fail to emerge for lack of adequate representation in items. It is quite clear, however, that the present factor analysis revealed some very meaningful modes of variation that merit consideration as fundamental dimensions of the *Weltanschauung*. It is hoped that the present factors will serve as a guide and a basis for hypothesizing in further explorations of this realm. The seventeen factors may be described as follows:

Factor 1

Although the items were designed to tap a variety of viewpoints regarding religion, most of the items pertaining to religion were drawn together by a single factor that contrasts a conventional outlook with various alternatives. Factor 1 may be called *conventional theistic religion* v. *non-theistic viewpoint*. Items 87, 97, 125, and 128 are among the many items with high positive loadings, while items 9, 28, 38, and 122 lie closer to the negative pole.

Factor 2

At the positive pole of this factor, we find an emphasis on the constructive utilization of time, on working toward future goals—a value central to the Puritan ethic (see items 4, 41, 54, and 57). The negative pole is characterized by a present orientation, a stress on doing what one feels like at the moment—in some senses, a hedonistic or sensualist orientation (see items 2, 31, and 47). We may call this *productiveness* v. *spontaneity*.

Factor 3

The high scorer (as seen in items 33, 44, 79, and 84) prefers to avoid getting emotionally involved, while the low scorer (as seen in item 45) considers it important to make commitments and assume the concomitant risk of getting hurt. An appropriate title would be *detachment* v. *involvement*.

Factor 4

The high scorer professes a tolerant or liberal attitude in matters of value and truth, while the low scorer is inclined to insist more dogmatically on one proper system of beliefs, standards, and actions. The factor is best marked at the positive end, by such items as 6, 49, 58, 98, and 110. It is essentially *relativism* v. *absolutism*.

Factor 5
This factor contrasts determinism, materialism, and 'scientism' on the one hand with humanism, indeterminism, finalism, and 'religionism' on the other. It is best expressed in such positively loaded items as 14, 61, 88, and 114. A fairly accurate title would be simply *physical determinism*.

Factor 6
At the positive pole (as seen in items 21, 77, 83, 107, and 112), we find a stress on the importance of things in the subjective realm— ideas, reason, principles, feelings (particularly love). The negative pole combines a more cynical outlook with social determinism. The term *idealism* seems to fit the factor fairly well in several of its common meanings.

Factor 7
The high scorer (see items 20, 108, and 123) says that life is worth-while and believes in living fully or self-actualizing. The low scorer is more pessimistic and conservative (see items 3, 13, 37, and 115). He feels that the lot of mankind is either deteriorating or static. Since change means deterioration, he favors preservation of the *status quo* or turning to the ways of the past. We might call this *adventurous optimism* v. *resignation*. Perhaps it will prove to be just a specific expression of a more basic dimension of optimism *v.* pessimism.

Factor 8
This factor is not clearly interpretable. At the positive pole it combines pantheism, chance or acausality, and a stress on the value of direct experience (items 27, 34, and 116). Several of the weakly loaded items suggest that a pleasure orientation tends to go with the positive pole, while an acceptance of suffering for the sake of remote fulfilment goes with the negative pole. A tentative title might be *orientation to immediate experience* v. *ultimate goals*.

Factor 9
The few well loaded items are consistent with an interpretation of this factor as *human nature viewed as basically good* v. *needing*

restraint. Items 91, 94, and 106 are loaded positively, while 55 and 65 have negative loadings.

Factor 10
The most prevalent theme in the items loaded by this factor is will or personal control. A title that fits the best three items (56, 69, and 82) is *possibility of self-mastery*.

Factor 11
This is concerned more with potential control or power on the part of mankind in general. The best loaded positive and negative items are 103 and 53 respectively. We may call this *potential human supremacy* v. *human limitation*.

Factor 12
This contrasts a faith in the ultimate triumph of 'good' with a stress on the value of human intervention or creative effort. The best loaded items are 22, 66, and 105, which mark the positive pole of this factor. We may call it *acceptance of benign fate* v. *emphasis on human creativity*.

Factor 13
This factor has at its negative pole some of the features found at the positive pole of factor 12. It loads items 11 and 35 positively. It may best be called *perilous world situation*.

Factor 14
Here the main idea seems to be that events in this world are relatively devoid of sense. This is expressed particularly well in items 50 and 68. An appropriate title would be *life viewed as incomprehensible and unpredictable*.

Factor 15
The term that best fits the two items of substantial loading (29 and 111) is *mechanism*, and the remaining items can at least be reconciled with this interpretation.

Factor 16
The best items (30, 36, 77, 120, 124) fit an interpretation of *personal responsibility*, implying both that the individual should assume responsibility for his life and that he should be held accountable for his actions. Supporting this main theme is the

idea that self-determination is essentially possible, as opposed to the idea that one's life is governed by forces beyond personal control.

Factor 17
The positively loaded items (39, 76, 121) emphasize personal or private religious experience and finalism. The negatively loaded items (24, 109) invoke the notion or one true religion and stress one's duty to others. There are few items on which to base an interpretation, and it is not clear to what extent religious experience is really central to the factor. A tentative interpretation would be *individualism* v. *group adherence or social responsibility*.

Like the factors of the Experience Inventory and the Personal Opinion Survey, these are arranged in order of decreasing variance. Here, as in the other factored questionnaires, therefore, the factors near the beginning of this list are the ones best represented by substantial numbers of items, the ones most readily interpretable, and the ones most likely to prove replicable in future studies. Most readers will probably agree that the factors as a whole embrace a wide range of continua that are logically quite distinguishable from one another. Among certain of these factors, to be sure, we would expect interaction or interdependence, and since this is an oblique system, our expectations are matched to some extent by correlations. Thus, we are not surprised to find that factor 1 correlates positively with factors 2 and 12 and negatively with factors 4 and 5. On the whole, however, this system of factors approaches orthogonality. Most of the factor intercorrelations are close to zero.

Significant sex differences have been found on eleven of the factors. Women tend to score higher than men on factors 1, 4, 8, 9, 12, and 16, while men tend to score higher on 3, 5, 11, 13, and 15. These findings seem consistent with sex differences that have long been recognized. We can largely summarize them by saying that women are more oriented toward conventional religion, human values, and harmonious relationships, while men are more concerned with power relationships, independence, and the maintenance of control over the environment. The difference found on factor 13, where men are more inclined to perceive the present state of the world as perilous, is reminiscent of the responses of male and female subjects to Story Completions.

The correlations of the General Beliefs factors with other battery variables serve to augment our understanding a bit. Wherever these correlations are high, they seem quite consistent with the interpretations presented above. Factors 1 and 12, the most closely related factors in the total set ($r_{1\cdot12}=$ 0·57), share a common pattern of correlates that points to a generalized tendency on the part of the high scorer to accept conventional modes of thought. As one might expect, the subject who scores high on factor 2 shows varied evidence on other measures of an emphasis on order, planning, and self-control. Factor 4 is the one that proves most highly related to the variables measured by the Experience Inventory. The relativistic subject proves to be open to experience both in terms of the total *a priori* score for openness and in terms of most of the individual factors derived from the Experience Inventory as well. Several of the General Beliefs factors display low correlations with measures of experienced control. The relationship is most marked for factor 7, which is positively related to control, and factor 14, which is negatively related. On the whole, the correlation patterns for these two factors are very similar (but opposite in sign).

In view of the heterogeneous content and the Likert format of General Beliefs' items, it seemed worthwhile to score this test for two possible types of response bias—tendency to agree and extremity of response—although neither of these was of central interest in this research. The marking of extreme categories ($+2$ and -2) proves to be a fairly consistent response tendency within General Beliefs—the corrected split-half reliability is 0·93. Its correlations with other battery measures are all quite low, however, and can be reasonably attributed to chance.

The agreement response bias—or acquiescence, as it has sometimes been construed—has received much more attention in the literature, and there is considerable disagreement as to its meaning and importance. It has been viewed as a negligible influence in well designed items, as a potent response bias that must be controlled through balanced item selection, and as a potentially useful measure of personality variables in its own right. In the present study, the agreement tendency is substantially correlated with most of the General Beliefs factors, but of course, these correlations are all spurious. They vary directly with the balance of positive and negative loadings found in the various factors. It is instructive to note these correlations, however, for they underscore the fact that the overall pattern of external correlations for the agreement bias cannot be attributed to its dependence on any single component of General Beliefs. This overall pattern strongly suggests that the tendency to agree reflects a basic disposition to conform and to accept conventional ideas even when they are unrealistic or logically inconsistent. We must proceed with caution, however, for some of the highest correlations (between tendency to agree and score variables derived from other instruments in the battery) may depend on the presence of the same or a related response bias in other instruments.

In research conducted since the analysis of the battery, Hanson (1970) and also Coan, Hanson, and Dobyns (1972) tested the replicability of six of the General Beliefs' factors—factors 1, 2, 3, 4, 5, and 7—and developed expanded and refined scales for them. Each of the revised scales contains approximately equal numbers of items that contribute positively and negatively to the scale scores. The relationships which Hanson reports between the six factors and other variables are clearly consistent with our interpretations of them and with the evidence provided by the battery correlates. High scores on the first two scales went with a general response pattern and life style that were conservative. When subjects were asked to indicate religious preferences, it was found that Roman Catholics scored highest on these scales, followed by Protestants, Jews, and finally subjects who indicated no preference. The reverse order was found for the scale of physical determinism. On the fourth scale, however, Jews proved to be most relativistic on the average, while Protestants had the lowest mean score. Frequency of church attendance was positively related to scores on the first and second scales and negatively correlated with scores on the fourth and fifth scales.

When subjects were asked to indicate their political preferences, those who classified themselves as conservative Republicans scored highest on the first two scales, while those who classified themselves as liberal independents scored lowest. The reverse pattern was found on the fourth scale. The third scale was also related significantly to political preference, but here a different component of political philosophy was evidently involved. Liberal Republicans scored highest, followed by conservative Republicans, liberal independents, conservative Democrats, and finally liberal Democrats. Perhaps this order represents in part a dimension of rejection versus acceptance of what has been called 'custodial liberalism'. Subjects who view social welfare as a major responsibility of government would tend to score toward the involvement end of the third scale. When subjects were asked for their specific views on the Vietnam war, those who favored military escalation tended to score high on conventional theistic religion, productiveness, and optimism, while those who favored immediate withdrawal of American forces scored low on these scales. Those who favored an intermediate position, stated in terms of a gradual reduction of involvement and corresponding more closely to announced Administration policy, scored higher than either of the other two groups on the third scale. This suggests that the subject who tended toward detachment was least inclined to take a very definite independent stand on this issue.

Scores on the fourth and fifth scales also showed some expected relationships to the chosen majors of student subjects. The highest scores on relativism were found among students in the humanities and fine arts. Engineering students proved to be most absolutist, followed by students in the natural sciences. Averages for other majors lay fairly close together in the middle of the scale. On the fifth scale, we see a partial reversal of this order. Engineering students were the most deterministic, while students in the social sciences and nursing were also high. Students in the fine arts scored near the other extreme, while those in the humanities and education also tended to have rather low scores.

Reality contact

Realistic thinking assumes a role of major importance in the psychoanalytic view of personality. In Chapter 4, we considered an attempt to measure realism of self-appraisal. Our concern now is with realism in general. There have been many more attempts to measure this, though none of them has yet led to a standard instrument that would be likely to gain widespread approval. It seems a fairly simple matter to construct a true-false or multiple-choice item for which the alternative responses will differ in realism. Indeed, we could rapidly construct items in large numbers if we employed statements like these:

'Clouds are composed of marshmallows and whipped cream.'
'The average cat has three eyes and two horns.'

If we are not content with a score distribution of zero variance, however, we must compose items that will discriminate within whatever population we may hope to test. We must have items for which a fair proportion of the population will endorse the answer we have keyed as unrealistic. When we construct such items, we find that some of our colleagues regard the answers we have so keyed as quite realistic. If those in our own department agree with our keying, we may find that people in other disciplines see our notion of reality as the perverted outlook common to clinicians and personality theorists, an outlook grounded perhaps in the metaphysical presuppositions shared by nineteenth-century physics and twentieth-century psychology. In short, in writing items that will effectively discriminate, we are confronted by the awkward fact that there is no absolute standard of reality on which we can rely, nor is there a method that can reveal a picture of reality free of the assumptions that we made prior to employing it. At best, we can compose items that will reflect a view of reality shared by most psychologists or most scientists. In interpreting the data that these items yield, it behoves us to remember that there is nothing eternally sacred about this viewpoint.

Of the extant scales for assessing reality contact, the one that has probably been subjected to the greatest amount of research application is one that has been used in Cattell's research batteries. When we examine the accumulated findings for this scale, it is interesting to discover that the factors to which it seems most closely related are those that Cattell calls *comention* (herd conformity) v. *abcultion* and *superego asthenia* v. *rough assurance* (see Cattell and Warburton, 1967). There is little indication that scores on this scale are governed by factors that have a more central bearing on overall adjustment or integration. By and large, similar scales that have been designed for lower age levels have met with a comparable fate.

It is possible, but by no means certain, that such a scale would act more in the way that theory would lead us to expect if item selection were improved. Of course, there is no certain means of improving item selection. Perhaps a good item for a reality scale might be expected to meet the following criteria:

1. It should be relatively free of the influence of general intelligence (but not completely free since realistic thinking of any sort presupposes a necessary capacity).
2. It should not depend on specialized information, but on information derivable from observations that almost everyone has made.
3. The unrealistic alternative should be one chosen most often because of emotional factors that override objective consideration of the content domain of the item.
4. The realistic answer should be one endorsed by people who actually do view the world realistically.

The fourth criterion is the most slippery one. It is subject to variable application, since in practice the class of realistic people is simply taken to mean those who think the way the test constructor does. At any rate, many of the items in extant scales seem, in the author's view, to fall short with respect to the last criterion as well as the other three. It is for this reason that the author undertook afresh to construct a reality contact scale.

In method, the author introduced nothing novel. The items chosen are all of an *a priori* character. They reflect a view of reality that most psychologists are likely to accept in each case but which is likely to be rejected by a fair percentage of people in general. A number of the items are borrowed from earlier scales. Some of them were contributed by graduate students in two or three classes in which the problem of assessing reality contact was discussed. All of them have survived sufficient discussion to forestall their being attributed to the idiosyncratic viewpoint of one eccentric author. In compiling the total set of items, the author sought to avoid overloading it with ingredients favorable to any one narrow conception of reality. At the same time, items were selected in such a way as to avoid overconcentration of unrealistic responses in any one form of bias.

It would be naïve to suppose that the present effort to construct a general measure of reality contact was overwhelmingly successful or that the present items are even free of obvious shortcomings. They do not fully meet the criteria set forth above, but as a composite they may come closer than previous scales. (In actual use, all the items were well spaced in a true-false test that contained items for several other scales in addition to this one. The answer keyed for realism in each item is indicated in parentheses.) Perhaps some reader will be inspired to develop something better after studying the following 41 items selected for the present scale:

1. Most people of normal intelligence who are determined to get a Ph.D. can succeed if they try hard enough. (F)
2. It is reasonable to believe that intelligent life exists in millions of places throughout the universe. (T)
3. There is scientific evidence that God does not exist. (F)
4. It is reasonable to believe that man gradually evolved from lower forms of life. (T)
5. Racial groups differ appreciably from one another in inborn intelligence. (F)

6. People of very high intelligence tend to be emotionally unstable. (F)
7. The civil rights movement is largely inspired by Communist agitators. (F)
8. Human beings will probably be scientifically capable some day of controlling their own evolution extensively by biochemical means. (T)
9. Scientists will probably succeed some day in producing living organisms in a laboratory from non-living matter. (T)
10. There is sound evidence that cigarette smoking greatly increases the risk of lung cancer and other diseases. (T)
11. Most automobile accidents are caused by women drivers. (F)
12. The children of racially mixed marriages are more likely to be defective than children of unmixed marriages. (F)
13. Dogs can hear many sounds that people cannot hear. (T)
14. A person who does not look you in the eye is probably untrustworthy. (F)
15. Extremely bright children tend to be bigger and stronger than average children. (T)
16. The intermarriage of people who are very closely related frequently results in children of low intelligence. (F)
17. People with long, slender hands tend to be artistic. (F)
18. People in general tend to grow more conservative after age 40. (T)
19. Cats can see in complete darkness. (F)
20. All men are created equal in capacity for achievement. (F)
21. Little boys instinctively play with mechanical things, whereas little girls instinctively prefer dolls. (F)
22. Half the people in this country are below average in intelligence. (T)
23. A child comes into the world with a knowledge of good and evil which is his inborn conscience. (F)
24. You can tell what a person is really like by looking at his eyes. (F)
25. While people have always cried and shouted that we will destroy ourselves and that the world is coming to an end, it is true that we have reached a stage of scientific and technological development where we can destroy mankind. (T)
26. History shows that oppressed peoples have always succeeded in liberating themselves in the end. (F)

27. Every man is a genius at something and deserves our respect and admiration. (F)
28. Some of the restrictions on sexual behavior imposed in earlier Victorian times are still necessary today. (T)
29. Cities are spreading out into the country, but it should be possible for every house to be on an acre of land without having suburbs go farther than they do now. (F)
30. Society supports conflicting standards of conduct so often that it is sometimes impossible to act in a way people consider right. (T)
31. The Russians are not only wrong, but they are an inevitable menace to the world because they believe in immoral and unethical dogmas and are, further, themselves basically perverted and evil. (F)
32. Only a person who has led a sheltered life could really believe that most people can be trusted. (F)
33. Most highly creative people are emotionally stable. (T)
34. Behind most noble and outwardly righteous acts is a selfish or exploitative motive. (F)
35. There are many people who are better off single and should not get married. (T)
36. The inability of Latin America and other backward and underdeveloped regions to follow our way of life is responsible for their eternal frustrations and hardships. (F)
37. Since love is purely an emotional experience, we should accept it as it comes and not try to be rational and objective about it. (F)
38. It is consistent to believe the Communist system has created a mass of people who are dedicated to the removal of the capitalist societies and it should be destroyed before they destroy us. (F)
39. The only true measure of success in life is the degree of prestige one has attained. (F)
40. Most people who perform noble and humanitarian deeds do so because they derive personal satisfaction from these acts. (T)
41. College students should not marry until they have some degree of economic security. (T)

Considering the data thus far obtained with this scale, it seems fair to say that it shows a bit of promise. In the context of the battery, it correlates most highly ($r = -0.38$) with the measure of logical inconsistency of attitudes and beliefs. Both of these measures were designed, of course, to tap distortions in thought of an 'emotional' origin. It is interesting to note, further, that reality contact correlates with many of the same variables as logical inconsistency. We can summarize most of its correlations above the 0·20 level by saying that a high reality subject tends to be a critical, independent thinker who is inclined to reject conventional ideas on many subjects. This suggests that the reality contact measure shares a bit of contamination with logical inconsistency, since conventionality is conducive to unfavorable scores on both variables. Two comments are in order. First, the 'contamination' is inevitable in both variables if we are to construct items that discriminate within a normal population. Second, the correlation between the two measures cannot be explained this easily. Reality contact correlates more highly with logical inconsistency than it does with any of a number of variables that reflect conventional thinking more directly.

As we might expect, reality contact also correlates substantially with the best indicators of general intelligence in our battery. Whether these correlations, which range from 0·25 to 0·33, reflect too much confounding from this source is hard to say, but it is evident that general intellectual ability is not the main source of variance in reality contact scores.

Other scales

In any large-scale multivariate study of personality, it is wise to include some measures that will provide a bridge to the findings of earlier research. The main instrument selected for this purpose was Form C of the Sixteen Personality Factor Questionnaire (Cattell, Saunders, and Stice, 1957). This test is designed to yield scores on the following variables, which Cattell regards as the major personality dimensions to be found in the realm of questionnaire measurement. Both the letter symbol and the technical label are given here to facilitate reference to relevant literature. The popular description suggested on the test profile sheet is shown in parentheses.

1. Factor A: Affectothymia (outgoing, warmhearted, easy-going, participating) v. Sizothymia (reserved, detached, critical, cool).
2. B: Intelligence.

E*

3. C: Higher Ego Strength (emotionally stable, faces reality, calm) *v.* Lower Ego Strength (affected by feelings, emotionally less stable, easily upset).

4. E: Dominance (assertive, independent, aggressive, stubborn) *v.* Submissiveness (humble, mild, obedient, conforming).

5. F: Surgency (happy-go-lucky, heedless, gay, enthusiastic) *v.* Desurgency (sober, prudent, serious, taciturn).

6. G: Stronger Superego Strength (conscientious, persevering, staid, rule-bound) *v.* Weaker Superego Strength (expedient, a law to himself, by-passes obligations).

7. H: Parmia (venturesome, socially bold, uninhibited, spontaneous) *v.* Threctia (shy, restrained, diffident, timid).

8. I: Premsia (tender-minded, dependent, over-protected, sensitive) *v.* Harria (tough-minded, self-reliant, realistic, no-nonsense).

9. L: Protension (suspicious, self-opinionated, hard to fool) *v.* Alaxia (trusting, adaptable, free of jealousy, easy to get on with).

10. M: Autia (imaginative, wrapped up in inner urgencies, careless of practical matters, bohemian) *v.* Praxernia (practical, careful, conventional, regulated by external realities, proper).

11. N: Shrewdness (shrewd, calculating, worldly, penetrating) *v.* Artlessness (forthright, natural, artless, sentimental).

12. O: Guilt Proneness (apprehensive, worrying, depressive, troubled) *v.* Untroubled Adequacy (placid, self-assured, confident, serene).

13. Q_1: Radicalism (experimenting, critical, liberal, analytical, free-thinking) *v.* Conservativism (conservative, respecting established ideas, tolerant of traditional difficulties).

14. Q_2: Self-sufficiency (self-sufficient, prefers own decisions, resourceful) *v.* Group Adherence (group-dependent, a 'joiner' and sound follower).

15. Q_3: High Self-Concept Control (controlled, socially precise, self-disciplined, compulsive) *v.* Low Integration (casual, careless of protocol, untidy, follows own urges).

16. Q_4: High Ergic Tension (tense, driven, overwrought, fretful) *v.* Low Ergic Tension (relaxed, tranquil, torpid, unfrustrated).

The Sixteen Personality Factor Questionnaire is designed to provide a global picture of the personality. By virtue of its broad coverage, it might be expected to throw light on any factor that might emerge from the present battery. The following additional scales were included in the battery because they were more focally concerned with variables in the area of the present research and promised to provide a link to related studies:

1. Barron's independence (Barron, 1963).
2. The Manifest Anxiety Scale (Taylor, 1953).
3. Rehfisch's rigidity scale (Rehfisch, 1958).
4. Barron's ego strength scale (Barron, 1953b).
5. A set of items found by Crutchfield to distinguish independent from conforming subjects (Crutchfield, 1955).
6. The Dogmatism Scale (Rokeach, 1960).

One further questionnaire that was freshly constructed for inclusion in the battery was a one-page test called the Health Inventory, which yields an overall score for psychosomatic symptoms. The Health Inventory contains 42 brief items of the sort that appear in inventories like the Cornell Medical Index. In each item, the subject indicates whether he has a given symptom. The symptoms in the present test all involve physical disorders, but ones which are frequently psychogenic. It was the basic purpose of the present research, of course, to analyze constructive functioning rather than pathology, but we can hardly afford to ignore the relationship between the two. It was hoped that the limited information about emotional and physical problems provided by the Health Inventory and other scales noted above would enable us to see constructive processes in a somewhat broader perspective.

Chapter 8

Other measures included in the research battery

Measures of cognitive functioning

Common observation, theory, and past research all point to important relationships between cognitive efficiency and the extent of optimal functioning in the personality as a whole. When there is a disturbance in the personality, there may be some general performance decrement in intellectual tasks or there may be selective impairment. Furthermore, because of peculiarities in overall development, intellectual abilities may fall below—either generally or selectively—the individual's potential. A man may display a knack for concocting novel ideas but lack the orderliness requisite for a high level of rational analysis; he may be adept at logical reasoning and analysis but be unable to think creatively; or he may be skilful in applying logic to numbers but not to people.

The desirability of securing information about the intellectual functioning of the subjects taking the personality battery was obvious from the outset. Yet a thorough assessment that would reveal all major patterns of performance was beyond practical reach. It seemed far better, however, to devote a small portion of testing time to cognitive measures than to neglect such variables altogether. For a global estimate of general ability we turned to college records. Since students normally take scholastic aptitude examinations before or shortly after entering college, it was felt that scores from these might be added to the information derived from the battery, permitting us to devote available testing time to more specific aspects of intellectual functioning.

This course was not free of pitfalls. As it turned out, entrance examination scores were available on a little less than 80 per cent of the battery sample. The records yielded a mixture of scores obtained locally and scores transferred from records at other institutions, and they were based on five different instruments— the American College Testing Program Examination (the ACT), the College Qualification Tests (CQT), the College Entrance Examination Board Scholastic Aptitude Test (SAT), the American

Council on Education Psychological Examination for College Freshmen (ACE), and the Cooperative School and College Ability Tests (SCAT). As a further complication, for some of these tests the scores were derived from more than one edition. Wherever such scores were available, however, it was possible to secure some indication of linguistic ability and some indication of quantitative ability. For the former, the relevant score was variously designated verbal, linguistic, or English usage (on the ACT); for the latter, it was called quantitative, mathematical, numerical, or mathematics usage.

Undoubtedly the above tests do not yield strictly equivalent information, but for the sake of correlating other measures with basic ability variables, it seemed worthwhile to assume that they do. The most likely effect of pooling data from non-equivalent ability tests would be a lack of correlation between the ability scores and anything else. Pooling scores from different instruments required use of a common scale. For this purpose, the scores were all transformed to T scores on the basis of whatever was available in the way of local normative data. To an unknown extent, the effects of non-equivalent tests were compounded with those of non-equivalent normative samples, but this was unavoidable. In any case, we thereby obtained a linguistic T score and a quantitative T score for most of our subjects.

There is reason to believe that the over- and under-development of either of these broad abilities relative to the other one is bound up with certain aspects of the individual's overall mode of adjustment. As a rough measure of aptitude discrepancy, we took the difference between the two T scores. For purposes of analysis, this was expressed in two forms—as the excess of linguistic over quantitative ability (i.e. the difference obtained by subtracting the latter from the former) and as an absolute discrepancy (the difference treated without regard for its direction).

The aptitude discrepancy scores might be expected to reveal some of the long-term effects of disturbances in personality development and organization. Of equal importance, however, is the immediate effect of distress on any given performance. Perhaps the ideal way to assess this would involve placing subjects individually in stressful or anxiety-arousing conditions and examining the effects of various kinds of stress on various kinds of performance. By using a multiplicity of conditions we could determine which things are specifically disturbing or threatening for any given subject and, at the same time, ensure the uniformity of stimulus context that we need to get normatively meaningful performance-decrement scores.

For the sake of economical group testing, we resorted to a simpler and less satisfactory procedure. We sought a simple performance task that would be sensitive to disruption under timed group administration and in which threatening stimuli or content could be easily incorporated. A scrambled sentences test seemed to offer the best prospect. Two sets of scrambled sentences were constructed, a set A and a set B. These are roughly comparable with respect to sentence lengths and grammatical complexity, but set A contains presumably neutral material, while set B items contain a liberal sprinkling of words that should tend to be threatening or disturbing for many subjects. The words denote or suggest content in the realms of sex, violence, common objects of disgust, and threats to self-esteem.

The A set contains the following items:

1. RODE THEY SAID A HE HORSE
2. FRIED IN I A THE PAN BACON FRYING
3. MANY PICTURE VERY PEOPLE IS THE GOOD THINK
4. GROCER A SAW HE CUSTOMER THE THOUGHT
5. WAS HAPPY ALMOST BECAUSE THE WORK WAS I DONE
6. BE GLAD THEY TO THEY WHEN WILL START GO
7. ATE OFF DINNER THE RADIO AND TURNED I
8. OF TO WHEN A READ I BOOKS LOT SCHOOL WENT I
9. THEM WHEN I WAS SAID THEY HEARD I HERE
10. THE TO FLOWERS BLOOM BEGAN IT AFTER RAINED
11. LUCK I FIND GOOD WILL IT BRING IT CAN IF
12. THE CAN IF IT SEWS WEAR QUICKLY VERY SHE DRESS SHE
13. WORK HOT COFFEE THE HE DRANK WENT AND TO
14. SAY THAT IN WAS PLEASANT HE NOT I A DID MOOD
15. RANG STRUMMED BELL OLD THE YOU THE GUITAR ON UNTIL I
16. THE FLOOR DUSTY IN SWEEP HALL THE THEY TO TOLD HER
17. THE BEGAN RAIN TO WHEN THE POUR I WINDOW CLOSED
18. THE TWINS SONG AND PLAYED ON SHE DUET PIANO A SANG THE A
19. DOOR AND DROVE HONKED IN HE WHEN I HIS CAR THE OPENED UP
20. FROM CAUGHT HE TO BENT PIN FISH ORDER WITH A IN STARVING KEEP

The B set contains the following items:

1. HE I GUTS NO SAID HAD
2. I THE MESS SPIT ROTTEN A INTO CROCK

3. THINK MANY QUEER PEOPLE A AM I BIT
4. A I FATHER MY THOUGHT COWARD WAS
5. MY ASHAMED PANTS BECAUSE I WAS SO WERE DIRTY
6. FAIL WILL LAUGH THEY I IF COME TO
7. HER CALLED HER A AND SLUT SLAPPED I
8. WAS BABY WHEN I I AT WAS A BREAST THE NURSED
9. WHEN CRAZY THEY HATE AM SAY I THEM I
10. TEASED PUNCHED HE ME IN WHEN THE ME SHE NOSE
11. BE MAKE WILL IT A LOW I BLOW IT IF CAN'T
12. TOUCHES SHE SHE PRICK QUICKLY FINGER TOO IF IT HER WILL
13. SICK I YELLOW AND GOT JUICE THE SLIMY DRANK
14. I SUCH DO THING MOTHER NOT KNOW STUPID MY WOULD DID A
15. PAIN I FELT SUCKED ON I NIPPLE THE UNTIL RUBBER
16. ASKED FRAME TO HE SCREW ME BROAD THE WALL TO THE
17. BEGAN OUT SPURT FORTH UNTIL BLOOD THE TO SQUEEZED I PUS
18. COCK EGG AND AN AND THE HEN CROWED LAID FLOOR THE ON BARE
19. THROUGH FLESH MY EXPOSED LAY WHILE I STILL AND BULLET THE CUT HE
20. I GET IN HOLE BALLS THEM STICK WITH THE THE HARD THE HIT TO

The task of the subject, of course, was to rearrange the words in as many items as possible within a given time period. The two sets were administered on different occasions, set A being given first. Two scores were employed in subsequent analyses—a scrambled sentences skill score, based on set A performance alone, and a score for performance decrement, based on the difference in performance between the two sets.

It also seemed worthwhile to explore the realm of creative ability, since the traits of creative people and the characteristics of the optimal personality have been frequently linked in past theoretical treatments and because there are many reasons for expecting subtle relationships between the personality traits that underlie creativity and performance in tasks designed to tap creative ability. Unfortunately, creative ability is a rather complex composite. It seemed practical to include only one pertinent test, the Consequences test of Christensen, Merrifield, and Guilford (Guilford, 1959). This test yields two scores, one for originality and one for ideational fluency. The former has frequently been cited as a good measure of one of the factors most central to creative ability.

There were also reasons for suspecting that Witkin's dimension of field dependence-independence might be related to some of the variables assessed by the battery (see Witkin *et al.*, 1954, and Witkin *et al.*, 1962). It seemed impractical, however, to employ any of Witkin's individual apparatus tasks in the present study. The obvious alternative was a measure of ability to identify embedded figures, since this has been found to be highly related to the variables measured by the apparatus tasks. As a convenient group test of this ability, we chose the Closure Flexibility test of Thurstone and Jeffrey (1965).

Another feature of perceptual functioning that seemed of possible importance for our purposes is the extent to which the perceptual field is precisely articulated and organized. Organization and form-level scores applied to Rorschach responses have been regarded as measures of this, and Thomas (1955) has found a relationship between such a measure—his scale of perceptual maturity—and a measure of ego strength. For the present battery, the author's own inkblot test (see Coan, 1959) was converted to a group instrument. The inkblots were reproduced by photo-offset processing and presented in the form of a booklet in which the subject has ample space to record his responses. Of primary interest in the present research was a score for form level based on the overall organization of the blot into components of definite form. Since the blots were originally designed for the study of movement responses, each protocol was additionally scored for presence and type of movement concept. In later analyses, we used scores for non-popular manifest human movement, non-human movement, popular movement, movement tendency, and unenlivened concepts (simple form concepts or blot rejections).

We employed one other instrument that might be considered an ability test, the Barron–Welsh Art Scale (see Welsh, 1959). This is composed of design preference items which were found to differentiate between artists and people in general. On the whole, figures preferred by artists tend to be relatively complex in composition, and scores on this test have been found to be related to independence and originality.

Correlates of the cognitive measures

The correlations obtained for the various ability measures with one another and with other battery measures contain no startling surprises. Many cognitive performance measures have been regarded from time to time as useful indices of personality characteristics, but almost invariably they have proved to correlate more highly with other abilities than they do with independent measures of the personality traits which they are alleged to tap. Substantial correlations are to be expected among most of the present cognitive performance measures. Linguistic ability, quantitative ability, closure flexibility, and scrambled sentences skill all prove to be appreciably inter-related, but predictably, closure flexibility correlates most highly with quantitative ability, while scrambled sentences skill correlates most highly with linguistic ability.

The correlations between these abilities and other battery variables show patterns that are broadly consistent with previous research findings. Subjects who score high in linguistic ability tend to be relatively independent and to display aesthetic interest and sensitivity. The findings for scrambled sentences skill are similar but less marked. High scores for quantitative ability and closure flexibility, on the other hand, are more likely to be accompanied by scientific and mechanical interests and a confidence in one's capacity for intellectual analysis and mastery. The most prominent features of these trends are all consistent with sex differences found in the abilities, though they cannot be fully explained by such sex differences. A marked performance difference between men and women is most evident in quantitative ability, in which men score higher on the average, and scrambled sentences skill, where women score higher.

If present correlations are an adequate guide, the difference between verbal and quantitative ability does not have much bearing on personality organization. The absolute discrepancy is essentially uncorrelated with other battery variables. The algebraic difference (verbal minus quantitative), on the other hand, yields correlations that are predictable from those for the two ability measures considered independently. Thus, it is positively related to artistic and linguistic interests and negatively related to scientific and mechanical interests. The difference tends to be positive for women and negative for men.

The other ability discrepancy score—performance decrement for threatening scrambled sentences content—also proved un-related to other battery variables. On the average, subjects scored about one point higher on the second set of sentences than they did on the first. Although the two sets were not precisely equated in difficulty, this suggests that any disruptive impact the supposedly threatening content may have had on most subjects was more than offset by a practice effect. It is possible that a few subjects with large positive discrepancy scores suffered a genuine disruption in their performance, but the correlational evidence throws no light on this matter. It is likely that the content of the second set of sentences was not sufficiently disturbing for most subjects to permit satisfactory discrimination throughout most of our sample with regard to the disruptive effects of threat. It is also quite possible that the present measure would prove more useful in a different population. In a sample of university students who volunteer from psychology classes to take psychological tests, we are not likely to find many individuals who are easily shocked by words presented in a group-administered test form.

The other tests that we described in the preceding section of this chapter yielded information that was largely independent of that afforded by the measures of linguistic ability, quantitative ability, closure flexibility, and scrambled sentences skill. The originality score derived from Consequences showed low correlations (between 0·15 and 0·25) with all four of these, but it displayed an additional tendency to accompany a set of variables that suggest a freedom to speculate or entertain unusual or unconventional ideas. The correlates of ideational fluency, on the other hand, were confined to other fluency measures (which will be discussed in later sections of this chapter). The originality score was also correlated with these fluency variables, but less markedly.

The form level of inkblot responses also proved to be very independent of other cognitive performance measures and, to a great extent, of the rest of the battery as a whole. If anything, its correlates seem to entail an openness to varied perceptual experience. The basic score from the Barron–Welsh Art Scale yielded a far more extensive set of correlations. The correlated variables seem in general to involve independence of thought, a tendency to reject the conventional and commonplace, aesthetic interest and sensitivity, and openness to various kinds of experience. A design rejection score derived from the Barron–Welsh Art Scale was found to be more related to the experience of control. Subjects who indicate a dislike for many designs show a slight tendency to report a lack of personal confidence or control.

Measures of temporal orientation

The utilization and experience of time are probably closely interwoven with many other aspects of the individual's total system of behavior and experience, and it is not possible to deal thoroughly with the issue of successful personality organization without considering temporal variables. There are many temporal variables that we might consider, however, and they are not all of equal importance. Perhaps the easiest to measure is temporal judgment—the extent to which the individual can judge the length of a given interval or produce one of prescribed duration— but it is not likely that variations within the normal range in this ability are of great significance for the personality theorist.

Of greater importance is the extent to which position and order in time are meaningful to the individual, so that he keeps track of the timing of events in his own life and is prone to accumulate temporal information about historical events. Possibly related to this is the internalization of conventional time divisions and the maintenance of contact with the 'world time' expressed in clocks and calendars. Here we are confronted with a time-sense dimension in which there is probably wide cultural variation, with those of us who are products of northern European culture lying near one extreme.

A variable that may be of still greater importance is the apparent speed of passage of time. We all know that this changes with advancing age, and it undergoes fluctuations depending on our current emotional states. It is also said to be characteristically fast in mania and slow in depression, while certain schizophrenics feel as if time were arrested altogether. Much has been said about the phenomenal speed of time, but little careful research has been done on the matter for the obvious reason that the variable is rather resistant to adequate quantification.

The variables that seemed of particular significance for our research lie in the realm of temporal orientation. It is convenient to use this term to embrace a variety of interrelated variables. These include the length of the time span with which the individual typically deals, his temporal direction (whether he is primarily concerned with events in the past, present, or future), his retrospective orientation (the extent to which he dwells on things in the immediate or remote past, the order and clarity of personal events recalled from various points in the past, etc.), and his prospective orientation (the extent to which he is concerned with the immediate or remote future, the extent to which he anticipates events at various points in the future in a clear, orderly, or realistic way, etc.).

A number of tests have been devised for assessing aspects of temporal orientation. For the present research, three instruments were designed to measure the variables that seemed most relevant. Thematic tests—story telling, story completion, and TAT productions—have been used by a number of people to assess temporal span, or the length of the time period with which the individual is typically concerned. Since a thematic test, Story Completions, was destined for use anyway in the study of experienced control, it seemed preferable to adapt this test for a second purpose rather than construct a separate test to measure temporal span. This required only one additional step in administration. After all subjects had completed the eight stories, they were asked to record next to each story an estimate of the amount of time the events in it would actually take. For most subjects, these time estimates tended to form a rather skewed distribution, since several of the stories were structured in such a way that they tended to elicit stories involving very brief periods. If a mean of the time estimates had been used as a temporal-extension, or time-span score, it would have been unduly affected by these short time values. On the other hand, the longest period given by a subject could easily be atypical and could also distort any average value, while providing an unsatisfactory indication by itself of the total set of estimates. In view of these considerations, it was decided that the second longest time value given by the subject would be used as a rough but hopefully more stable measure of temporal extension.

A second test, Future Events, was designed to deal with future time extension in the context of the subject's own life. It is a modified version of a test originally introduced by Wallace (1956). In its present form, the subject is given two minutes to write a list of events that may happen to him during the rest of his life. At the end of the two minutes, he is asked to go back over the list and indicate for each listed item what his age will be when the event occurs. The test yields two scores: fluency on future events, and future time extension. The first of these is simply the number of items recorded in the time allowed. The second is the difference between the average of the highest three age values recorded and the subject's present age.

Future Events might be expected to reveal the extent to which the subject is concerned with events of the remote future as opposed to the fairly immediate future. It would not indicate the extent to which the subject is concerned with the future rather than the past or present, however, though this would be one determinant (probably a minor one) of the fluency score. Perhaps the ideal way to determine the individual's characteristic temporal direction would be to sample his thoughts by asking him on a large number of occasions what he is thinking about at the moment. For the sake of practical large-scale testing, it is obviously necessary to use a less direct procedure. The test called Conversational Topics is a modification of a procedure introduced by Eson (1951). In this test, the subject was given three minutes to write a list of things he had thought about or talked about within the past two weeks. At the end of the time allotted, he was asked to indicate whether each listed item referred primarily to something in the past, present, or future. In many cases, this appeared rather difficult or arbitrary, since many of the items produced were intellectual topics with no clear reference to points in the subjects' lives, but it was still assumed that the overall pattern of temporal positions would be meaningful for most subjects. Three scores were obtained: fluency on conversational topics; future time perspective; and past time perspective. The first is again a simple item count. The second is the ratio of the number of items marked *future* to the total number of items, and the third is the ratio of the number marked *past* to the total number.

The temporal measures were included in the battery because there was good reason to believe they might yield information pertinent to the basic problem of the optimal personality. Since temporal orientation was not a matter of primary interest in its own right, however, the tests employed to assess it were designed with an eye to convenience and economy, rather than reliability. It was assumed that the findings for the present brief instruments would indicate whether it would be worthwhile to seek more adequate measures of the time variables for use in later research. As it turns out, the present temporal measures prove to have little correlation with other battery variables.

Of the measures we have just described, the ones that prove most predictive of scores on other instruments are the rather incidental fluency measures—fluency on conversational topics and fluency on future events. These correlate 0·39 with each other and yield similar correlations with similar measures derived from other instruments. This set of interrelationships is not surprising, nor is it of great theoretical importance. Productivity on tests like Future Events and Conversational Topics is presumably governed by a variable mixture of ability, motivation, and willingness to produce. The subject is not told on either test that extensive production is desirable, but he may draw this conclusion on his own. A slight difference in correlation pattern between the two measures may be of some interest. Fluency on future events proves much more highly related to the originality and ideational fluency scores derived from Consequences. It appears, therefore, to be somewhat more governed by an ability to produce ideas within a specified content domain. Fluency on conversational topics, on the other hand, proves to be related to several variables in the realm of openness to experience. Perhaps it reflects a greater freedom to think loosely or a greater willingness to record thoughts with limited personal censorship.

The measures more directly concerned with temporal orientation —future time perspective, past time perspective, future time extension, and temporal extension in story completions—yield no correlations above 0·18 with measures with which they are not interdependent. There is nothing in the present data to indicate that they merit further use in research in this area. We must weigh our evidence, however, in the light of the total composition of the present battery and the subject sample. The battery may lack adequate measures of the facets of behavioral organization for which temporal orientation would prove most predictive. Furthermore, a college sample may be too homogeneous in temporal orientation to reveal relationships that would emerge if one tested, say, a mixture of normal and schizophrenic subjects. Many of the promising findings for similar measures in the past have come from comparisons of groups that might be expected to differ widely in temporal perspective (normals *v.* schizophrenics, younger *v.* older subjects, etc.).

Another look at the self-concept

In the view of many theorists, one of the most important features of the personality is the way in which the individual pictures himself. Despite the recognized significance of the self-concept, however, surprisingly little effort has been devoted to the development of instruments that will provide an overall summary of the subject's self-concept. There have been many attempts, of course, to assess specific aspects such as self-esteem or self-acceptance, and we have considered measures of this sort in Chapter 4.

It can rightly be argued that much of what is effectively measured by most self-report inventories, or questionnaires, lies in the realm of the self-concept, and many of the scales they contain are commonly interpreted in terms of qualities of self-description.

But by and large, the psychologists who have constructed such instruments have not sought to provide just an overview of the self-concept. They have typically included many items that do not pertain directly to it, and in many cases they have even attempted to devise 'subtle' scales that will furnish insights that penetrate the haze of misleading self-description to the 'true' personality. If we seek to get a clear picture of the self-concept *per se*, we thus find that most extant questionnaires are not properly designed to do this, although they provide a great deal of relevant information.

It would undoubtedly be worthwhile to develop questionnaire scales with this specific objective in mind. At the same time, we should note that questionnaire scales can yield only a certain kind of pre-structured information. Perhaps more than any other feature of the personality, the self-concept is subject to highly individualized styling. For many purposes, therefore, it might be useful to employ a more open-ended measuring operation that could provide a view of the unique facets of a subject's self-definition.

The best known such procedure is the 'Twenty-Statements' test of Kuhn and McPartland (1954). They ask subjects to write 20 answers to the question 'Who am I?' They cite as a special advantage of this approach over more structured questionnaires the fact that it provides an indication of the salience of any particular attitude that the individual maintains toward himself—the more salient the given attitude or idea, the earlier it appears in the list of answers. This assumes, of course, that the various ideas an individual consciously maintains about himself are not subject to differential suppression when a verbal report is called for.

In analyzing responses to the Twenty-Statements test, Kuhn and McPartland categorize each one as consensual or subconsensual. A consensual response would be one in which the subject defines himself in terms of a consensually defined status or class —i.e. he identifies himself as a member of a group or class 'whose limits and conditions of membership are matters of common knowledge.' The response would be subconsensual if it does not refer to a generally recognized class or if the reference to a consensual class is 'obscured by ambiguous modifiers.' Examples of consensual responses given by Kuhn and McPartland include 'student,' 'girl,' 'husband,' 'Baptist,' 'from Chicago,' 'pre-med,' 'daughter,' 'oldest child,' and 'studying engineering.' Examples of subconsensual responses are 'happy,' 'bored,' 'pretty good student,' 'too heavy,' 'good wife,' and 'interesting.'

In the present battery, we included a test simply called the WAY (or Who Are You?). In this test, the Kuhn–McPartland procedure was modified for reasons of administrative economy. Instead of requesting 20 responses, we asked the subject to write as many answers to the question 'Who are you?' as he could in the space of two minutes. Four scores were derived from the WAY for use in the analysis of battery variables:

1. Fluency on self, based on the total number of responses given.
2. Consensual self-references, the Kuhn–McPartland variable scored as a proportion of total responses.
3. Salience of sexual identity, the extent to which a response indicating sexual identity occurs early in the list. (In scoring, a distinction was made between primary and secondary sexual identity responses. In the latter, sex is only a part of the basis for classification. Both the position and the type of response were taken into account in scoring salience.)
4. Salience of name, the extent to which the subject gives an early response that consists of his name, initials, nickname, etc.

It is by no means certain that these are the most useful scores that could have been derived from the WAY responses. The information they provide is certainly limited. As might be expected, fluency on self proves to be most highly related to the other fluency measures we have considered in earlier sections. Like them, it reflects some mixture of ability and willingness to record varied ideas of a prescribed type within a specified time period. There is nothing in the present data to indicate that a fluency measure based on self-defining responses is different in meaning from one based on responses involving other kinds of content. The score for consensual self-references yields its highest correlation (-0.25) with the Barron–Welsh Art Scale. The relationship is not marked, but it indicates some tendency for subjects who define themselves in terms of consensual categories to prefer simplicity. The total pattern of correlations suggests that subjects with low scores—whose responses on the whole are probably more idiosyncratic—tend to be more independent and more open to varied experience.

Salience of sexual identity proved significantly higher on the average for female subjects than for male subjects, and most of its correlates appear to reflect the sex difference. High salience of sexual identity—at least in a mixed sample—tends to go with various qualities one might characterize in terms of feminine orientation. Salience of name was found to be essentially un-correlated with other battery variables, but it might prove more meaningful under different testing conditions. In the present research, to ensure confidentiality, subjects were instructed to employ code numbers rather than names on all test forms. While name responses were fairly common on the WAY, there is little doubt that a set to suppress personal identification was carried into this test by many subjects. Presumably the name response would have a somewhat different meaning if the subject knew at the outset that his personal identity would already be known to anyone who might happen to look at his test form.

The two salience scores represent some guesses made early in the present research as to content categories that might prove useful. There are many possible ways of classifying responses, however, and there are many other categories that might prove to have greater significance. Casual inspection of the test forms reveals a fair incidence of responses pertaining to each of the following: formal group membership, physical characteristics, personality characteristics, present emotional state, characteristic activities, and goals and interests. All of these categories merit further study, though they do not all lend themselves conveniently to the kind of correlational analysis we have attempted thus far. It is possible that some of the most revealing kinds of responses will be ones that are given very infrequently. A good example of a test form containing information we were not able to utilize in the present research is provided by a subject whose entire production on the WAY form reads: 'Confused, angry, and sensitive. I don't know who I am and I don't think anyone else will know in the near future either.' The subject is probably not altogether unique in his reaction to our test nor in his present existential predica-ment, but it would be rather foolish of us to dispute his statement.

Undoubtedly we have merely begun to tap the riches that might be unearthed by an open-ended approach to the self-concept. In future work, however, we must certainly recognize the inherent limitations of the one question that we have employed. It is true that we have not yet exploited adequately the material that it yields, but still we can hope to do only so much with it. The question 'Who are you?' tends to evoke response sets that are of slight significance in themselves. In particular, it tends to evoke nouns. For this reason, there are many aspects of the self-concept that are likely to be revealed more readily in response to other questions. It would be useful to compare the responses elicited by this question to those obtained with others. Some of the alternatives would be: 'What kind of person are you?' 'What do you want out of life?' 'What are the most important things you do?' 'What are the most important things you have done?' 'What sort of person do other people think you are?' (Perhaps followed by: 'In what ways are they right or wrong?' 'Is there anything about you that most people don't realize?') A simple alternative to 'Who are you?' that should evoke a different grammatical set would be 'Describe yourself.'

Chapter 9

An analysis of the battery as a whole

We have discussed all the tests employed in the research under consideration except one—the Smoking Survey. This was a questionnaire designed to illuminate the habit patterns of the cigarette smokers in our sample. One of the basic purposes underlying much of the work we are reporting in this book was an investigation of the personality characteristics of smokers in general and of specific types of smokers. The relationships we have found between smoking and the variables we have discussed in the preceding chapters, however, tell us much more about the former than they do about the latter. For this reason, it seems appropriate to forego any further treatment of smoking here and reserve this matter for separate publication (see Coan, 1973).

The battery as a whole is concerned with a wide assortment of variables that are contained in or related to common concepts of the optimal personality. It includes measures pertaining to phenomenal consistency, cognitive efficiency, the experience of control, the scope of awareness, independence, the experience of time, and general beliefs and attitudes. The most fundamental question that we raised at the outset of this research was whether all the variables that most clearly bear on optimal functioning would point to a common general dimension. Should this prove not to be the case, it would then be appropriate to ask which independent components of optimal functioning might be distinguishable. We have already considered pertinent evidence in the analyses of three questionnaire instruments, but the obvious method for obtaining a more direct answer to our basic question is a factor analysis of the entire battery. This was the next major undertaking in data analysis, and for this purpose we had essentially complete sets of data for 361 subjects, including 170 men and 191 women.

On a variety of methodological grounds, the wisdom of factoring the entire battery in its present form is subject to question. Its ingredients vary considerably in reliability and in clarity of meaning. We might expect to obtain more meaningful factors if we first refined many of our instruments, improving them with respect to stability, internal consistency, and construct validity. Furthermore, the total battery represents a much more obscure sampling of variables than does any of the single questionnaires that we factored. The battery variables probably vary appreciably in level of referent generality (see Coan, 1964a) and in the density of coverage of component content areas. Further separate exploration of these component areas would enable us to devise a battery of better defined coverage.

These are indeed important considerations, and they point to a need for caution in interpreting our results, but they do not constitute a sound argument for not undertaking the present factor analysis. It is always incumbent on any researcher who employs factor analysis to take into account all relevant characteristics of his battery in interpreting factors. After all, factor analysis is not a magic tool designed to reveal the one true set of essences under any circumstances. It is merely a systematic procedure for re-arranging correlational data so as to reveal trends that would not otherwise be readily apparent. What it reveals depends on what we feed into it, but it still serves this basic function whatever we feed into it.

If we maintain our sights on our basic scientific aim of making orderly sense of the area we have set forth to investigate and avoid getting sidetracked by arbitrary methodological proscriptions, it is obvious that factor analysis and other multivariate techniques may be fruitfully employed at various stages of exploration and hypothesis testing in a given area. The results of such an analysis can augment our understanding of the overall structure of the area at any point, but they must always be interpreted in the light of our current knowledge of the area and of the specific variables we are measuring. Often, one analysis sets the stage for later, more adequate analyses. In the present case, we can hope through factor analysis to increase our understanding of the components of the battery and thus be in a better position to refine them for future use. To some extent, it should clarify the constructs that need to be measured and point to contaminants for which control is needed.

Similar reasoning may be applied to a methodological issue that many would consider more serious than those noted above, the issue of subject sample size. The productions elicited by our six-hour battery surely constitute a sizeable mass of test material, but some researchers would question whether 361 subjects constitute a sufficient sample on which to base an analysis of the 123 variables that were ultimately factored. To be sure, there have been many published analyses in which the subject sample was far smaller relative to the variable sample, but in recent years there has been a growing recognition that the effects of sampling error become increasingly serious as the size of the variable sample increases and can markedly affect the mathematical structure of the factors. It is now generally agreed that it is best for the subject sample (the number of units across which we run correlations) to be considerably larger than the variable sample (the number of elements to be intercorrelated). The matter is not as simple as many writers would have us believe, however, and it is not subject to the imposition of any absolute rule regarding a necessary ratio between the two numbers. The meaning of such a ratio would vary with the actual size of the two numbers. In any real-life research context too, there are likely to be competing practical considerations that will determine the feasibility of securing a subject sample of any particular size. Moreover, those who like to prescribe numbers frequently overlook the fact that the distorting influence of sampling error varies systematically with the variance magnitude of the factors. In general, it will most drastically affect the composition of the smaller variance factors—within both the rotated and the unrotated solutions. Sampling error is a matter we must always consider in examining a given set of factors and making predictions on the basis of it. In interpreting any one factor, we must make some estimate of the extent to which it is likely to prove replicable. To the extent that it is governed by sampling error, it will not. To the extent that it is of large variance and accords with both theoretical expectations and past research, we can place some confidence in it.

The variables analyzed

The following list contains all the variables ultimately included in the present analysis except those derived from the Smoking Survey. Where possible, we have noted a consistency coefficient value in parentheses. In each instance, this is a Spearman–Brown-corrected split-half reliability estimate based on the responses of 291 subjects.

1. Sex (male = 1, female = 0).
2. Age.
3. Miscellaneous activity.
4. Barron–Welsh Art Scale ($r_{tt} = 0.95$).

5. Design rejection ($r_{tt} = 0\cdot93$).
6. Closure flexibility.
7. Originality ($r_{tt} = 0\cdot70$).
8. Ideational fluency ($r_{tt} = 0\cdot76$).
9. Fluency on conversational topics.
10. Future time perspective.
11. Age of earliest memory.
12. Number of specific early memories.
13. Variety of revived impressions.
14. Fluency on future events.
15. Future time extension.
16. Tendency to agree ($r_{tt} = 0\cdot84$).
17. Extremity of viewpoint ($r_{tt} = 0\cdot93$).
18. Psychosomatic symptoms ($r_{tt} = 0\cdot80$).
19. Form level of inkblot responses.
20. Human movement in inkblot responses.
21. Consistency of interests ($r_{tt} = 0\cdot89$).
22. Artistic interest ($r_{tt} = 0\cdot79$).
23. Musical interest ($r_{tt} = 0\cdot85$).
24. Linguistic–literary interest ($r_{tt} = 0\cdot84$).
25. Scientific interest ($r_{tt} = 0\cdot86$).
26. Mechanical interest ($r_{tt} = 0\cdot89$).
27. Social welfare interest ($r_{tt} = 0\cdot92$).
28. Social ascendance interest ($r_{tt} = 0\cdot88$).
29. Outdoor interest ($r_{tt} = 0\cdot81$).
30. Differentiation of interest pattern.
31. Logical inconsistency of attitudes and beliefs ($r_{tt} = 0\cdot70$).
32. Dogmatism (Rokeach) ($r_{tt} = 0\cdot86$).
33. Performance decrement for threatening content.
34. Consistency of self-rating ($r_{tt} = 0\cdot70$).
35. Independence $v.$ yielding (adjective choices) ($r_{tt} = 0\cdot79$).
36. 16PF: A (affectothymia $v.$ sizothymia).
37. 16PF: B (intelligence).
38. 16PF: C (ego strength).
39. 16PF: E (dominance $v.$ submissiveness).
40. 16PF: F (surgency $v.$ desurgency).
41. 16PF: G (superego strength).
42. 16PF: H (parmia $v.$ threctia).
43. 16PF: I (premsia $v.$ harria).
44. 16PF: L (protension $v.$ alaxia).
45. 16PF: M (autia $v.$ praxernia).
46. 16PF: N (shrewdness $v.$ artlessness).

47. 16PF: O (guilt proneness).
48. 16PF: Q1 (radicalism *v.* conservatism).
49. 16PF: Q2 (self-sufficiency *v.* group adherence).
50. 16PF: Q3 (self-concept control).
51. 16PF: Q4 (ergic tension).
52. Temporal extension in story completions.
53. Internal control in story completions ($r_{tt} = 0.57$).
54. Unrealism of self-description.
55. Self-ideal discrepancy for personality traits ($r_{tt} = 0.75$).
56. Self-ideal discrepancy for physical traits.
57. Reality contact ($r_{tt} = 0.55$).
58. Independence (Barron) ($r_{tt} = 0.58$).
59. Manifest Anxiety Scale (Taylor) ($r_{tt} = 0.83$).
60. Rigidity (Rehfisch) ($r_{tt} = 0.72$).
61. Ego strength (Barron) ($r_{tt} = 0.93$).
62. Independence (Crutchfield) ($r_{tt} = 0.81$).
63. Consistency of value choices ($r_{tt} = 0.86$).
64. Fluency on self.
65. Consensual self-references.
66. Salience of sexual identity.
67. Salience of name.
68. Response idiosyncrasy ($r_{tt} = 0.49$).
69. Consistency with correlation ($r_{tt} = 0.86$).
70. Linguistic ability.
71. Quantitative ability.
72. Aptitude discrepancy: absolute difference between linguistic and quantitative standard scores.
73. EI 1: aesthetic insensitivity *v.* aesthetic sensitivity.
74. EI 2: unusual perceptions and associations.
75. EI 3: openness to theoretical or hypothetical ideas.
76. EI 4: constructive utilization of fantasy and dreams.
77. EI 5: openness to unconventional views of reality *v.* adherence to mundane material reality.
78. EI 6: indulgence in fantasy *v.* avoidance of fantasy.
79. EI 7: deliberate and systematic thought.
80. EI 8: unrealistic fantasy content.
81. EI 9: preference for predictable constancy *v.* excitement.
82. EI 10: need for involvement.
83. EI 11: ability to relax personal identity and control.
84. EI 12: experience of alienation.
85. EI 13: experience of unconventional impulses *v.* motivational restraint.

86. EI 14: relaxation of conscious control of thought and action.
87. EI 15: passive enjoyment of imagery.
88. EI 16: scientific analysis and speculation.
89. GB 1: conventional theistic religion *v.* non-theistic viewpoint.
90. GB 2: productiveness *v.* spontaneity.
91. GB 3: detachment *v.* involvement.
92. GB 4: relativism *v.* absolutism.
93. GB 5: physical determinism.
94. GB 6: idealism.
95. GB 7: adventurous optimism *v.* resignation.
96. GB 8: orientation to immediate experience *v.* ultimate goals.
97. GB 9: human nature viewed as basically good *v.* needing restraint.
98. GB 10: possibility of self-mastery.
99. GB 11: potential human supremacy *v.* human limitation.
100. GB 12: acceptance of benign fate *v.* emphasis on human creativity.
101. GB 13: perilous world situation.
102. GB 14: life viewed as incomprehensible and unpredictable.
103. GB 15: mechanism.
104. GB 16: personal responsibility.
105. GB 17: individualism *v.* group adherence or social responsibility.
106. POS 1: achievement through conscientious effort.
107. POS 2: personal confidence in ability to achieve mastery.
108. POS 3: capacity of mankind to control its destiny *v.* supernatural power or fate.
109. POS 4: successful planning and organization.
110. POS 5: lack of self-control over internal processes *v.* self-control.
111. POS 6: lack of control over large-scale social and political events.
112. POS 7: people viewed as undependable *v.* dependable.
113. POS 8: academic grading viewed as just *v.* capricious.
114. POS 9: dependence of success on luck.
115. POS 10: impossibility of willed actions and decisions *v.* possibility of successful assertion of the will.
116. POS 11: control in immediate social interaction.

117. POS 12: dependence on others for direction *v*. self-sufficiency.
118. POS 13: defensive self-reliance.
119. POS 14: emotional vulnerability.
120. POS 15: personal responsibility.
121. POS 16: personal control over thought and action.
122. POS 17: nervous tension.
123. POS 18: carefree acknowledgment of shortcomings.
124. (X1) smoker *v*. non-smoker (smoker = 1, non-smoker = 0).
125. (X2) past time perspective.
126. (X3) non-human movement in inkblot responses.
127. (X4) popular movement in inkblot responses.
128. (X5) movement tendency in inkblot responses.
129. (X6) unenlivened inkblot concepts.
130. (X7) scrambled sentences skill.
131. (X8) detrimental external control in story completions ($r_{tt} = 0.55$).
132. (X9) benign external control in story completions ($r_{tt} = 0.42$).
133. (X10) aptitude discrepancy: excess of linguistic over quantitative.
134. (X11) EI: total openness to experience (*a priori* score).
135. (X12) POS: total experienced internal control (*a priori* score).

This list, it will be noted, includes the factors derived from the questionnaires that were analyzed initially. That is, the factors of the Experience Inventory, General Beliefs, and the Personal Opinion Survey were treated as variables to be further analyzed. For this purpose, factor scores were derived for these three instruments by multiple-regression procedures and included in the battery score matrix. This seemed an appropriate step because it was assumed that the total battery, by virtue of its sparser and more diverse variable sampling, would yield factors on a higher level of referent generality—comparable to those that might be found at the second-order level in the individual questionnaires.

Only the first 123 variables in the above list were subjected directly to factor analysis. From these, 19 factors were extracted by the principal-axis method and rotated to an oblique simple-structure solution. Variables 124–135 (also numbered X1–X12 to indicate their separate status), as well as the variables derived from the Smoking Survey, were treated as extension variables. After analysis of the first 123 variables was completed, reference-vector correlations, factor loadings, and variable-factor correlations were obtained for the extension variables by the Dwyer method. Some of the extension variables proved central to battery factors. The basic purpose in excluding them from the initial analysis was to reduce, within the set of variables to be factored, the amount of statistical interdependence inherent in the measurement procedures. Some interdependence remains and must be taken into account in factor interpretation. Probably the most serious case is the eight interest variables. These form an ipsative set, since each Interest Inventory item contains alternatives keyed for two interest scales. The factor scores derived from each of the three new questionnaires included in the analysis are interdependent in so far as they are all derived by the application of regression weights to the entire set of items, but their intercorrelations can be regarded as more nearly a function of 'true' covariation. What we mainly sought to reduce was artificial interdependence that might tend to generate factors that could not otherwise appear.

The battery factors

We can best indicate the nature of the factors derived from the battery by first listing for each the variables that are loaded most highly by it and then noting the trend that seems to be common to the total loading pattern. Ideally, the interpretation of a factor takes into account not only its loadings but also its correlations both with the individual variables and with other factors. In the lists below, we have noted two values in parentheses for each variable. The first is a factor-pattern-matrix value (i.e., a factor loading), and the second is a factor-structure-matrix value (a factor-variable correlation).

Factor 1
    59. (0·78, 0·87) Manifest Anxiety Scale.
    51. (0·76, 0·73) 16PF: Q4 (ergic tension).
    18. (0·70, 0·59) psychosomatic symptoms.
  110. (0·69, 0·81) POS 5: lack of self-control over internal processes *v.* self-control.
    60. (0·50, 0·42) rigidity.
  119. (0·44, 0·66) POS 14: emotional vulnerability.
    44. (0·43, 0·37) 16PF: L (protension *v.* alaxia).
    82. (0·40, 0·54) EI 10: need for involvement.
    72. (0·39, 0·13) Aptitude discrepancy: absolute difference

between linguistic and quantitative standard scores.
47. (0·34, 0·28) 16PF: O (guilt proneness).
80. (0·34, 0·48) EI 8: unrealistic fantasy content.
122. (0·34, 0·61) POS 17: nervous tension.
78. (0·33, 0·48) EI 6: indulgence in fantasy v. avoidance of fantasy.
38. (−0·85, −0·52) 16 PF: C (ego strength).
61. (−0·66, −0·74) Ego strength.
42. (−0·65, −0·50) 16PF: H (parmia v. threctia).
54. (−0·56, −0·52) Unrealism of self-description.
50. (−0·45, −0·47) 16PF: Q3 (self-concept control).
113. (−0·35, −0·39) POS 8: academic grading viewed as just v. capricious.
40. (−0·33, −0·34) 16PF: F (surgency v. desurgency).
94. (−0·33, −0·10) GB 6: idealism.
X12. (−0·39, −0·77) POS: total experienced internal control (*a priori* score).

This factor clearly distinguishes between symptoms of maladjustment on the one hand and those indicative of adjustment on the other. At the positive pole in particular are variables indicating an acknowledgment or awareness of distress. In addition, there is at least one sign of cognitive dysfunction, in the absolute discrepancy between levels linguistic and quantitative performance. This discrepancy does not actually correlate highly with any of the present factors, but it is loaded more highly by this one than by any other. In a college population, of course, such a discrepancy could easily be a source as well as a result of disturbance. This factor probably corresponds fairly closely to Eysenck's neuroticism dimension, as well as to Cattell's anxiety dimension. It is interesting to note that all the appropriate markers of Cattell's second-order questionnaire factor of anxiety are present and properly loaded.

It should be noted that the variables at the negative pole indicate not only a relative stability and invulnerability, but a sort of blissful unawareness as well. It takes but scant consideration of the instruments involved to recognize that the low scorer generally provides more favorable self-description than does the high scorer. The loading for variable 54 suggests that he tends to do this at the expense of realism. This finding is consistent with the notion that existential anxiety is an inevitable consequence of accepting the responsibility for being aware.

Perhaps some would dismiss this as a factor that merely reflects a social desirability response bias. It is difficult, however, to reconcile the entire loading pattern with this interpretation. Of course, the response bias is involved in the sense that we can effectively tap such things as maladjustment or anxiety with questionnaire instruments only to the extent that the individual is willing to acknowledge their presence. In line with earlier comments of the author, to be sure, it is reasonable to conjecture that the present factor, with its heavy concentration of questionnaire scales, is yielding information most effectively with respect to the phenomenal realm. If we construe it in terms of anxiety, it refers particularly to anxiety as a quality of experience. If we interpret it more directly and narrowly in terms of test behavior, it is a factor reflecting the subject's tendency to report experienced emotionality in general and symptoms of distress in particular, as opposed to a tendency to describe himself as stable, controlled, and adequate.

Of the factor labels in common use, *anxiety* seems the one most suitable for this factor, but this term is probably a bit too specific. It is clear from the composition of the loaded variables that they are concerned more with a *trait*, involving a predisposition to distress, than with the immediate, present *state* of the subject. It is possible to distinguish a variety of disturbed states, such as anxiety, depression, guilt, shame, and embarrassment, but so far these diverse qualities have not been shown to be particularly separable at the trait level. Undoubtedly the crudeness of our measuring techniques is one reason, but it is also possible that being prone to one form of distress is tantamount to being prone to all of them—i.e. that most of the variance at the trait level can be ascribed to a single dimension. We obviously need more research on the relationship between states and traits in the affective realm. For the moment, it seems best to think of the present factor in terms of a general *distress proneness* or *perturbability*.

Factor 2

26. (0·76, 0·77) Mechanical interest.
85. (0·50, 0·59) EI 13: experience of unconventional impulses *v.* motivational restraint.
 1. (0·46, 0·65) Sex (male = 1, female = 0).
107. (0·45, 0·54) POS 2: personal confidence in ability to achieve mastery.
29. (0·43, 0·15) Outdoor interest.

3. (0·38, 0·29) Miscellaneous activity.
112. (0·38, 0·40) POS 7: people viewed as undependable v. dependable.
86. (0·36, 0·21) EI 14: relaxation of conscious control of thought and action.
44. (0·31, 0·08) 16PF: L (protension v. alaxia).
39. (0·29, 0·22) 16PF: E (dominance v. submissiveness).
27. (—0·70, —0·57) Social welfare interest
43. (—0·57, —0·67) 16PF: I (premsia v. harria).
30. (—0·53, —0·44) Differentiation of interest pattern.
24. (—0·46, —0·43) Linguistic–literary interest.
21. (—0·38, —0·38) Consistency of interests.
94. (—0·33, —0·15) GB 6: idealism.
38. (—0·29, 0·00) 16PF: C (ego strength).

This factor correlates more highly with sex than does any other, and we might be tempted to call it *masculinity* v. *femininity*. Such an interpretation would be overinclusive, however, for many of the appropriate constituents of such a broad dimension are not present, and there has never been any good evidence that a very unitary general dimension of this sort can be found. In the present case, we find mechanical and outdoor interests at the positive end and social welfare and linguistic-literary interests at the negative end. Scientific and artistic interests, however, do not appear here. The overall pattern at the positive pole suggests a confident, impersonal, and perhaps aggressive attitude, with some tendency to experience incongruence with the social environment. At the negative pole, we see more sensitivity, in particular a sensitive concern for other people—a more humanistic outlook. The high scorer is oriented toward control, manipulation, and mastery while the low scorer is oriented toward relationship. In Buber's terms, we have the I–it relationship opposing the I–thou. We have also some ingredients of the conscious masculine and feminine attitudes which Jung distinguishes in some later writings in terms of Logos and Eros. Let us call this *object orientation* v. *personal orientation*.

It may be useful to note that there is evidence of a better defined and organized pattern of interests at the negative pole (as indicated by variables 21 and 30). This is consistent with the fact that the interests at this end of the factor are of a type known from Strong's research to relate positively to interest maturity, while the reverse is true of those at the positive pole. Age, however, is essentially unrelated to factor 2 in our sample. Perhaps a personal orientation entails a greater sensitivity to, and awareness of, the inner realm, which might be conducive to a more evolved system of tastes on the part of the low scorer.

Factor 3

108. (0·70, 0·80) POS 3: capacity of mankind to control its destiny *v.* supernatural power or fate.
 92. (0·56, 0·48) GB 4: relativism *v.* absolutism.
 93. (0·48, 0·42) GB 5: physical determinism.
 57. (0·44, 0·43) Reality contact.
 24. (0·35, 0·34) Linguistic-literary interest.
 85. (0·30, 0·38) EI 13: experience of unconventional impulses *v.* motivational restraint.
 58. (0·28, 0·46) Independence.
 48. (0·26, 0·36) 16PF: Q1 (radicalism *v.* conservatism).
 89. (−0·86, −0·88) GB 1: conventional theistic religion *v.* non-theistic viewpoint.
100. (−0·60, −0·69) GB 12: acceptance of benign fate *v.* emphasis on human creativity.
 31. (−0·47, −0·53) Logical inconsistency of attitudes and beliefs.
 40. (−0·40, −0·17) 16PF: F (surgency *v.* desurgency).
 97. (−0·29, −0·24) GB 9: human nature viewed as basically good *v.* needing restraint.
 42. (−0·26, −0·08) 16PF: H (parmia *v.* threctia).

Liberalism v. *conservatism* embraces the main features of this factor, though further investigation might show that it is too broad an interpretation. At the positive pole, we find a faith in human potential, a tolerance for varying views of reality and ethical standards, and scientific realism. At the negative pole, we see a conventional theistic outlook, less tolerance of diverse viewpoints, and an acceptance of commonplace notions despite their inconsistencies.

Factor 4

 75. (0·75, 0·66) EI 3: openness to theoretical or hypothetical ideas.
 76. (0·72, 0·62) EI 4: constructive utilization of fantasy and dreams.
 74. (0·55, 0·75) EI 2: unusual perceptions and associations.

82. (0·50, 0·59) EI 10: need for involvement.
87. (0·49, 0·52) EI 15: passive enjoyment.
48. (0·48, 0·35) 16PF: Q1 (radicalism *v.* conservatism).
88. (0·45, 0·32) EI 16: scientific analysis and speculation.
84. (0·41, 0·52) EI 12: experience of alienation.
58. (0·39, 0·49) Independence.
105. (0·32, 0·29) GB 17: individualism *v.* group adherence or social responsibility.
92. (0·30, 0·43) GB 4: relativism *v.* absolutism.
107. (0·30, 0·08) POS 2: personal confidence in ability to achieve mastery.
109. (0·29, −0·10) POS 4: successful planning and organization.
83. (0·28, 0·31) EI 11: ability to relax personal identity and control.
121. (0·27, −0·07) POS 16: personal control over thought and action.
XII. (0·74, 0·91) EI: total openness to experience (*a priori* score).
73. (−0·65, −0·71) EI 1: aesthetic insensitivity *v.* aesthetic sensitivity.
28. (−0·30, −0·25) Social ascendance interest.
113. (−0·28, −0·37) POS 8: academic grading viewed as just *v.* capricious.

This factor evidently corresponds to a general dimension among the Experience Inventory factors. While that questionnaire taps many distinct aspects of openness, its factors intercorrelate, as we noted before, in a manner consistent with the operation of a general openness factor on a higher level of generality. It is reasonable simply to designate this factor *openness to experience*. The loadings for variables from other parts of the battery all accord with this interpretation, but we should note that the emphasis is on experience *per se*. There is nothing here to indicate that the high scorer would be more likely than others to indulge in exploration that requires active movement into the environment.

Factor 5
96. (0·80, 0·74) GB 8: orientation to immediate experience *v.* ultimate goals.
16. (0·71, 0·82) Tendency to agree.
97. (0·61, 0·54) GB 9: human nature viewed as basically good *v.* needing restraint.

104. (0·59, 0·61) GB 16: personal responsibility.
100. (0·49, 0·52) GB 12: acceptance of benign fate *v.* emphasis on human creativity.
 92. (0·46, 0·47) GB 4: relativism *v.* absolutism.
 94. (0·38, 0·30) GB 6: idealism.
 17. (0·36, 0·24) Extremity of viewpoint.
106. (0·35, 0·50) POS 1: achievement through conscientious effort.
101. (0·29, 0·36) GB 13: perilous world situation.
 31. (0·25, 0·34) Logical inconsistency of attitudes and beliefs.
 90. (0·24, 0·41) GB 2: productiveness *v.* spontaneity.

This bears some resemblance to Cattell's factor of 'comention,' but we can best label it *acceptance* on the basis of the overall combination of content apparent in the highly loaded variables. The high scorer displays an accepting attitude toward the immediate situation, toward people, toward varied views of right and wrong, and toward the ideas he encounters—even if they are mutually discordant. Thus, the high scorer might be expected to adapt more easily and to relate more satisfactorily to other people, but he may tend to accept people and ideas at the expense of his freedom to think independently. The low scorer would display more intolerance but would be freer to respond independently and to explore ideas not generally accepted.

As the writer has interpreted it, this factor seems to possess a fair degree of psychological unity, but one note of caution must be sounded. The variable that correlates most highly with this factor is tendency to agree, and it will undoubtedly occur to some critics that this may simply be a factor of agreement response bias. Consistent with this notion is the fact that all the General Beliefs factors that are loaded here display very marked positive manifold —i.e. there is a heavy preponderance of *agree*, over *disagree*, answers that go with the positive pole of each these factors. The same is true for the Personal Opinion Survey factor in the above list, if we construe *true* answers as equivalent to *agree* answers. Furthermore, as we noted earlier, the answers keyed for our measure of logical inconsistency of attitudes and beliefs are predominantly *agree* answers. On the other hand, a considerable amount of research has been devoted to the agreement response bias, and it seems a fair summary of the evidence to say that this bias is not likely to generate a factor of sizeable variance by itself. Where we find a factor that seems to involve this bias, we will normally have to consider the common content of the statements with which the subject agrees to arrive at a proper interpretation.

The present situation, however, is a little more complicated, since the score for tendency to agree is derived from the General Beliefs questionnaire. The correlation of this variable with each of the General Beliefs factors thus contains a spurious component. Of course, the factor cannot be dismissed as an artifact of spurious correlation, since these correlations form only a portion of the set actually generating the factor. We must take particular note of the prominent loadings for two variables derived from other instruments. But needless to say, if we wish to secure sound evidence for a psychological dimension corresponding to the above interpretation, acceptance, we should first determine whether we can reproduce this factor with a set of variables free of the shortcomings of the present set.

Factor 6

103. (0·62, 0·62) GB 15: mechanism.
  91. (0·61, 0·70) GB 3: detachment v. involvement.
102. (0·54, 0·44) GB 14: life viewed as incomprehensible and unpredictable.
  32. (0·49, 0·61) Dogmatism.
114. (0·48, 0·44) POS 9: dependence of success on luck.
101. (0·45, 0·58) GB 13: perilous world situation.
118. (0·37, 0·25) POS 13: defensive self-reliance.
  16. (0·37, 0·52) Tendency to agree.
112. (0·36, 0·44) POS 7: people viewed as undependable v. dependable.
111. (0·31, 0·32) POS 6: lack of control over large-scale social and political events.
  93. (0·28, 0·41) GB 5: physical determinism.
  95. (−0·56, −0·52) GB 7: adventurous optimism v. resignation.
  17. (−0·43, −0·29) Extremity of viewpoint.
X12. (−0·27, −0·31) POS: total experienced internal control (a priori score).

The high scorer regards life as meaningless and unpredictable and considers it better not to get too involved in things. The low scorer finds more meaning in life and is more hopeful and willing to make commitments. Perhaps *pessimism* v. *optimism* comes as close to the central theme of loaded variables as any available set of labels, and we may use this for the present. The factor entails a bit more than this label denotes, however. With the optimism goes a willingness to act and take stands, while the grim outlook of the pessimist seems to be accompanied by a defensive avoidance of involvement.

Factor 7

50. (0·61, 0·50) 16PF: Q3 (self-concept control).
41. (0·60, 0·59) 16PF: G (superego strength).
79. (0·55, 0·53) EI 7: deliberate and systematic thought.
90. (0·51, 0·58) GB 2: productiveness *v.* spontaneity.
109. (0·50, 0·49) POS 4: successful planning and organization.
81. (0·47, 0·56) EI 9: preference for predictable constancy *v.* excitement.
17. (0·39, —0·02) Extremity of viewpoint.
33. (0·33, 0·07) Performance decrement for threatening content.
104. (0·31, 0·17) GB 16: personal responsibility.
86. (—0·59, —0·46) EI 14: relaxation of conscious control of thought and action.
4. (—0·43, —0·51) Barron–Welsh Art scale.
62. (—0·41, —0·54) Independence-creativity.
77. (—0·38, —0·54) EI 5: openness to unconventional views of reality *v.* adherence to mundane material reality.
78. (—0·32, —0·44) EI 6: indulgence in fantasy *v.* avoidance of fantasy.

The high scorer tends to be conscientious, well controlled, deliberate, planful and production-oriented, while the low scorer prefers a more relaxed and less systematized life. The core of the factor seems quite clear, but there are several possible labels (with slightly different shades of meaning) that seem almost equally appropriate. The central thread might be described in terms of a need for order. A label that would better capture the active expression of such a need would be *deliberateness* v. *spontaneity*.

Factor 8

14. (0·70, 0·68) Fluency on future events.
9. (0·56, 0·59) Fluency on conversational topics.
8. (0·55, 0·50) Ideational fluency.
64. (0·54, 0·57) Fluency on self.
7. (0·42, 0·43) Originality.
15. (0·30, 0·32) Future time extension.

29. (0·29, 0·10) Outdoor interest.
6. (0·25, 0·17) Closure flexibility.
35. (−0·22, −0·16) Independence v. yielding (adjective choices).
47. (−0·22, −0·19) 16PF: O (guilt proneness).

We can best call this *ideational fluency*, since the high loadings all involve fluency measures derived from various instruments in the battery. We must bear in mind, however, that each of our fluency variables reflects the graphic productiveness of the subject, which is certainly dependent partly on his willingness to comply with test instructions to produce maximally. In this light, the low negative loading for one of our independence variables is not surprising.

Factor 9
39. (0·64, 0·62) 16PF: E (dominance v. submissiveness).
28. (0·61, 0·66) Social ascendance interest.
40. (0·45, 0·42) 16PF: F (Surgency v. desurgency).
36. (0·39, 0·39) 16PF: A (affectothymia v. sizothymia).
46. (0·34, 0·31) 16PF: N (shrewdness v. artlessness).
45. (0·28, 0·23) 16PF: M (autia v. praxernia).
42. (0·25, 0·27) 16PF: H (parmia v. threctia).
29. (−0·62, −0·46) Outdoor interest.
60. (−0·39, −0·48) Rigidity.
94. (−0·27, −0·24) GB 6: idealism,
113. (−0·27, −0·19) POS 8: academic grading viewed as just v. capricious.

The obvious label for this factor is *extroversion* v. *introversion*, for it has the principal 16PF markers for the second-order questionnaire factor so identified, and the remaining loadings can be reconciled easily with this interpretation. It probably does not correspond well to the Jungian polarity, but it may be consistent with the concepts of Cattell and Eysenck. There is, however, a bit more emphasis on social control and manipulation at the positive pole and maladjustment at the negative than one might expect.

Factor 10
71. (0·77, 0·75) Quantitative ability.
70. (0·56, 0·52) Linguistic ability.
6. (0·55, 0·52) Closure flexibility.

7. (0·38, 0·33) Originality.
25. (0·36, 0·45) Scientific interest.
57. (0·33, 0·42) Reality contact.
37. (0·25, 0·29) 16PF: B (intelligence).
48. (0·25, 0·33) 16PF: Q1 (radicalism v. conservatism).
X7. (0·25, 0·26) Scrambled sentences skill.
29. (−0·37, −0·22) Outdoor interest.
123. (−0·26, −0·24) POS 18: carefree acknowledgment of shortcomings.

This is undoubtedly *general intelligence*. It draws together all the variables that would seem inevitably related to this dimension. The one minor surprise here is that the radicalism scale of the Sixteen Personality Factor Questionnaire correlates a little more highly with this factor than does the intelligence scale of that test. In the light of past research, however, a positive correlation for radicalism is to be expected.

Factor 11
98. (0·67, 0·62) GB 10: possibility of self-mastery.
94. (0·42, 0·40) GB 6: idealism.
104. (0·38, 0·34) GB 16: personal responsibility.
93. (0·28, 0·30) GB 5: physical determinism.
120. (0·27, 0·22) POS 15: personal responsibility.
121. (0·26, 0·51) POS 16: personal control over thought and action.
106. (0·25, 0·39) POS 1: achievement through conscientious effort.
90. (0·24, 0·24) GB 2: productiveness v. spontaneity.
X12. (0·38, 0·66) POS: total experienced internal control (*a priori* score).
115. (−0·50, −0·54) POS 10: impossibility of willed actions and decisions v. possibility of successful assertion of the will.
111. (−0·37, −0·49) POS 6: lack of control over large-scale social and political events.
117. (−0·36, −0·48) POS 12: dependence on others for direction v. self-sufficiency.
29. (−0·23, −0·23) Outdoor interest.

This factor loads a variety of General Beliefs and Personal Opinion Survey variables that involve will, control, and responsibility. It loads total experienced internal control more highly than does any other factor except 1, but it falls short of being a general experience-of-control factor. As we could have predicted from the interrelationships among components of the Personal Opinion Survey, such a factor does not appear in this series. In fact, the emphasis in the present factor is not on the experience of control so much as the recognized possibility of control. Essentially the high scorer is telling us that people can assume control over their lives and over events in the world around them and that they should accept the responsibility for doing so. Perhaps the term *responsibility* would fit this dimension as well as any available brief title, but many of the connotations of this broad label are probably irrelevant to the present continuum.

Factor 12

99. (0·70, 0·63) GB 11: potential human supremacy *v.* human limitation.
25. (0·43, 0·51) Scientific interest.
105. (0·33, 0·26) GB 17: individualism *v.* group adherence or social responsibility.
106. (0·33, 0·36) POS 1: achievement through conscientious effort.
103. (0·29, 0·33) GB 15: mechanism.
23. (−0·59, −0·44) Musical interest.
102. (−0·38, −0·37) GB 14: life viewed as incomprehensible and unpredictable.
70. (−0·37, −0·33) Linguistic ability.
72. (−0·26, −0·17) Aptitude discrepancy: absolute difference between linguistic and quantitative standard scores.
X10. (−0·40, −0·45) Aptitude discrepancy: excess of linguistic over quantitative.

This factor, like most of those that remain, is of doubtful identity. The positive pole combines scientific interest with a belief in the ability of mankind to understand and control nature. The negative pole combines musical interest with a view of life as incomprehensible. In the high scorer, quantitative ability tends to exceed verbal ability, while the reverse is true of the low scorer. Perhaps the basic contrast is between two alternative intellectual attitudes—one directed toward analytical understanding, the other emphasizing appreciation of unanalyzed totalities. Perhaps the factor has something to do with need for achievement or need for control. For the present, let us tentatively call this *analytic* v. *global orientation*.

Factor 13

65. (0·54, 0·54) Consensual self-references.
66. (0·39, 0·41) Salience of sexual identity.
34. (0·35, 0·21) Consistency of self-rating.
107. (0·31, 0·32) POS 2: personal confidence in ability to achieve mastery.
121. (0·30, 0·43) POS 16: personal control over thought and action.
49. (0·26, 0·22) 16PF: Q2 (self-sufficiency v. group adherence).
5. (−0·51, −0·54) Design rejection.
4. (−0·31, −0·42) Barron–Welsh Art Scale.
1. (−0·28, −0·20) Sex (male = 1, female = 0).
111. (−0·26, −0·41) POS 6: lack of control over large-scale social and political events.
X8. (−0·29, −0·33) Detrimental external control in story completions.

This factor, and several of those remaining, are less clearly identifiable than those above. If the first two variables in the present list are construed in terms of simple and commonplace self-description, the high scorer might be described as a person with a relatively simple and internally consistent self-concept, who reports confidence in his ability to master himself and problems that he encounters. The low scorer tends both to perceive and to prefer to perceive complexity and dissonance. Perhaps we can encompass the main features of this factor with the tentative title of *organized simplicity* v. *uncontrolled complexity*. This is probably related to Barron's (1953a) complexity dimension.

Factor 14

55. (0·61, 0·54) Self-ideal discrepancy for personality traits.
123. (0·49, 0·45) POS 18: carefree acknowledgment of shortcomings.
56. (0·42, 0·36) Self-ideal discrepancy for physical traits.
15. (0·30, 0·12) Future time extension.
119. (0·29, 0·58) POS 14: emotional vulnerability.
116. (−0·52, −0·62) POS 11: control in immediate social interaction.
109. (−0·33, −0·54) POS 4: successful planning and organization.

63. (−0·29, −0·17) Consistency of value choices.
5. (−0·27, −0·07) Design rejection.

We can label this *self-dissatisfaction* v. *self-satisfaction*. It is logically related to factor 1, where negative self-description also plays a prominent role. That feature takes a variety of forms in factor 1. Here it is focused on discrepancies between phenomenal-self and ideal-self trait rankings. The emotional vulnerability factor of the Personal Opinion Survey fits easily into the present picture in so far as it involves items symptomatic of shame reactions. Anxiety indicators, on the other hand, are prominent in factor 1 but absent here. Variables pertaining to experienced control figure in both factors. In factor 14, however, the emphasis is on control in work and social interaction, while in factor 1 there are higher loadings for variables more directly concerned with affect management.

Factor 15
12. (0·67, 0·70) Number of specific early memories.
13. (0·47, 0·53) Variety of revived impressions.
11. (−0·51, −0·48) Age of earliest memory.
34. (−0·33, −0·20) Consistency of self-rating.
63. (−0·30, −0·19) Consistency of value choices.

On the basis of the highest three loadings, we can title this *scope of early memory*. For some reason, the individual low in this characteristic tends to manifest higher consistency in self-description and values, but the reason is not clear. Perhaps the person whose childhood experience is highly accessible (because he dwells on it) tends to be immature. On the other hand, perhaps over-organization or systematization in the phenomenal realm inhibits the free flow of thought that would otherwise enable early impressions to emerge into consciousness. A broad generalization on this matter would not be warranted, since the early memory and consistency variables actually have little variance in common.

Factor 16
19. (0·47, 0·43) Form level of inkblot responses.
20. (0·33, 0·37) Human movement in inkblot responses.
15. (0·25, 0·21) Future time extension.
53. (0·25, 0·19) Internal control in story completions.
23. (−0·54, −0·39) Musical interest.

81. (−0·27, −0·26) EI 9: preference for predictable constancy
    v. excitement.
118. (−0·25, −0·33) POS 13: defensive self-reliance.
97. (−0·24, −0·17) GB 9: human nature viewed as basically
    good v. needing restraint.
X6. (−0·42, −0·48) Unenlivened inkblot concepts.

The prominence of the inkblot variables suggests that this
factor may have something to do with perceptual organization.
The fact that musical interest has the highest negative loading is
difficult to explain, but it suggests that some sort of visual v.
auditory contrast underlies the factor. A tentative identification
that takes more loadings into account would be *conceptual elaboration* v. *preference for constancy*.

Factor 17

77. (0·50, 0·39) EI 5: openness to unconventional views of reality
    v. adherence to mundane material reality.
80. (0·27, 0·18) EI 8: unrealistic fantasy content.
113. (0·27, 0·20) POS 8: academic grading viewed as just v.
    capricious.
83. (0·25, 0·18) EI 11: ability to relax personal identity and
    control.
68. (−0·69, −0·64) Response idiosyncrasy.
69. (−0·29, −0·14) Consistency with correlation.

On the basis of the chief positive loadings, we can call this
openness to unreality, but the high negative loading for response
idiosyncrasy is hard to reconcile with this interpretation.

Factor 18

2. (0·62, 0·67) Age.
113. (0·29, 0·34) POS 8: academic grading viewed as just v.
    capricious.
42. (0·27, 0·18) 16PF: H (parmia v. threctia).
83. (0·27, 0·13) EI 11: ability to relax personal identity and
    control.
81. (0·24, 0·47) EI 9: preference for predictable constancy v.
    excitement.
15. (−0·39, −0·28) Future time extension.
67. (−0·31, −0·23) Salience of name.

112. (−0·28, −0·24) POS 7: people viewed as undependable *v.* dependable.

X9. (−0·25, −0·20) Benign external control in story completions.

Age is the dominant variable in this factor, and it is accompanied by a motley assortment of variables that correlate with it. A rough attempt at an overall label would be *age stabilization*.

Factor 19

  22. (0·64, 0·72) Artistic interest

  24. (0·36, 0·46) Linguistic–literary interest

   5. (0·25, 0·26) Design rejection

104. (0·25, 0·18) GB 16: personal responsibility.

  33. (0·25, 0·14) Performance decrement for threatening content.

X7. (0·36, 0·33) Scrambled sentences skill.

  27. (−0·54, −0·24) Social welfare interest.

  25. (−0·31, −0·44) Scientific interest.

  57. (−0·25, −0·13) Reality contact.

This factor apparently serves to isolate a component of the Interest Inventory that is not accounted for by any of the previous factors. We might call this *aesthetic* v. *practical interest*, though many of the variables that would logically be governed by such a dimension are not loaded by this factor.

An overview of the factors and their interrelationships

From the present evidence, it is clear that the characteristics commonly attributed to the optimal personality do not form a broad common dimension. Many of these characteristics are statistically independent of one another. Some of them apparently tend toward mutual incompatibility. At least, they are negatively associated in the present sample.

The factor that accounts for the greatest amount of variance in battery scores is the first factor. Perhaps this could be construed in terms of a dimension of general adjustment, but the emphasis is clearly on *self-reported* distress or an absence thereof. We are tapping a dimension the content of which is largely confined to the experiential realm. We certainly cannot regard this as a general dimension of integration or constructive functioning. There are other distinct factors concerned more with the individual's mode of relating to people and to the world and with the regulation of behavior, thought, and affects.

In the other factors, we find various mixtures of characteristics commonly deemed desirable and undesirable. In most cases, we find trait combinations that do not align neatly with most conceptions of the optimal personality. There are a few instances, however, where the main thrust of a particular viewpoint seems well represented at a single pole. Thus, the 'personal' pole of factor 2 might seem the ideal position for some recent theorists who stress a capacity for genuine relatedness. The high end of factor 4, openness to experience, corresponds still more clearly to a quality valued by many humanistic psychologists.

It is interesting to find that the indices of intellectual functioning, which represent a fairly obvious desideratum, tend to be related to one another but to remain fairly independent of the other variables studied. Since intellectual impairment is probably the most generally recognizable feature of psychopathology, it is possible that we would have obtained different results in a population manifesting more maladjustment and instability. Within a reasonably 'normal' and well functioning population, there seems to be little relationship between intellectual performance and other characteristics attributed to the optimal personality. Perhaps the picture would change a bit, however, if we had better evidence pertaining to common patterns of selective impairment and functional loss under conditions of stress. Only a generalization about gross intellectual functioning is strictly warranted by our data.

We can gain a few further insights by considering the inter-correlations among the battery factors, which are shown in Table 1. On the whole, these correlations are low. The few correlations of size are readily interpretable, but they do not form a simple general pattern. Thus, we could not expect to encompass them satisfactorily with, say, one broad second-order factor, but there are patterns worth noting. There is a tendency for the various factors that involve discomfort to be interrelated. The highest correlation of all is between factor 1 and factor 14. Factor 6 is related to both of these but is a bit more independent.

A second evident trend is for the 'open' or 'spontaneous' ends of the factors that entail some kind of openness to go together. Thus, factors 3, 4, and 15 are positively correlated with one another and all negatively correlated with factor 7. Furthermore, in accordance with some of our earlier observations on the composition of individual factors, there is a tendency on the inter-factor level for openness and distress to go together. This is best shown

Table 1 Correlations among battery factors

Factor	1	2	3	4	5	6	7	8	9	10	11	12	13	14	15	16	17	18	19
1		-32	-03	36	21	19	-19	-01	-16	-18	-34	-36	-27	58	13	-28	-04	-09	39
2	-32		18	-19	-07	28	00	-02	05	23	18	44	-02	-07	-14	-21	-26	-01	-36
3	-03	18		27	-14	04	-46	01	31	17	-04	12	-17	04	09	10	-15	08	13
4	36	-19	27		08	-05	-45	18	07	12	-01	-14	17	25	39	10	13	-08	31
5	21	-07	-14	08		25	09	11	-04	-22	05	05	07	13	06	08	25	-13	12
6	19	28	04	-05	25		13	-01	-07	-25	00	12	-02	23	-07	-12	-18	03	-14
7	-19	00	-46	-45	09	13		-03	-24	-11	07	09	30	-22	-21	-12	05	34	-31
8	-01	-02	01	18	11	-01	-03		31	-06	08	06	04	-02	12	05	10	-03	-04
9	-16	05	31	07	-04	-07	-24	31		-05	14	13	-03	-23	00	16	00	-06	-07
10	-18	23	17	12	-22	-25	-11	-06	-05		04	15	15	04	06	06	06	05	-06
11	-34	18	-04	-01	05	00	07	08	14	04		25	19	-30	-05	-06	06	07	-13
12	-36	44	12	-14	05	12	09	06	13	15	25		16	-19	-03	-30	-16	-02	-28
13	-27	-02	-17	17	07	-02	30	04	-03	15	19	16		-14	11	-13	14	12	-17
14	58	-07	04	25	13	23	-22	-02	-23	04	-30	-19	-14		09	07	-10	00	24
15	13	-14	09	39	06	-07	-21	12	00	06	-05	-03	11	09		05	21	-25	13
16	-28	-21	10	10	08	-12	-12	05	16	06	-06	-30	-13	07	05		-06	-09	16
17	-04	-26	-15	13	25	-18	05	10	00	06	06	-16	14	-10	21	-06		-08	-02
18	-09	-01	08	-08	-13	03	34	-03	-06	05	07	-02	12	00	-25	-09	-08		-01
19	39	-36	13	31	12	-14	-31	-04	-07	-06	-13	-28	-17	24	13	16	-02	-01	

in the positive correlations manifested by factor 4 with factor 1 and with factor 14.

In view of the complex pattern of interrelationships among the battery factors, we might hope to gain a clearer picture of the total system through a second-order analysis. Such an analysis was applied to the matrix shown in Table 1, and it is worth noting. In view of the amount of uncertainty present in the first-order solution, however, we must regard the second-order solution as a very rough chart that may be amended appreciably in the course of further exploration. As expected, the second-order variance distributes itself over a number of factors. Seven factors in all were extracted and rotated to an oblique simple-structure solution. We can get a fair picture of each rotated factor by noting the variables with loadings of 0·25 or greater. In each list below, both the factor loading and the factor-variable correlation are noted in parentheses for each of the salient variables.

Factor I

2. (0·73, 0·71) Object orientation v. personal orientation.
6. (0·61, 0·37) Pessimism v. optimism.
12. (0·61, 0·62) Analytic v. global orientation.
16. (−0·34, −0·35) Conceptual elaboration v. preference for constancy.
19. (−0·34, −0·48) Aesthetic v. practical interest.
17. (−0·28, −0·25) Openness to unreality.

The positive pole involves an objective, analytical, and impersonal outlook that suggests an effort to maintain a perceptual order characterized by a clear separation of the individual from a discretely organized environment. At the negative pole we see a more willing involvement and participation in the total field of experience. Although we are not dealing with quite the same variables here, there is a striking similarity between this factor and the most general dimension among the theoretical variables discussed in Chapter 1. We may tentatively call this *restrictive* v. *fluid orientation*. It will be interesting to see whether the constituents of the present factor are among the basic determinants of a psychologist's outlook on theoretical issues.

Factor II

14. (0·76, 0·69) Self-dissatisfaction v. self-satisfaction.
1. (0·75, 0·82) Distress proneness.

6. (0·53, 0·27) Pessimism *v.* optimism.
5. (0·32, 0·23) Acceptance.
11. (−0·31, −0·39) Responsibility.
9. (−0·27, −0·25) Extroversion *v.* introversion.

There are several terms that would serve equally well, but the common ingredient of the most highly loaded variables is obviously *general discomfort*. Perhaps acceptance (factor 5) is loaded here because it represents a pattern of adjustment that often serves as a passive mode of coping with distress, but this variable is loaded more highly by factor III. Responsibility, on the other hand, is negatively loaded because it embodies the assurance that successful active coping is possible. The negative loading for extroversion is consistent with the maladjustive content which we found to be associated with the introversive pole of that factor in the present battery.

Factor III

17. (0·45, 0·50) Openness to unreality.
5. (0·44, 0·37) Acceptance.
4. (0·41, 0·37) Openness to experience.
15. (0·41, 0·47) Scope of early memory.
8. (0·34, 0·27) Ideational fluency.
13. (0·32, 0·29) Organized simplicity *v.* uncontrolled complexity.
11. (0·25, 0·17) Responsibility.

This is one of two second-order factors to which some kind of openness appears to be central. Perhaps we can approximate the specific character of the present factor by calling it *uncritical openness*.

Factor IV

3. (0·59, 0·62) Liberalism *v.* conservatism.
4. (0·51, 0·55) Openness to experience.
19. (0·40, 0·40) Aesthetic *v.* practical interest.
7. (−0·67, −0·68) Deliberateness *v.* spontaneity.
13. (−0·26, −0·32) Organized simplicity *v.* uncontrolled complexity.

In contrast to factor III, this seems to involve an openness that is more a product of active choice and perhaps more intellectually developed in content. It entails less of an easy conformity and more of a willingness to entertain the unconventional. Of course, the distinction between factor III and factor IV is not altogether free of ambiguity, but for the present we might designate the latter *refined openness*.

Factor V

18. (0·63, 0·63) Age stabilization.
7. (0·45, 0·44) Deliberateness *v.* spontaneity.
13. (0·25, 0·19) Organized simplicity *v.* uncontrolled complexity.

Here we find a consistent emphasis on order and simplicity. We may call this *stability*.

Factor VI

10. (0·65, 0·65) General intelligence.
5. (−0·28, −0·33) Acceptance.
6. (−0·25, −0·31) Pessimism *v.* optimism.

This is presumably just the *general intelligence* factor reappearing at the second-order level with small loadings for the correlates of the first-order factor.

Factor VII

9. (0·51, 0·60) Extroversion *v.* introversion.
16. (0·48, 0·37) Conceptual elaboration *v.* preference for constancy.
8. (0·35, 0·32) Ideational fluency.

Expressiveness seems a fair label for this final pattern of loaded variables.

Examining relationships among the second-order factors, we find confluences that are largely predictable from what we have already observed. Thus, factor II correlates negatively with factor I and positively with factor IV, indicating once more that a certain amount of distress tends to accompany a willingness to face new and complex experiences. Factor III, on the other hand, is essentially uncorrelated with factor II. It relates most highly to factor V ($r = -0·30$), with which it presumably shares an emphasis on the presence or absence of a certain kind of order. In Chapters 10 and 11, we shall consider at greater length the implications of the analyses described in the present chapter.

Chapter 10

Masculine and feminine modes of functioning

Sex differences observed in the present battery

As many people have long suspected, there is a difference between the sexes. As a matter of fact, there are many differences between the sexes. Sex differences in psychological traits are dismissed by some psychologists as rather trivial and unimportant cultural artifacts, but anyone who has examined much behavioral or personality test data is bound to be impressed by the pervasiveness of these differences. To be sure, the differences are often small in relation to variance within the sexes, but it is still interesting to see how persistently significant differences appear whether we expect and predict them or not. The present data are no exception.

The present battery was not primarily designed for the specific purpose of illuminating sex differences, and the subjects, being mostly volunteers, were not selected in a way that would ensure representativeness with respect to well defined male and female populations. Still, significant differences turned up in most of our factors, and in the main they are sufficiently consistent with trends that have been observed independently in other samples to justify a number of broad tentative generalizations about masculine and feminine patterns of personality organization.

A consistent pattern of differences appeared with respect to the components of the second-order factor that we called restrictive *v.* fluid orientation. On the average, men are appreciably higher on battery factors 2, 6, and 12, while women are higher on factor 19 and, to a slight extent, on factors 16 and 17. Thus, men in general display an orientation that is more impersonal, more pessimistic, more analytical, and more practical. Women tend to display the more fluid orientation. They show a more personal and more aesthetic quality that suggests greater willingness for a certain kind of emotional participation. This picture is in keeping with observations that have been made regarding the related dimension of theoretical orientation. The tenderminded, Leibnizean, 'fluid' outlook has often been viewed as feminine, while the toughminded, Lockean, 'restrictive' outlook has been seen as more masculine.

The former tends to go with an interest in the arts and humanities, while the latter goes with a stronger interest in the natural sciences.

This total pattern corresponds well to sex differences that Jung has described in terms of the thinking and feeling functions and more recently in terms of the logos and eros principles. As we suggested in Chapter 6, women seem more inclined than men to seek a harmonious relationship with the environment or to blend in with their surroundings, while men are more inclined to reinforce the line that separates them from everything else. They more often seek experiences that accentuate their individual distinctiveness. Similarly it seems more important to them to formulate logical distinctions and to perceive separations and distinctions in the environment.

This basic difference in disposition is probably responsible for certain trends that recur in ability data. Since the male is more inclined to regard the physical world as something to be analyzed, mastered, and manipulated, he is likely to surpass the female in various kinds of mechanical tasks. The most striking effect in the present data is in quantitative ability. The analytical attitude of the male favors mastery of mathematical operations. There is a significant sex difference in the battery factor of general intelligence that is almost entirely attributable to the higher average scores of males in quantitative ability. Perhaps the best way of characterizing the situation would be to say that a selectively deficient performance on mathematical problems is much more common in women than in men. This is reflected in present data as a positive average algebraic difference between linguistic and quantitative standard scores. As we have noted, of course, women tended to surpass men in our sample in the various tests that involved verbal skills. In men we are more likely to encounter a selective handicap with respect to tasks that require a global apprehension of verbal content or a flow of ideas not bound to strict logical progressions.

It is obviously pointless to ask whether there is really a basic difference in general intelligence between the sexes. Sex differences are known to appear regularly in a host of intellectual tasks. Some of these differences favor men and some favor women. The overall difference found in a test or set of tests that contains a mixture of tasks will depend on the composition of the mixture and the weight attached to its various constituents. The sex difference found in the present battery factor is a function of the variables that were available for high loadings.

In effect, we have suggested that many of the specific differences that we see between men and women in intellectual performance may be viewed as an expression of basic differences in attitude or mode of relating to the world. Presumably the effects that we find here in paper-and-pencil tests reflect a more pervasive difference in the adequacy with which men and women can cope with various aspects of the world around them. On the average, men can probably deal more constructively with the concrete physical environment, while women, on the other hand, may be better able as a rule to grasp emotional subtleties in the interpersonal realm. Perhaps women will tend to excel in situations that require a relatively global or intuitive approach, while men will do better in those that demand a more focal, articulated, or analytical mode of apprehension. At least some of the differences that we find psychometrically may be aptly summed up in the words of the poet James Stephens: 'Women are wiser than men because they know less and understand more.'

In Chapter 6, we discussed sex differences in the context of the experience of control. It is clear that it is more important for men than for women, as a rule, to feel capable of controlling themselves and the world with which they interact. They may be less inclined, however, to attribute this capability to other people, and they are more likely to view the world as fraught with antagonistic forces. Roughly speaking, men in general have a greater need for control than women. In a few respects, however, the reverse is true. While men may stress successful action, it may be more important to women to achieve self-control through restraint of action. On the average, the responses of women indicate greater compliance and conventionality, while those of men suggest greater emphasis on independent and individualized action.

As we noted in Chapter 5, women on the whole display greater openness to experience than men in terms of the total contents of the Experience Inventory. The specific differences found on that instrument and on the Activity Checklist led us to conclude that women tend to be more open in the realm of feeling and thought, while men tend to be more open in the realm of action. This contrast is further borne out by the fact that men score significantly higher on the present factor of extroversion $v.$ introversion. (It would be a mistake to assume that men are more extroverted than women in all respects. There are other factors, such as 2, in which the average position for women might be considered more extroverted than that for men.) As it is constituted in the present battery, this factor seems to emphasize social interaction at the positive pole. The second-order factor that we called uncritical openness also supports this picture, since women score higher on nearly all of its positively loaded constituents—first-order factors 17, 5, 4, 15, 8, and 13. Men score higher on the more peripheral component of responsibility (first-order factor 11) because of its emphasis on the possibility of exerting control.

A possible exception to this overall picture of patterns of openness is the battery factor of liberalism v. conservatism. The fact that men score higher on this on the average might suggest that they are more open to varied stimulation in the realm of thought. When we examine the ingredients of this factor, we can see that this is true in some senses. Men are more likely to espouse a novel or unconventional idea, and they are more likely to accept a scientific view in preference to a widely accepted traditional view. There are a number of indications that men tend toward greater radicalism of thought than do women. Perhaps this is another manifestation of their emphasis on independence and individuality. But it does not follow that they are more tolerant of diversity. Having adopted a deviant position, one may cease to be open to alternative viewpoints. As it happens, women—despite their greater conservatism—have a significantly higher average score on the variable of relativism. Thus, with respect to openness in the realm of thought, the picture is not a simple one, but it does make sense.

One salient component of liberalism on which men achieve a higher average score is reality contact. We may interpret this to mean that men by and large have a more 'objective', scientific view of the world. The Trait Ranking test furnishes a rather interesting contrast, for we find there that women manifest greater self-objectification—i.e. greater realism in self-description. Thus while men may have a more realistic view of the universe, women—who are less intent on maintaining an unblemished self-image—have a more realistic view of themselves. It is possible that the advantage of the gentler sex extends to certain forms of social perception as well, but this is a matter on which the present data cannot enlighten us.

The feminine self-concept tends also to possess greater internal consistency. We found earlier that the measures we called consistency of interests, consistency of self-rating, and consistency of values did not correlate substantially with one another or with other battery variables. Nevertheless, in each of these measures we find a significant sex difference involving greater consistency on the part of the women. This could simply mean that women, being more compliant subjects, are less careless in marking test forms. More likely, this finding, along with those for openness and self-realism, indicates that women on the average are more self-reflective than men. They therefore spend more of their time thinking about who they are, and about what things are meaningful and important to them. As a result, they evolve better defined pictures of themselves and their interests and values. Having a clearer basis for responding to the Interest Inventory, Self-Rating Pairs, and Value Choices, they respond more consistently. By the same token, we might expect men to respond more consistently to questions about the external world that involve no personal reference.

There is one remaining major sex difference that appears in various forms in our data. The female subjects consistently report more distress or discomfort—more self-dissatisfaction, more anxiety, more neurotic symptoms, more psychosomatic problems. This is true not only for the first battery factor, which we called distress proneness, but for all the other components of the second-order factor of general discomfort—except for pessimism *v.* optimism. Men are significantly more pessimistic than women, because they perceive more fault in the environment. It appears that the female members of our college population, in general, suffer from greater emotional disturbance than do the male members. But undoubtedly one source of the sex difference we are observing is the fact that women, being on the average more self-aware and self-realistic, are better able and more willing to acknowledge personal difficulties. Men tend to be less self-aware, less willing to admit weakness, more disposed to maintain a self-concept that is generally favorable, and more inclined to perceive the source of any discomfort as lying outside themselves.

If we construe the observed differences here in terms of a sex difference in emotional disturbance or maladjustment, it is doubtful that we can generalize it beyond the college population. Some might argue that we cannot generalize even to that population, since we lack a representative sample of it, but it is quite unlikely that a sampling bias explains the consistent sex difference we are observing. It is worth noting that the data on school children, particularly in the elementary school years, point overwhelmingly to greater emotional disturbance among males than among females. If the situation is truly reversed at the college level, this would indicate a rather interesting sex difference with respect to the stages in the life cycle that are maximally stressful—or stages in which the masculine and feminine life styles are maximally adaptive. The age effect is probably due in part to differences in mode of measurement. The child data depend mostly on the ratings or evaluations of adults, who tend to see greatest disturbance in the child with the most obvious outward symptoms, in particular symptoms that create problems for supervising adults. The adult data depend more on self-report. Thus, the observed age effect may stem from the greater willingness of female subjects to admit emotional disturbance and from the fact that emotional disturbance at any age level is more likely to be expressed in conflict with the environment in the male and in subjective distress in the female.

The basic nature and source of sex differences

Very often the author has had occasion to discuss sex differences in personality traits in class. Over the years, he has grown accustomed to receiving an almost automatic initial reaction from students who are prepared to object very strongly if there is any sign that these differences are assumed to be universal and biologically based. Most often the adverse reaction comes from female students. This is understandable in the context of a culture that has traditionally accorded women an inferior status—and a culture within which many female college students are preparing to compete in traditionally masculine fields of endeavor. Perhaps the reaction seems a little more surprising, however, when we note that from the bulk of the accumulated evidence we could make a pretty fair case for female superiority. But then, it still depends on what traits one chooses to value, and all we can really say with certainty is that there is some difference between the sexes.

If we are to consider the general problem of masculine and feminine personality characteristics, it seems wise to start with certain broad and basic observations. First of all, we are certainly not talking about a single all-important dimension. We are talking about a great variety of characteristics that are interrelated in certain respects but which vary semi-independently of one another. Second, it is absurd in most cases to assume that these traits are either of strictly biological origin or pure and simple products of learning within a given culture. We are talking about the characteristics of biological organisms that learn things, and what they learn is very much a function of their species and sex. To the extent that we can meaningfully distinguish sources of total variance, we may reasonably assume that biological sexual identity is a determinant whose importance varies widely with the trait. But if we had access to all the facts of development, we might be hard-pressed to find any feature of the total personality for which this determinant made no difference whatsoever.

It may clarify things a bit to spell out more specifically the classes of psychological variables that might be regarded as masculine or feminine. It is convenient to think of these under four main headings.

Sexual identity

This is essentially a matter of the sex to which an individual regards himself as belonging—whether one is felt to be basically a male or a female. This is a very central part of a person's experience of self or identity, and according to Stoller (1968), who speaks of it in terms of *gender* identity, it is largely formed within the first two or three years of life.

Sexual identification

This is related to the first category and probably not completely distinguishable from it, but the concern here is with what the individual would like to be and the extent to which he regards himself as being *like* either sex. In any individual, this will tend to be somewhat more complex and more ambiguous than mere sexual identity. It may even contradict sexual identity. Thus, a man may have no doubt that he is physically a male but feel that in some essential way he is more like a woman than a man. It might be argued that what we are really talking about in these first two categories is self-perceived biological status in the one case and self-perceived psychic status in the other. In any event, the latter is probably governed to a greater extent by later development and subject to greater variety in form. For example, one may identify strongly with both sexes or little with either, and one may identify with men in respect to some characteristics and with women in respect to others.

We have called this category sexual *identification* in deference to common usage, but to distinguish it more clearly from the first category, we could adopt some other term, such as alignment, congruence, or confluence. One might argue that, since the first category is more directly concerned with sex *per se*—i.e. biological status—we should call the second category *gender* identification. Perhaps this would only promote further confusion now, however, since Stoller has applied the term *gender identity* to the first category.

Sexual behaviour predisposition

Two major aspects must be distinguished: first, sexual object choice; and second, preferred mode of sexual behavior. With respect to the first aspect, several basic orientations are possible. One may be physically attracted mainly to members of his own sex, mainly to members of the opposite sex, to both, or to neither. Any of these possibilities may be combined with various preferences regarding the mode of sexual behavior. We commonly think of a mode that is basically passive and receptive as opposed to one that is more active, aggressive, exploitative, and intrusive. In view of the wide range of activities in the human erotic repertoire, this is undoubtedly an oversimplification. Furthermore, it is evident, especially from the accounts of male homosexuals, that the preferred mode need not be a static thing. One may prefer to alternate between markedly different modes of behavior.

General behavioral–experiential variables in which sex differences occur

This is obviously a very broad class, since it potentially encompasses the whole gamut of psychological variables not already subsumed under any of the categories above. One justification for listing this as just one category is that it serves to emphasize the arbitrariness of any subdivisions we may choose to introduce. Having said this, let us proceed to one reasonably convenient but overlapping set of subcategories.

(a) Cognitive–perceptual variables: Men and women tend to attend to different things in interpersonal situations, to different things in the physical world, and to different aspects of things that they perceive (such as color as opposed to form). They differ somewhat in the manner in which they organize perceptions, in the manner in which they proceed to form judgments, and in the kinds of judgments they seek (e.g. those of truth as against those of value). Thus we find a host of differences on tests involving abilities and cognitive and perceptual styles. We could roughly characterize most of the important differences by saying that men tend to be analytical, while women tend to be more global or synthetic in their thinking and perception.

(b) Mode of relating: Women tend towards greater personal involvement or participation, while men tend toward more active but more impersonal interplay with a greater range of physical and social objects. Sex differences in needs for independence and control are expressed in differences with respect to social behavior involving dominance and submission, nurturance and succorance, and the quest for subordinate or superordinate status. In close, cooperative relationships, women tend to experience greater empathy or unity with the other person. Thus, for women, love typically involves more conscious identification with the partner.

(c) Affective variables: There appear to be many sex differences in both the quality and expression of emotions. In so far as an affective state is a response to an external condition, these differences are a function of the basic mode of relating to other people and to the world. Thus, on the average, women can more readily experience and express positive feelings toward other people and objects in their environment.

(d) Behavioral style: This would include a great variety of stylistic variables not covered by (a) and (c), most obviously those in the realm of expressive movement. There are clear sex differences in the style of walking, speaking, smiling, laughing, gesturing, writing, etc.

(e) Preferences, interests, values: Differences in these enter into many of the differences in other subcategories, but we are concerned here with variables whose effects may not be so immediate and momentary as those of the other variables we have covered. The present variables would underlie basic choices that govern activity over extended periods of time. Some of the most obvious differences here are those commonly manifested in vocational choices. Thus, men tend to have greater interest in scientific and mechanical pursuits, while women tend to have greater interest in aesthetic and socially helpful activities.

It should be obvious that we are not dealing here with universal distinctions between the sexes. The only characteristic that is likely to prove capable of universally differentiating the sexes is one that we would employ in the first place to define sex—the most likely possibilities being chromosomal composition of cells and presence of a given type of gonad. Since the concomitant psychological traits display widely varying degrees of inter-correlation, we cannot even properly regard them as forming a single broad dimension of masculinity-femininity.

Obviously some of these traits distinguish the sexes better than others. Experienced sexual identity nearly always conforms to biologically defined sex, while many of the variables we might list under the category of general behavioral–experiential variables represent barely significant group differences in mean. We also find varying degrees of cross-cultural variation among the traits under consideration. Again this is probably minimal for experienced sexual identity and maximal for some of the general behavioral–experiential variables. It is tempting to adopt a general rule that the less the overlap between the sexes within a given population and the less the cross-cultural variation, the greater the extent to which sex differences in the trait are governed by strictly biological forces. To adopt such a rule without considering the various ways in which traits may be formed, however, could easily lead us astray, and its inadequacies are readily apparent. Clothing and hair style may provide highly reliable indicators of sex within a given population at a given time, but they are obviously not biologically dictated. On the other hand, within every species of primate, males tend to be more aggressive than females, and there is good reason to believe that biological factors are operating here at the human level as well as the sub-human level. At the same time, it must be granted that aggressiveness may be enhanced or suppressed within a given culture and that it varies considerably cross-culturally. Of particular interest in this case is the fact that, in the face of cross-cultural variation, the direction of the sex difference remains fairly constant (though not quite universal) across cultures.

There are many ways in which sex differences can come about. A strictly biological factor would presumably be either neurological or biochemical in nature. There seems to be no evidence of important sex differences in the structure of the nervous system. In lower mammals, sexual behavior as such seems to be largely under the control of biological influences, but the data strongly suggest that the structures required for both the male and the female patterns of behavior are incorporated into the nervous system of every individual organism. Hormone balance determines which behavior pattern actually appears, and this is subject to experimental manipulation as well as a certain amount of natural cyclic variation. As we go up the phyletic scale, we find that sexual behavior is increasingly subject to additional influences, probably because of the greater development of the higher brain centers. Thus, the most 'natural' pattern of sexual behavior is more susceptible to subversion and modification and has to be learned— or at least discovered—in the course of the individual's development.

Hormone balance—more specifically, the balance of male and female hormones—may continue to affect behavior to an important degree even at the human level, but its role is surely more easily masked and countermanded here than at lower levels in the phyletic scale. At the human level, it clearly has more to do with the overall level of the sex drive than with the direction that sexual behavior assumes. Of the behavioral variables in which sex differences are apparent in early childhood, the one most likely to be affected by the minor variations in hormone balance then present is sheer activity level. The extent to which the direction of sexual behavior—in particular, the choice of a homosexual or heterosexual object—is governed by strictly biological influences remains a matter of dispute. Many psychologists consider learning to be all-important, while others cite various kinds of indirect evidence for an inborn heterosexual bent in the human organism. Biological determinants as yet undiscovered—perhaps in the realm of brain chemistry—may eventually prove to be operative.

All forms of sexual behavior may be said to be biologically determined in the sense that they express an instinctual urge which in itself is relatively non-specific with respect to mode of expression. The fact that heterosexual intercourse is the preferred mode of expression in other primates and in nearly all human societies argues, though perhaps not conclusively, in favor of the notion that most people are biologically predisposed toward this mode. In view of the commonness of homosexual behavior, we might conclude either that it is an alternative mode for which most people have a somewhat weaker biological predisposition, or that it is merely an obviously accessible mode of expression for an instinctual force for which no particular direction is innately specified. Of course, if we assume that the direction of the instinct is specified only in the sense that the individual can most easily learn or discover that one particular form of expression is particularly satisfying, any argument regarding the innateness or 'naturalness' of any specific form of expression becomes rather tenuous.

Biological differences between the sexes may govern psychological traits indirectly, by providing the foundation for inevitable differences in experience. Of obvious importance here are differences in skeletal and muscular development that determine which things can be done forcefully, skilfully, or gracefully. Anyone is likely to seek activities that are pleasurable or that bring satisfying results, and this depends a bit on the anatomy. Thus, boys may show a greater preference for vigorous sports and rough-and-tumble play simply because they can experience greater success in them.

External reproductive anatomy plays a similarly indirect role in development. The awareness that one has the genitals appropriate to a given sex is undoubtedly a major factor in the early formation of sexual identity. Furthermore, the child who regards himself as deviating markedly in anatomical construction from what is normal for his sex may feel grossly inadequate in his basic sex role and develop in a deviant way with respect to many associated characteristics.

At birth, the sex of the newborn is ordinarily (and sometimes erroneously) determined by the appearance of the external genitalia. The adult world is quite aware that the child belongs to the male sex or the female sex long before the child is aware of this, and it is possible that through early childhood the parents' perception of the child's sexual status outweighs the child's perception of it as an influence on many emerging traits. Since adults step into the role of parents with many already formed ideas about what boys and girls are like, a 'sex-typing' influence usually enters into development via parental behavior within the first year of life. Parents may assume that girls need gentler handling and perhaps more verbal interaction, while boys need more vigorous play. Various actions of the child are encouraged or discouraged depending on their assumed appropriateness to the sex of the child. Girls are expected and encouraged to show an interest in dolls, and boys an interest in mechanical toys. Boys are expected to be somewhat noisy and boisterous, while girls are expected to be more quiet and ladylike.

Some significant sex differences in behavior have been reported within the first year, and it is possible that parental handling is partly responsible for these. Under ordinary circumstances, however, it is impossible to weigh accurately the actual importance of this source of variance in child behavior. Parents see their behavior as a response to the child. From a parental standpoint, restrictions, protectiveness, and affection are accorded to the extent that the child seems to need them, and there is unquestionably some validity to this view. The actions of even the most imperceptive parent are governed to some extent by the actions of the child. Thus, the differential handling of boys and girls may well be prompted to some extent by inherent variations in the dispositions of children. No doubt, in many instances the interaction of child constitution and parental response will create effects that neither of these determinants would produce by itself.

In the kind of parent–child interaction we have just considered, psychologists have probably tended in most cases to overemphasize the parent as a source of variance. In the sort of interaction stressed more by Freudian theory, the tendency has been to place much greater emphasis on constitution—at least as a determinant of normal development. Freud accounts for the differential development of the two sexes primarily in terms of the events of the phallic stage, in particular the Oedipus complex. It is assumed for all children—both boys and girls—that the phallic region assumes major importance as an erogenous zone at this stage, that the child discovers the basic anatomical difference between the sexes, and that the child concludes from this that it is better to be male. In the case of the boy, the attachment to the mother has taken on an erotic coloring and hostility is experienced toward the father, who is perceived as a rival for the mother's love. The boy is forced by castration anxiety, however, to achieve a resolution, or semi-resolution, of this situation. Recognizing that the female lacks a penis, he fears he may lose his own at the hands of the father. His basic solution of this problem is to acknowledge the father's claim on the mother and to settle for the vicarious satisfaction possible through identification with the father. The girl, on the other hand, sees herself as already castrated and views the mother as the source of her deficiency. As a consequence, she tends to shift her affection from her mother toward her father. At the same time, she is envious of the father, since he possesses the organ that she herself would like to have. Her love for the father is assumed to involve a stronger element of identification than does the love of the boy for his mother. In the course of time, the attachment to the father normally weakens, the girl develops a stronger identification with her mother, and ultimately finds new male love objects. In general, Freud assumes that the Oedipus complex is resolved less completely in girls than in boys and that girls retain a greater mixture of masculine and feminine identifications.

This classical Freudian view has a number of glaring logical flaws, particularly as it applies to feminine development. These shortcomings are widely recognized now, and we need not examine them in detail. It is more important to recognize what psycho-analytical theory adds to the overall picture of masculine and feminine development. It focuses on a kind of romantic interplay between the child and the parent of the opposite sex in the final phase of early childhood. We should note that this is a period when the divergence of the sexes is particularly marked. Thus, we may not see a great difference in activity on the average between boys and girls in a nursery school class of three-year-olds. The dramatic sex difference observable in any first-grade classroom, however, is hard to ignore. We must note, too, that the romantic interplay does commonly occur, though non-psychoanalytical writers usually say nothing about it. Freudian theory probably attempts to account for too much here on the basis of factors intrinsic to the child and to neglect the role of the parent as a source in the normal sequence of events. The fact is that parents in our culture tend to expect children to form romantic attachments to them. They encourage this to the extent that the father accords a special kind of affection to his daughter and the mother accords a special kind of affection to her son. Obviously there are wide variations in this among different cultural groups and among families in our own society, but the net importance of this aspect of parental behavior is commonly underestimated. It is not fashionable to recognize it because it suggests that the sexual needs of parents (however thoroughly disguised) affect their handling of their children to a greater extent than they usually wish to admit. Of course, the needs involved are probably essentially sexual only in a very broad sense of the word. In any case, it is clearly unnecessary to accept all ingredients of the Freudian formulation in order to appreciate the specific character of the affectional relationships between children and parents as a source of masculine and feminine patterns of development. These patterns probably result, however, from the interplay of many contributing factors, and as yet we have only limited information concerning the relative importance of any one factor.

Optimal modes of functioning in men and women

We began this work with questions about the nature of the optimal personality. We found that the qualities commonly attributed to the optimal personality form a motley assortment of independent and semi-independent variables that sometimes work at odds with one another. Now we have also seen that there are sizeable sex differences in many of these variables. We can hardly avoid asking whether the optimal mode of functioning for either sex is not a bit different from what it is for the other. If we think of the optimal mode as that conducive to the greatest realization of an individual's potentials for expressing, for understanding, for relating, and for experiencing joy, we are likely to find that the overall composition of this optimal mode differs a bit from one person to another. To the extent that men and women are differently constituted, it would follow that what is optimal on the average for one sex will differ from what is optimal on the average for the other. It would make little sense, however, to prescribe a single standard for all members of either sex. It may be quite natural for some men to be more feminine in various ways than some women are.

We may assume that to some extent individual differences and sex differences in the general behavioral and experiential traits we have touched on in this chapter have a constitutional basis. This foundation, however, is overlain with a host of cultural prescriptions and proscriptions regarding what is appropriate for either sex. Culturally defined sex roles may serve to magnify the effect of a biological determinant, or they may minimize, cancel, or even reverse that effect. These sex roles not only differ from one society to another; they change over time. In a given variable, culture may prescribe a sharp sex difference in one generation but not in the next.

There is reason to suspect that sharply differentiated sex roles within a society act as a barrier to individual development, since they accord each person reduced opportunity to discover what course is most appropriate to his individual makeup. Whichever way the individual turns, he is too aware that he is either conforming or failing to conform to be able to act spontaneously.

Some of the limiting effects of the differentiated sex role are apparent when the sex roles prescribed by our society are carried to their logical extremes. In the hypermasculine male, we see a strong emphasis on toughness and self-assertion and a rigid denial of weakness and tender feelings. In the hyperfeminine female, we may find an undue emphasis on sensitivities and such a reluctance to assert herself as an independent individual that she cannot function competently in most life situations. Of course, there are other facets of the sex roles that may assume more prominent importance and be exaggerated instead of these. Whatever precise form these lopsided sex roles may assume, we see here two individuals with a very limited capacity for satisfactory relationships, communication, and living in general. If they should marry each other, they might maintain a traditional kind of marital partnership, but they could never understand each other to any great degree.

The situation is obviously no better if either individual adopts the role assigned to the opposite sex. In the highly effeminate male, we find a failure to realize all the potentialities associated with the masculine role. This is most likely to occur in a man who is afraid of asserting himself for some reason or who is convinced that he is basically incapable of functioning adequately as a man. The highly masculine woman, on the other hand, rigidly denies many feminine qualities in an aggressive effort to prove she is equal to men in what she views as a man's world. Consciously or unconsciously, she is likely to regard herself as biologically inferior; her assertiveness represents a strenuous effort to overcome her inferiority.

The sharply differentiated sex role is a limiting one because it is inevitably one-sided. It excludes the qualities assigned to the opposite sex. Of course, special problems may arise as sharp distinctions are reduced. There has been such a trend in our own society in recent decades, and it has been viewed by many people with alarm. (It is unfortunate that we have little in the way of psychometric data pertaining to this trend. It would be interesting to study sex differences in a variety of traits over time. Perhaps many of the presently observed sex differences are much smaller than the ones we would have found had we conducted such a study thirty or forty years ago. If we merely compared different age groups at the present time, of course, we would be compounding the effects of changes that normally occur with advancing age with the changes that have occurred from one generation to the next.) The need for change is certainly apparent. The role assigned to women in particular has been a very limiting one in the past. Women must be permitted to move beyond a conventional homemaker role if they wish to and realize the potentials afforded by a more varied assortment of social roles.

Evidently this prospect is very threatening to many men. They are fearful of women who are able to demonstrate their intelligence and compete effectively with them. If they are willing to tolerate this competition in their vocational lives, they may yet insist that the women they marry be more conventionally feminine and subservient creatures who greatly admire their husbands and consider themselves a bit less wise. Many women, fearful of reducing their prospects for marriage, are reluctant to appear too assertive, too intellectual, or too intelligent and cling to a fairly conventional role despite a lack of genuine satisfaction in it.

Sometimes a concern has been expressed—probably much more often by men—that there are serious dangers in a loss of sex-role differentiation—that children will grow up confused regarding their sexual identities, that our society will be plagued with problems in sexual adjustment, etc. There is no compelling reason to believe that such alarm is warranted. Most children acquire a basic sense of sexual identity before much of the culturally defined sex role has been imposed on them, and they will continue to do so. We are discarding distinctions that are relatively artificial, but the alarmist believes that we need them to maintain distinctions that are presumed to be less artificial. Why should this be? If we impose no particular mold on men and women just because they are men and women, we can better determine what is artificial and what is not. In the process, we may re-discover a few natural tendencies that will guide us a bit in our search for self-definition and sexual orientation and in our relationships with others of our own and the opposite sex. If instead we really find ourselves lost in an instinctual vacuum, then it would seem that the human species has been badly shortchanged in the course of evolution.

The basic reason for welcoming some breakdown in sex-role differentiation, of course, is that whatever qualities we may regard as masculine or feminine, these are all qualities that each of us possesses to some extent. To understand ourselves adequately, we need to recognize and experience all these qualities. In the course of this exploration, we may discover that some of these qualities are in some fundamental way more masculine and others more feminine—i.e. it is somehow more 'natural' for men to manifest more of some and women more of others. At the same time, if we do find all these qualities within ourselves to some extent, all our relationships can rest on a firmer foundation. A man can better understand women and relate more completely to them if he can freely experience the feminine elements in his own makeup. Similarly, a woman can better understand and relate to men if she is in touch with her own masculine qualities.

A common assumption that tends to obscure some of the issues here is that masculinity and femininity are opposite ends of a common continuum. To the extent that one is masculine, one cannot be feminine, and vice versa. For some variables, this assumption is appropriate. More often, it probably is not. Yet it underlies most of our devices for measuring masculinity and femininity, and it is bound up with the fear that many people have of moving in the one direction or the other. It would be more fruitful in most instances to think of masculine and feminine qualities as complementary traits that are not inherently incompatible, even if they cannot be simultaneously expressed in the same instant. Thus, the ability to solve mechanical problems is not intrinsically incompatible with the capacity for intense aesthetic experience. The ability to think in a systematic and logical fashion is not hopelessly inconsistent with the ability to weigh values or to rely on a rapid intuitive process in which the steps are not all consciously articulated. Maximal understanding and appreciation require the flexible use of many qualities. In the people who seem to us best developed and most creative, we are likely to find that so-called masculine and feminine characteristics are both abundantly developed. In the individual whose development is most deficient—e.g. the severe process schizophrenic who remains fixed at a childhood level in many respects—we see little fulfilment of either kind of potential.

Chapter 11

Toward a general theory of the optimal personality

The nature of the issue

In Chapter 2, we surveyed the realm of variables bound up in concepts of optimal functioning. In later chapters we considered a body of research data pertaining to these variables and their inter-relationships. We can learn a great deal about the realm of the optimal personality from this and other kinds of research, and in this chapter we shall pursue the implications of the empirical findings a bit further. It should be recognized at the outset, however, that no kind or amount of empirical data can yield a simple and clear answer to the question: What is the optimal personality? The term *optimal personality* implies a value judgment, some decision as to what traits are more or less desirable. All the extant concepts of maturity, normality, and self-actualization embraced by the term rest on value judgments, though the most basic judgments are not often stated very explicitly.

To some extent, the various concepts considered in Chapter 2 represent different decisions about valuable qualities. These concepts may also be seen as expressions of a limited variety of models of the 'good person' that have dominated twentieth-century thought in psychology and psychiatry. For much of Freud's thinking on the matter, the model was that of the realistic and rational scientific observer. To this model, which underlies his view of development as ego growth, he added the element of altruistic love, which was expressed in his concept of object-cathexis.

The theorists who departed from the psychoanalytical main-stream in the early decades of the movement tended to reject this model just as they rejected other basic assumptions of Freud. For Rank, the prototype of the mature man is the creative artist, who successfully asserts his own will. The most important character-istics of the Rankian model are independence and creativity. From the standpoint of Jung, most theoretical systems—including those of Freud and Rank—rest on too narrow conceptions of human potential. For Jung, the well developed or individuated person would be one who functions in a natural, spontaneous manner. Such a person would be open to all parts of his being in the sense that he would let all inherent psychic functions, attitudes, and archetypal forces express themselves, rather than over-asserting those functions that are most highly developed on a conscious level.

In American psychology, one can find still other models of the good person. In the mental hygiene literature, an adjustment model has long competed with a model emphasizing self-expression. The latter may be viewed as a variant of the Rankian notion. In recent years, the 'humanistic' movement in this country has ushered in a new set of emphases. Perhaps most of them center around a model of the natural, spontaneous person and are thus reminiscent of the Jungian view. The proponents of the humanistic version of the model differ from Jung in that they operate with a less explicit conception of human personality. They also introduce some elements that are rather novel—e.g. emphases on joy, love for people in general, community, transparency and physical expression.

It is apparent that no absolute answer can be given to the question of what the optimal personality is. In describing the optimal condition, we are defining what we choose to value, and psychological theorists do not all make the same choices. The traits that seem supremely important to any one of us may seem inconsequential to others. To the extent that we are simply dealing with a question of values, a relativistic position seems most defensible. It is not difficult, after all, to perceive merit in many sharply contrasting styles of life. For the most part, we surely perform a better service for other people by letting them decide for themselves what they wish to do with their lives than by trying to impose our own standards on them. Within the humanistic movement, we see frequent expression of this sort of relativism, along with various contrasting viewpoints.

Relativism sometimes serves as a convenient mode of evading awkward questions, and despite its obvious merits, it can easily assume this role in the present issue. It is clear that the question of the optimal personality is not simply a question of empirical truth, and thus it cannot be answered definitively by the amassing of research data. At the same time, however, there is more involved in the question than values alone, since the models of the optimal tend to incorporate various assumptions about the nature of personality organization. In particular, they tend to incorporate assumptions about which qualities go together and assumptions about which qualities are most intrinsic to the species. Thus, the value question becomes thoroughly intertwined with empirical research questions. The research data now available cannot provide final answers for us, but they contain pertinent information that must be heeded.

Empirical approaches to the issue

Several basic research strategies have been employed in studies designed to illuminate the realm of the optimal personality. One strategy consists of selecting a sample of subjects recognized at the outset as people who approximate a certain ideal and then examining their actual characteristics in some detail. This is the research strategy employed by Maslow (1970) in his study of 'self-actualizing' adults. Altogether the subjects studied by Maslow included personal acquaintances and friends, public and historical figures, and college students. The basic criterion for inclusion was a a loose and general one that Maslow describes as 'full use and exploitation of talents, capacities, potentialities, etc.' People with clear evidence of psychopathology were excluded. Maslow describes his study of the self-actualizers in terms of a 'slow development of a global or holistic impression of the sort that we form of our friends and acquaintances.' Though many might criticize Maslow for the impressionistic style of his research, his work culminated in a rather comprehensive picture of the self-actualizer that will probably continue to stimulate the thinking of other theorists and researchers for some time to come. Among the characteristics that Maslow found in his sample were an efficient perception of reality and comfortable relations with it, acceptance (of self, others, and nature), spontaneity, problem centering, a need for privacy, autonomy, continued freshness of appreciation, peak experiences, *Gemeinschaftsgefühl*, deep and profound relationships with a few people, democratic character structure, an unhostile sense of humor, clear discrimination between means and ends, creativeness, and a transcendence of the particular culture.

The same basic strategy has been employed on a larger scale in the study of creativity. Barron (1963), in particular, has become known for his studies of creative people, but similar work has been done on a smaller scale by a number of investigators. There is now a fair body of data on the personality correlates of creativity based on biographical and psychometric analyses of productive people in the arts and sciences.

Another instance of this research strategy is Heath's (1965) study of mature and immature college men. Heath's subjects were selected from a college population on the basis of nominations by a panel of eighteen judges, which included faculty members, administrators, and students. *Maturity* was defined for the judges as 'personal, social, and intellectual effectiveness,' while *immaturity* was defined as 'personal, social, and intellectual ineffectiveness.'

The studies we have noted here have all contributed to our understanding of the realm of the optimal personality. Each has yielded a picture of the traits that converge in a sample of people selected by some criterion of successful functioning. In some respects they all yield similar findings. But there are also fundamental differences that evidently stem from differences in selection criteria. Heath's mature college men tended to be stable and well organized, but only some of them could be characterized as creative. This is not surprising in view of Heath's definition of *maturity* and his method of selection by multiple nomination on a college campus.

Obviously, creativity is not an inevitable characteristic of the ideal person, provided we do not incorporate creativity in our definition of the ideal. There is considerable correspondence, however, between the characteristics of Maslow's sample and the characteristics found in various samples of creative scientists, artists, and writers. Maslow's subjects proved without exception to be very creative people. If we consider Maslow's list of public and historic figures, it is not difficult to discern the reason for this. What they most obviously have in common is a high level of intelligence and a pronounced tendency to be intellectually or socially innovative. Maslow started with a list of people he admired, and he apparently admired creative people. Of course, it is not difficult to read creativity into his initial definition of self-actualization.

The most serious weakness of the research strategy we have thus far considered is that it tends toward a kind of circularity. The characteristics we most clearly find are those encompassed by the initial selection criterion. At the least, however, this kind of research may yield a refined conception of the characteristic chosen for study, and it may also reveal some trait associations that could have been predicted. Its most salient virtue is the depth of examination that is possible when one is able to isolate a 'pure specimen' and study it as a totality.

A second basic research strategy is to note the changes that occur in people in general in the course of psychotherapy. Two assumptions seem important for those who use such changes as a basis for conceptualizing the optimal condition. The first is that the optimal condition is the end product of a course of development that we all tend naturally to go through. The second is that the therapeutic situation is essentially a situation that facilitates natural development, circumventing the characterological and environmental barriers that otherwise hinder this development.

The most elaborate description of the optimal condition and of the process leading to it is Jung's treatment of the individuation process. This is based in large part on changes that Jung observed in patients undergoing analysis, though Jung does not set forth his observations in the form of scientific research data.

Rogers (1961) also sees his therapeutic method as one that permits natural growth to occur, and he has endeavored to describe the changes that occur in his clients and the characteristics that emerge in the course of client-centered therapy. These characteristics include such things as self-direction, accepting oneself as a changing process, openness to experience, trust of self and acceptance of others. Although the terminology is not identical, Rogers acknowledges a great similarity between the qualities that emerge in his clients and those that Maslow attributes to the self-actualizer.

Encounter groups, too, are a change medium that many writers have viewed as one that facilitates natural growth, although one may or may not wish to classify encounter groups as a method of psychotherapy. They have been credited with bringing about all the kinds of change that Rogers describes. Among the benefits most often attributed to encounter groups are spontaneity, open expression of feelings, and an increased capacity for loving and relating to other people.

If we conceive of the optimal personality as the necessary consequence of unimpeded natural development, the second research strategy is a logical one to employ. It is always subject, however, to the criticism that the therapeutic medium itself is likely to be selectively conducive to certain effects. This objection may carry less weight to the extent that the therapeutic agent assumes a non-directive role, but even a non-directive agent may be viewed as a stimulus that tends to elicit a particular kind of response. There has been considerable argument over the idea that the encounter group serves to promote natural growth. Koch (1971), for one, sees the encounter group as a rather dehumanizing medium. It is to be hoped that his criticisms apply to a restricted subset of encounter groups, but they illustrate well the difficulties in determining the manner in which any social process affects developmental change.

The research reported in this book represents a third and somewhat more novel strategy for studying the optimal personality. Like the other two approaches, it cannot by itself tell us in a definitive way which personality pattern is optimal, but it can provide some information that the other approaches do not. The strategy in this case consists of applying multivariate analysis to a large number of variables observed in a large sample of subjects. By such a method, we can determine the manner in which traits covary in the general population and, hence, which trait patterns naturally occur there and which do not.

Much of the theorizing that has been done on the basis of observations involving the other two strategies assumes an underlying developmental process in which all the properties of the self-actualizing, individuated or liberated individual emerge conjointly. We can best determine the validity of this idea with the multivariate approach. The first strategy cannot serve this purpose, since the trait combinations that it reveals may be a function of the peculiarities of sample selection. In the case of the second strategy, it is difficult to rule out the shaping effect of the therapeutic procedure as a source of trait constellations. The multivariate strategy, however, is complementary to the other two. When the work reported in this book was begun, there was already a sizeable body of findings derived from other modes of research. These served as a foundation for the present research and they necessarily temper all the conclusions we are able to draw from this research.

An overview of present findings

The research reported here yielded a sizeable mass of data, and various parts of it are reported in some detail throughout this book, but we may summarize briefly the findings that bear most crucially on theories of the optimal personality.

1. The measures of phenomenal organization employed in this research proved to be fairly independent of one another and of other measures used. This suggests that different parts of an individual's total behavioral–phenomenal system may be sufficiently independent of one another to vary widely in level

of organization—at least within the members of a reasonably healthy population. There does not appear to be a common general dimension of phenomenal organization.

2. As measured here, reality contact, logical consistency of the attitude–belief system, and unconventionality of thought were interrelated, but they seemed to bear little relationship to most other aspects of adjustment that were studied.

3. Self-insight was related to openness to experience and to proneness to subjective distress.

4. It was possible to distinguish a number of semi-independent patterns of openness to experience, but there was some evidence of a weak general dimension of openness. Various forms of openness tended to be related positively to subjective distress.

5. The evidence did not support the idea of a general factor of experienced control. The control experienced in one area of life may be unrelated to the control in another. There was a general tendency, however, for various forms of experienced control to correlate negatively with both openness and subjective distress.

6. The ability measures used correlated much more highly with one another than with non-ability measures. Two measures of impaired intellectual functioning proved essentially unrelated to other measures in the battery. An originality score was found to be related to personality variables involving a freedom and willingness to speculate and to entertain unusual ideas.

7. An analysis of the battery as a whole yielded 19 obliquely rotated factors. The factors most pertinent to current theories of the optimal personality include distress proneness, object orientation v. personal orientation, openness to experience, acceptance, pessimism v. optimism, deliberateness v. spontaneity, responsibility, self-dissatisfaction v. self-satisfaction, and scope of early memory. There was no evidence at the first-order or higher levels of a unitary dimension that might be properly viewed as a general factor of personality integration, self-actualization, or positive mental health.

8. Sex differences were found in a large number of variables, many of them central to various concepts of the optimal personality. Men were more object-orientated, women more person-orientated. This and a number of related differences seemed to involve the thinking–feeling and logos–eros dichotomies of Jung. Men reported greater personal control, perhaps because they had a greater need to maintain a self-image of

mastery. They tended to emphasize independent and individualized action, while women were likely to be more orientated to harmony and relatedness. Women tended to be more open to experience, most notably in the realm of feeling and thought. Men were more open to experiences requiring action. Men scored higher on the measure of reality contact employed, but women scored higher on self-realism. Women reported much more subjective distress in various forms than did men. Characteristic differences in intellectual performance were also found.

The finding of greater overall significance here is that the variables commonly regarded as components of the optimal pattern do not covary in such a way as to support the notion of a common general factor. In addition, many instances were found in which desirable characteristics were inversely related, evidently tending to be mutually incompatible. The most pervasive evidence of this sort concerned measures of openness and measures of discomfort or distress—whatever their form, such measures tended to be positively intercorrelated. This trend, as well as the sex-linked adjustment patterns found, suggests that we might do better to stop thinking in terms of one optimal personality pattern and to think instead in terms of a variety of patterns that are desirable for a variety of purposes, each pattern being ideal when viewed from an appropriate perspective.

Theoretical implications

Is it possible that empirical, as well as ethical, considerations lead us to a relativistic position? In order to identify one well-defined adjustment pattern as the ideal one, we would probably have to agree on a single clear criterion of the successful life. For most contemporary theorists who deal with the optimal-personality issue, however, the criterion of a successful life is a very broad and amorphous one: one has led a successful life if he has realized his potentials as an individual and as a human being. These potentials embrace a vast territory of unknown boundaries—they include many possible modes of experiencing feelings, of being aware, of relating, and of expressing. It seems clear that one misses some of them by failing to be genuine, by trying to be something other than 'that self which one truly is' (in Kierkegaard's terms). But given a basic genuineness, does it follow that all parts of one's being will flow in such a way as to be fully realized? Or is it not inevitable that we will realize some parts at the expense of others? If so, are some parts more important to realize than other parts?

These are awkward questions indeed, and we lack an adequate basis for answering them all satisfactorily. Our research findings point to some of the choices that life poses for most of us. They show that certain alternative modes of experiencing and acting tend toward mutual incompatibility, though each of the alternatives may be viewed as a way of realizing a valuable human potential. The following are some of the contrasting modes that seem to call for value choices:

(a) a general openness to experience that permits richness or fullness of experience v. the stable organization that provides freedom from distress;

(b) an orientation toward harmony, toward relatedness, toward unity with other people and with the world v. a sense of clear differentiation from others and striving for autonomy, self-adequacy, mastery, and individual achievement;

(c) relating to oneself and others as persons v. the 'objective' orientation that permits technological efficiency;

(d) spontaneous expressiveness v. the order that permits planned, organized accomplishment;

(e) self-confidence, or a sense of control v. a realistic appraisal of one's own limitations; and

(f) an optimistic, confident attitude toward the world v. a realistic appraisal of world conditions.

It is not the contention of the author that we are confronted with utterly incompatible alternatives in any one of these cases. It is apparent, however, that these are polarities within which most people find it necessary under many circumstances to make a choice. Hence, in each of these pairs, the expressions associated with the two sides are found to be negatively correlated in the general population. They may, nonetheless, represent alternatives that can be reconciled. It was argued in Chapter 10 that to be fully human, every individual must realize both 'masculine' and 'feminine' qualities. Beisser (1971) describes the integration of the experiences of individual distinctiveness and of unity with the group that tends to occur in encounter and treatment groups. Maslow (1970) believes that self-actualizing people resolve in their experience many dichotomies of the sort we are considering here.

The polarities listed above are not totally independent of one another. Both logically and factually they are interrelated, and it is possible to recognize one theme that is common to most of them. We are dealing here with potentials that fall in many respects into two broad classes. On the one hand, there are potential modes of being that require a kind of openness, fluidity, permeability, or accessibility. For these modes to appear, we must be able to relax control over ourselves and the world around us. We must simply 'let go' and allow whatever is going to happen, happen. We must cease all concern with ourselves as individual persons. We must desist from trying to maintain a well-defined order in our actions or our experience. On the other hand, there are potential modes of being that require more in the way of deliberate control, restriction of attention, and systematic thought and action.

The open attitude underlying the first class permits a more spontaneous and direct response to all events. It permits us to relate to others and to act in general in a manner that is genuine and uncalculated. With it, we can feel everything intensely—we can experience supreme joy, but we can also be deeply hurt. A broad awareness of ourselves and of life and the world is possible in this state, for nothing is deliberately excluded, restricted, or unduly structured in the flow of impressions.

There are certain kinds of awareness and understanding, however, that require a bit of deliberate analysis or reflection, or at least a more persistent dwelling on particular segments of the total field of experience. A more structured attitude is needed if we are to find any order or meaning that transcends the experience of the moment. Through this attitude, we can relate the immediate sensation or impulse to things that have occurred at various points in the past and things that are likely to develop in the future. We thereby arrive at a relatively well-ordered view of ourselves and of things that are important to us over time. We can relate each action to an overall system of values or guiding philosophy. We can achieve the self-consistency of action that permits the achievement of long-term goals. We can progressively develop various abilities and skills; more broadly, we can develop a capacity for constructive action and problem-solving that would be impossible through spontaneous response alone. We can develop a sense of control, a certain degree of self-esteem, and a broad temporal perspective that make it easier to withstand the stress of the moment. Seeing beyond immediate difficulties, we can work more effectively toward future resolutions and maintain more stable relationships.

In the long run, the second basic attitude—directed toward order and control—is the one more conducive to stability and adjustment. It permits the greatest freedom from distress and the greatest self-satisfaction over time. The more open attitude, however, permits more spontaneity, more genuineness, more 'real living' of a kind. The need for some balanced combination of the two basic attitudes may be obvious, but apparently the ideal balance is not easily achieved. We have seen in this book that in a normal population the factors that involve spontaneity and openness tend to have a low negative correlation with those that involve adjustment, satisfaction, or freedom from distress. By and large, the people that best represent the first attitude are not, at the same time, the people who best represent the second attitude.

Later we shall explore both attitudes more thoroughly, but to complete our overview of the matter, let us consider further what is implied by a balanced combination. It is obvious that everyone displays both basic attitudes to some extent. Perhaps neither can persist very long without some movement toward the other. In any case, it is easy to see that both are essential for constructive growth. We may think of personality development as a creative process. Like any creative process, it depends on a balance of two kinds of subprocesses—on the one hand, those that lead to the breakdown of existing form, to change, to variety, to disorder, and on the other hand, those that lead to the emergence or imposition of an overall order or unity.

The idea that creative processes depend on the interaction of two opposing principles—destructive and constructive, diversifying and unifying, mutative and preservative, disordering and ordering—is hardly new. In one form or another, we can find this notion appearing repeatedly over many centuries in Western thought. In Oriental thought we might trace it back well over two thousand years. Such an idea has been applied theoretically at many times to the evolution of the physical universe, the evolution of living forms, the evolution of human society, the evolution of science and other forms of human thought, the development of the individual organism, and the development of an idea in an individual at a given time. The best known application of it to change in human society is the doctrine of dialectical materialism. In this, Marx and Engels borrowed the triadic dialectic commonly attributed to Hegel and employed it to explain historical change. Each point in the development of society was seen as a synthesis which resolved the contradictions contained in a previous stage but which generated its own contradictions and thus necessitated a new synthesis.

In biology, the best known application of the idea is undoubtedly the work of Darwin, who was influenced by a host of earlier evolutionists in biology and other fields of science. In the Darwinian and neo-Darwinian conceptions, evolution presupposes the interaction of a process that leads to increased variation in living forms and a process of natural selection whereby those forms most conducive to survival are selectively retained. The latter is an ordering process in so far as it preserves the organisms most in harmony with the environment and keeps all specimens of a given species or form within definable limits at any one time.

Historically, probably the most noteworthy effort to apply such a notion to the psychological realm was that of Herbert Spencer (1897), who saw a common evolutionary process in events ranging from individual thought, learning, and adjustment to the development of social institutions. In each realm, he saw a progression from initial homogeneous simplicity to complexity through combined processes of differentiation and integration. The interpretation of development in terms of this combination of processes has appeared subsequently in the work of so many different psychologists that it is impossible to trace all the lines of influence, but we may assume that Spencer is the common ultimate source of much of this theorizing.

Carmichael (1926, 1927) applied the concepts of differentiation and integration to motor development. On a grander scale, Gesell (1945) saw in the interaction of these two principles a basic key to behavioral development in general. In the work of Werner (1948) we see an application of the doctrine to the development of thought both from childhood to adulthood in individuals and from primitive to civilized stages within society. In the work of Harvey, Hunt, and Schroder (1961), it is applied once more to cognitive development. The first major and still the most comprehensive application of the doctrine to personality development is found in the work of Jung (1933, 1940, 1954) who sees differentiation and integration as the two basic components of the process of individuation.

Perhaps the most dramatic manifestation of the interplay of two such principles within the immediate experience of most of us is found in creative thinking. In the personal accounts of poets, artists, scientists, inventors, and other creative people, we see highly varied description but surprising agreement on certain basic features of the creative process. At some point, one must let go of an established order and yield to a flow of thoughts governed by forces beyond conscious control. This permits novel ideas to arise, which can then be sorted out, revised, and introduced systematically into a new order. Sometimes the first phase of the process is best accomplished in sleep or when conscious attention is directed elsewhere. Sometimes distinct stages of disorder or confusion and systematic construction or ordering are discernible. At other times, the subprocesses are so combined or so juxtaposed in intimate alternation that no distinguishable stages are apparent.

The sort of specialized activity that we call creative thinking is really just an instance of a type of process that underlies all personality growth. To grow, we must be willing to relinquish the security afforded by habitual modes of behavior and experience. We must permit the emergence of new ways of thinking, feeling, expressing, relating, etc. Those that prove valuable we will retain and incorporate into our overall pattern of living.

Our data suggest that some life styles emphasize the first principle—that of innovation or relaxed control—while others emphasize the controlling–ordering principle. In the one case, we see a life characterized by intensity, restless activity, and constant change. In the other, we see a more constant, less eventful existence. It is obvious, at the same time, that the balance of the two principles normally shifts in the course of any one life. There are periods—notably early childhood and adolescence—of great intensity and openness. New feelings and thoughts proliferate, and rapid change is possible in the entire mode of adjustment. Commonly through most of the adult years, the second principle increasingly predominates, and life becomes more stable and invariable.

The need for flexibility

No single response or set of responses is designed to meet all the needs or problems that arise in the course of a day. As we move from one situation to another and proceed to interact with different objects and different people, our behavior must change. From one day to the next, of course, we may continue to draw from various parts of a behavioral repertoire that is rather limited in its entirety. Over long periods of time, however, an individual's total life situation undergoes many changes, and these necessitate some alterations in the total repertoire. If we fail to make a few necessary replacements, our behavior becomes increasingly less adaptive.

It makes no sense to think of some ultimate stage of maturity when we cease to change, when our mode of adjustment remains static. If we were to formulate a list of desired goals of development, flexibility would have to be one of them. We must be able to act differently in different situations, and we must be prepared for long-term changes. For better or worse, the world changes. We may justifiably resist some of the novel horrors it sets before us, but in many respects we had better be prepared to change with it. If we have not lost the ability to perceive and remember, we will gain new understandings of ourselves and of the world around us in the process. Surely, the most mature person is one who has never stopped growing.

Flexibility is both a pre-condition for growth and a consequence of growth. It is probably easiest to think of it as an aspect of the open attitude, or of the principle of differentiation. To be open to new experience is to permit shifts to occur in our ways of perceiving, feeling, expressing, and relating. But the constructive or integrative process that accompanies or succeeds open exploration should preserve much of our flexibility. We inevitably find in the course of exploring new modes of acting and experiencing that there is value in contrasts. To accomplish certain goals and to live a rich life in general, we must be able to shift from one mode of experience or expression to one essentially opposite. To achieve integration is to combine contrasting modes into a common life pattern in which they complement each other rather than conflict. If contrasting modes stand in a relationship of integrated complementarity, we can readily shift from one to the other when it best suits our needs.

We can better grasp these general principles, particularly the need for flexibility itself, if we consider more specifically some of the kinds of behavior and experience that are involved. People vary enormously with respect to the ways in which they attend, recognize, perceive, and understand. There is considerable variation with respect to the basic locus of experience. We may be concerned primarily with what goes on in the realm of internal sensation and feeling, with what goes on externally in the world around us, or with matters in a more abstract realm of thoughts. Proper adjustment in each of these three realms demands at least occasional attention. It is not essential that a great deal of time be devoted to each of these realms, and it is true that much of our adjustment can be handled through devices that become fairly automatic, but occasional conscious attention may be required for the maintenance of automatic mechanisms, if not for survival itself. Occasionally while driving down the road, we really must focus our attention on the traffic conditions, and we run the risk of various infirmities if we do not respond appropriately to the sensations from our own bodies and give particular heed to the more unusual ones.

We might think of the internal–external dimension of attention in terms of attending to the input from interoceptors or exteroceptors. There are additional variations in the use of different sensory modes that we have not considered. In the past, this matter has been treated primarily in terms of imagery types, but there is a close relationship between the use of a given sensory mode in perception and its use in imagery. Many people appear to be handicapped by a neglect of vision or audition. They fail to attend effectively to various qualities in one of these modes, have difficulty retaining the resulting impressions, and cannot utilize them constructively in imagery. A neglect of gustation and olfaction is probably more common and less crippling, though it may reduce the richness of experience a bit.

The selective over-emphasis or under-use of different sensory modes has not received nearly the attention that it deserves. The research of past decades on imagery types did not begin to exhaust the potential means of assessing individual patterns of preference or effective utilization. Much could be done, for example, by devising problems whose solution calls for use of a particular kind of sensation or imagery and perhaps securing an introspective report from subjects after they have been asked to solve the problems. Witkin's apparatus tests (Witkin *et al.*, 1954) might be construed as problems that require the effective utilization of somesthetic sensations, but even in this one realm there are many other kinds of tasks that might be devised. Whatever we may discover in the way of patterns of sense and image utilization, there is an obvious advantage in having flexible access to all available modes.

Jungian theory offers a different sort of subdivision of experiential modes. Jung (1933) speaks of four psychic functions— thinking, feeling, sensation, and intuition. The first two of these are regarded as opposing rational functions. They are both concerned with the formation of judgments, but the first is directed toward judgments of truth, while the second is directed toward judgments of value. Sensation and intuition are said to be opposing irrational functions. Both are concerned with perception, but one involves perception in terms of the immediate data of experience—

the sensation itself or the object that elicits it—while the other involves perception via unconscious processes, or perception in terms of possibilities or meanings implied by the immediate data. In the early stages of development, it is assumed that as a given function comes to be emphasized in our conscious life, its opposite tends to be suppressed and to operate primarily on an unconscious level. There are many noteworthy things we can accomplish through pronounced emphasis on any one of these functions, but we remain handicapped in being unable to use any of them effectively. A major goal of development from a Jungian standpoint is a conscious differentiation of all four functions and their integration into a harmonious system.

We have already touched on a third Jungian polarity—that of the basic attitudes of introversion and extroversion—in so far as this concerns the internal or external locus of attention. But these concepts have a number of additional implications in Jungian theory. From a Jungian standpoint, the introvert attaches greater value to the inner world, and his thinking and behavior are governed more by inner conditions. The extrovert attaches greater value to things in his environment, and his thinking and behavior are governed more directly by external conditions. In general, the extrovert responds more directly and hence more immediately to stimuli from without. The extrovert is likely, as a rule, to be more overtly expressive. The introvert is more inclined to withhold outward expression and indulge more in fantasy. Each basic attitude serves a constructive purpose under many circumstances, but it is possible to utilize one to the virtual exclusion of the other. Thus, an introvert may confine his attention to the fantasy realm and avoid various kinds of external involvement. Similarly, an extrovert may avoid the experiences that arise in a private, solitary setting by a constant search for new forms of intense external stimulation. In the one case, we may see great openness with respect to the inner realm, while in the other, we may see great openness to the outer realm, but in both cases a more basic sort of flexibility is lacking. Jung again regards the desired state in terms of an ultimately harmonious utilization of both attitudes, which would enable the individual to attend appropriately to both the inner and outer realms.

A distinction between two modes of knowing or understanding has been widely noted and has received increasing attention in recent years, particularly because of the efforts of the existentialists. It has been formulated in many different sets of terms with minor

variations in meaning. This is the distinction between an understanding in terms of abstract truth and an understanding in terms
of immediately experienced reality, between intellectual insight
and emotional insight, between essence and existence, between
knowing about something and knowing by direct acquaintance or
living-through. The existentialists have effectively exposed the
delusion in trying to comprehend reality in a purely abstract way,
and yet abstraction can afford us a broad perspective that is not
otherwise possible. In individual people we can readily see the
shortcomings of both over-intellectualism and total immersion in
the immediate reality. Neither mode of understanding can operate
very efficiently without the other.

We might also note some of the patterns of cognitive functioning
that are evident in performance patterns on ability tests. Some
tests require the subject to deal with relatively immediate, concrete
materials or situations. Others demand considerable use of
abstraction, and these tend usually to rely heavily on verbal or
mathematical content. As we have previously noted, some tests
call for relatively loose, global thinking, while others demand
precise, orderly, systematic analysis. In some tests, the subject
must confine his attention to the materials presented to him and
manipulate them in some specified way. In other tests, he must
produce content that goes beyond anything presented to him. It is
obvious that the individual's habitual modes of perceiving and
thinking will determine to some extent what functions he can
readily call into play when they are required in an ability test.
Being stuck in any particular cognitive rut may favor performance
on an occasional test, but it is likely to interfere with performance
on many others and restrict our ability to cope with many situations
outside the testing room. In the preceding chapter, we considered
some characteristic sex differences in cognitive functioning, but
there are obviously many possible patterns of selective cognitive
functioning and dysfunctioning beyond those typical of most men
or most women.

Thus far, we have considered the notion of flexibility primarily
in relation to modes of experiencing or thinking, but it obviously
applies to action as well. Some of the most pervasive kinds of
behavioral variation involve what we might call modes of impulse
regulation. Perhaps the most important dimension here is that of
productiveness, or future orientation, as against a persistent
emphasis on the present and on spontaneous action. On the one
hand, we find people whose lives are characterized by acting on

the impulse of the moment and constant self-indulgence. On the other hand, we find people who constantly sacrifice immediate pleasures for a future that never quite arrives. The disadvantages of both extremes are easy to see. To meet his own needs and those of others who depend on him adequately in the long run, everyone must perform some actions with an eye to the future. But there can be only limited pleasure, perhaps limited intense feeling of any sort, for a person for whom the events of the present instant are never very important in themselves.

People also vary with respect to their prevailing moods and their prevailing attitudes toward life and the world, and again it is easy to see that ruts have their shortcomings. There is value in both optimism and pessimism, but the value runs short when either outlook is too persistent. Without hope, we would never try to accomplish anything, but we must be able to recognize obstacles and trends that run counter to our hopes. Furthermore, to evaluate any matter adequately and perceive it in clear perspective, we should be able to consider it soberly and seriously, but we should also be able to view it with levity or amused detachment. If an individual maintains either attitude incessantly, we can usually suspect that there is something he is trying to avoid recognizing. To relate effectively to the world, we must have a certain basic trust in its benevolence and a willingness to accept it. We should probably be willing to risk being fooled on occasion, but there are desirable limits to gullibility. There are occasions when wariness makes more sense. To lead full lives, we must be able to commit ourselves, to invest faith in certain causes and certain people, but to do this promiscuously would be rather chaotic. Perhaps any general attitude can be carried too far if it is constantly maintained. Perhaps even the affirmation of one's own life can be maintained to excess. For each of us there comes a point in time when we should perhaps be willing—if not eager— to release our hold on life. On the whole, Western culture does not prepare us well for this moment.

Flexibility and experience of the self

Various attitudes toward the self are possible. Western attitudes toward life and death are linked, of course, to an emphasis on individuality. Separate individual being assumes an importance in the West that it apparently does not have in other parts of the world. To the extent that one's individual self is important, it becomes important to avoid its loss by any means and it becomes important to accomplish things as an individual, for our worth as individuals depends on what we produce as individuals. There is a rather general tendency in Eastern thought to regard the individual self as an illusion that must be overcome. The experience of unity with something universal is held to represent a deeper reality. In the West, this same idea runs through a large body of Judeo–Christian tradition, in which man's experience of himself as a separate self-aware entity is viewed as the original sin.

The more common self-oriented outlook in the West has borne palpable fruit, for it underlies the unparalleled, though lopsided, material progress that has taken place in the West. There is good reason to believe, however, that the Eastern tradition has yielded much more in the way of significant spiritual insight—including a more comprehensive understanding of the 'illusion', the experience of individual self. We are faced, then, with two sharply contrasting views of the basic relationship between the individual person and the universe. It would be futile to ask which view is correct and which is not. (Indeed, the question is utterly misleading.) Each view has yielded certain forms of cultural progress, but it is possible that each view leads to certain excesses if it is not tempered by the alternative view. It seems likely, too, that an individual can realize a wider range of his potentialities if he is able both to experience fully his individual separateness and to find at moments that sense of unity that all great mystics have stressed for ages in all parts of the world. It is debatable, of course, how much inherent worth there is in this sort of versatility, and it would be senseless to suggest that this two-fold path is the only proper course for all mankind.

Certain questions of determination arise when the individual personality is viewed as a separate entity. Each person is inclined to regard his own actions as personally willed, though he may see his own will as strongly or weakly opposed by external forces. From an extraspective standpoint, behavior may be seen more as a product of external stimuli, and it may be considered more or less predictable from these. Regardless of one's stand on the metaphysical issues pertaining to will and determinism, it seems essential for everyone to experience some personal control over his destiny so long as we are orientated in terms of individual particularity. Psychopathology is accompanied by a loss of this experience, and the disturbed person sees himself as the victim of agents external to his conscious ego. In the extreme case, one can no longer clearly distinguish between personal will and external agent or between self and not-self. In compulsives and paranoids, we may find energetic efforts to compensate for an experienced loss of control through actions and thoughts calculated to enhance feelings of separateness and power. Neither a sense of supreme mastery nor that of total lack of control appears to be a desirable state of affairs. One can function effectively only if there is a realistic correspondence between the personal experience of control and one's capacity for effective action.

If we adopt the view of a basic cosmic unity underlying all mental life, the metaphysical questions of will and determinism no longer arise—at least not in the form in which they are most familiar to us. Furthermore, if the individual self is an illusion, then our experience of individual will must also be viewed as an illusion. While we may all experience some discord between ourselves and the rest of the universe, the goal of development, from the standpoint of a doctrine of cosmic unity, is the attainment of perfect harmony with cosmic will or universal mind. At such a stage, we should see ourselves neither as individual masters nor as victims of events. Instead our actions and thoughts would be viewed as arising in a totally natural fashion from the same common source as all other events in the universe, and we would suffer from no confusion regarding the locus of control of the events in our lives. There are some people who are evidently able to achieve a mode of life that is pervaded by such an outlook. But again we may wonder whether it is realistic or even desirable to regard it as an appropriate course for everyone. The agonies that commonly attend the Western view, however, suggest that our customary perspective is an overly restricted one and that there are things we may profitably learn from the Orient.

We commonly find something akin to the cosmic-unity outlook in effectively creative people. The ordinary person who is relatively free of emotional disturbance and who constantly experiences a very high degree of control over the events of his life cannot function very creatively. He retains his firm sense of control by clinging to a well-ordered pattern of life in which all occurrences are highly predictable. To be creative, one must be open to the unknown, to the not-yet-experienced; one must relax the control achieved by habitual modes of thinking and acting and permit events and experiences that are not fully predictable to unfold. We are likely to find the highest levels of effectively creative work in the sort of individual who is often described as being 'in tune' or 'in touch' with his unconscious. What this sort of description essentially implies is that he finds it relatively easy to relinquish conscious wilful control because he is prepared to trust whatever forces may emerge when he does so. Given this underlying sense of harmony, a constant assertion of conscious will is unnecessary.

In American psychology, where a kind of individualism is taken for granted, there has been more discussion of attitudes toward the self than of the existential status of the individual self. There are many kinds of self-directed attitudes that we might consider for present purposes, but the most important ones are those that are essentially positive or negative. A person may be largely satisfied with himself as he sees himself or he may suffer from great dissatisfaction. On the positive side, he may manifest considerable pride or high self-esteem. On the other hand, he may display great humility, self-abasement, or guilt. We have come to expect an abundance of the negative attitudes in neurotics, and many writers equate the positive attitudes with successful adjustment. From the standpoint of many existentialists, however, we are all guilty to the extent that we fail to actualize certain potentials or live up to certain values, and we inevitably experience guilt as we become aware of our failure. This view, which has had an increasing influence on psychologists, is consistent with a theological tradition that stresses humility, in some senses, as a prerequisite for spiritual attainment.

When we view the matter of self-directed attitudes in isolation, it seems best for a person to be able to accept all those characteristics that are an inevitable part of being human, as well as those that are an inevitable part of being that particular person with whatever that implies in the way of a unique constitution and inherent limitations. At the same time, a sense of pride that is disproportionate to one's attainments or one's worth as evaluated by anyone else seems undesirable. The matter is a bit more complicated than these statements imply, however, since self-directed attitudes are closely bound up with self-awareness, self-reflection, and self-insight, and people vary enormously in these characteristics. It is possible for a person to direct his attention toward himself very infrequently and thus have little occasion for self-evaluation, while leading a life that is quite satisfactory and constructive. A productive life is possible with either extensive self-awareness or very meager self-awareness, but its overall style will differ accordingly.

We have seen some evidence that self-awareness tends to be

negatively related to self-satisfaction and emotional adjustment. The moderate correlations we have observed do not point to inevitable associations among the traits involved, but they help to direct attention to certain facts of development that we should bear in mind. At certain points in life, people tend to become much more aware of themselves. Inevitably they discover things that do not mesh with their previous views of themselves and things that may clash sharply with what they would like to believe. During these periods they may experience much more distress and dissatisfaction with themselves. In the course of time, the new perceptions may be assimilated into a revised and expanded but essentially consistent self-concept. To the extent that growth of this kind is likely to be episodic, we should expect some fluctuations over time in a person's attitudes toward himself and in various features of his self-concept. People vary, of course, in their tolerance of distress and inconsistency, just as they do in their concern with personal characteristics. For this reason, whatever the temporal fluctuation, there are also wide individual differences in characteristic levels of self-satisfaction and consistency of self-concept.

There is a fairly obvious virtue in a combination of characteristics that are not commonly found together: basic acceptance of oneself with a relatively high level of self-esteem in the presence of extensive and accurate self-knowledge organized into a consistent self-concept. But can we reasonably recommend this as an appropriate goal for everyone? It has been suggested that introspection and hence self-knowledge are almost always, if not always, a consequence of distress, because it is distress that prompts us to look inward. Undoubtedly we can find various patterns of self-knowledge and self-assessment in the context of productive and useful lives. We find such lives in people who maintain a thoroughly extroverted outlook and engage in little self-reflection. We can also find them sometimes in more inward-turning folk, such as creative writers and psychologists, who are much more concerned with making sense of themselves and who, as a consequence, manifest a great deal of self-awareness. Among occupational groups, people in the arts, particularly poets and novelists, seem most extensively self-aware. In psychologists one typically finds a greater emphasis on intellectually structured insight—and thus less extensive awareness but greater internal consistency. In some psychologists, a reliance on simple and orderly conceptual schemes seems almost calculated to guarantee very limited self-knowledge.

In the past few pages, we have examined the question of flexibility in the context of many aspects of personal functioning—the individual's characteristic locus of attention, basic modes of sensing, imagining, and understanding, cognitive skills, impulse regulation, and fundamental attitudes toward oneself and the world. For certain basic functions, flexibility is clearly necessary for satisfactory adjustment and may sometimes be essential for survival. With respect to those functions that distinguish the major life styles and general attitude patterns of people, flexibility may be less essential, for a one-sided life can be very useful and productive. Flexibility, however, makes possible a life of richer experience, and it is prerequisite for continuing growth.

Flexibility and interpersonal relationships

Many conceptions of the optimal personality stress social relatedness or social orientation. It is readily apparent that these are closely tied to various general attitudes toward the world and toward life, as well as attitudes toward the self. One may view either himself or others with 'objective' detachment, as objects to be understood in an intellectual or impersonal way, or one may view himself and others as 'subjects' or persons, as creatures with human feelings rather than automata. The former implies relationships characterized by aloofness and lack of involvement. The latter implies more intimacy, treating the other person as 'thou' rather than 'it'. Many writers have stressed the need for more personal concern on the part of people in our society. Newspaper accounts of bystanders in our big cities who witness crimes of violence and do nothing because they 'don't want to get involved' have generated the suspicion that non-involvement is a problem peculiar to our time. Yet historical accounts offer no indication that an active concern for the whole of mankind has ever been a widespread phenomenon. If we compare newspaper accounts with the novels of Charles Dickens, twentieth-century New York seems rather congenial when placed alongside nineteenth-century London. Turning to a story of an earlier era, we may note that the parable of the good Samaritan was particularly effective because both Jesus and his listeners clearly recognized that it described a man who did not act the way most others did. Throughout most of mankind's history, it has been customary to confine genuine involvement to the immediate members of one's own family, clan, or small village. But the world has changed. It has become possible for people to move easily over long distances and to come into contact with people over wide areas. We tend to live in more populous urban centers where we daily encounter many people we have not seen before and will not see again. And we live beside mushrooming military stockpiles that remind us that the whole of mankind really does have a common destiny, of harmonious coexistence or total obliteration.

It has long been evident that to attain the mere semblance of complete development an individual must be able to establish close personal relationships with at least a few other people. In addition, it now appears that the survival of the species may depend on the development of a greater concern for the rest of humanity as well. It does not follow that we should expect to enter into a deep personal relationship with everyone who crosses our path. The mere fact that personal relationships consume time makes it imperative that many of our transactions be conducted in a relatively impersonal way. The person who feels compelled to become intimately involved with too many people leads a life of unmanageable complications. We must be able to enter relationships with various degrees of closeness. If we have an underlying attitude of concern for others, we can respond with personal involvement when there is the greatest need to do so.

It should be noted that if any close personal relationship is to persist on a sound basis over time, we must be able to respond to the other person in a somewhat variable way. If we approach the other person with the same attitude and the same manner on every occasion, it is almost inevitable that our behavior will be inappropriate to his mood a good part of the time. To know another person fully, we must be able to view him from many perspectives —not only in the light of intimate involvement, but also from standpoints characterized by amused detachment, cold objective analysis, and even anger. If the relationship cannot bear the brunt of the insights that result from this, then we may suspect that it rests on a rather insubstantial foundation.

A need for flexibility is clear with respect to other aspects of interpersonal contact as well. Some writers—notably Otto Rank— have stressed independence as a goal of development. There are obvious reasons for thinking that a well-developed person should be able to stand on his own feet and assume control over the direction of his life. Yet independence can just as obviously be overdone. There are times in the life of each person when it is most sensible to recognize that one does not know all the answers, to admit that one needs help, and to be able to assume a dependent role. Only in a very rare circumstance would a rational man attempt to remove his own appendix.

Similar comments could be offered with respect to various other modes of relating. Whatever one's characteristic mode may be—one of dominance, deference, subordination, nurturance, comic entertainment, etc.—there will inevitably be some situations where it creates problems if it is maintained too rigidly. People often lose flexibility by adopting relatively complex social roles and identifying with them so closely that they are unable to distinguish the roles from their personal identities. The social role with which a person identifies is often one that is bound up with a particular social or occupational status. This problem is particularly common among professional people who have invested a great deal of time, energy, and thought in attaining a particular professional status. They become so involved with the role that goes with the status that they think of themselves primarily as physicians, professors, psychologists, scientists, etc. rather than as individual human beings who happen to be members of a particular professional group. In some cases, the role is a very useful and adaptable one, but no well defined role can fit all situations. There are times when one must cease to play it and act more spontaneously. At such moments a person may suffer great confusion if he cannot find an identity apart from the role. Indeed, the most adaptable professional roles—such as that of the actor—may prove most severely handicapping if one does not know how to step out of them and still function as a person with a clear identity.

One type of human relationship that poses special theoretical problems is love between the sexes, especially in its most dramatic form—romantic love. There is probably no other form of human experience that is so widespread and which has such profound effects on people that is, at the same time, so conspicuously ignored by psychologists. Very few general elementary textbooks (books intended to provide a representative overview of the science) contain any reference to it. Those written by staunch positivists may treat it very briefly as one manifestation of a biologically rooted sex drive. Those written by the champions of rationality and realism may treat it as a form of psychopathology fostered by conditions peculiar to Western society in recent times. Some recent treatments are a bit more sophisticated, but even the best of these do not come to grips with the phenomenal variety and complexity of the experience of love. The reader who is not too naïve himself may wisely infer that most psychologists lead emotionally insulated lives or that they indulge in a bit of deceit when writing textbooks.

If we view matters from a relatively abstract ethical standpoint, it is easy to agree with writers who contend that the best form of love is one that is realistic and altruistic—a love in which we genuinely accept our partner as he or she really is and try in a relatively unselfish manner to meet the needs of the other person. By such a standard, romantic love, as it is commonly manifested, falls far short and is dismissed as an inferior form of love. It is more difficult to pass judgment when we attempt to take into account the complexities of human nature. Admirable as it may be to be realistic, rational and altruistic, it is not at all clear that the human organism was designed to function that way all the time.

In relating to another person, it is possible either to respond directly to actual qualities of that person manifested in his behavior or to act strictly on the basis of qualities that we have projected on to him. There is probably no human relationship in which we do exclusively one or the other of these things. We tend always to develop images of the people we deal with and to interpret their behavior in terms of these. Our images may fit our acquaintances with varying degrees of accuracy, but they always involve at least a bit of oversimplification and artificiality. There are some human relationships where special needs enter in, where we project images dominated by ideal qualities that we need very much to find in people. Romantic love is perhaps the most common and dramatic case in point. It is a relationship in which we project an image that embodies the ideal characteristics that we need most strongly to find in a member of the opposite sex. Because it is essentially a form of idealization, romantic love is notoriously 'blind'. Hence, while it accords us the temporary power to walk on clouds and to perceive inspiring beauty where others find mere dross, we usually experience difficulties before long. Our expectations keep clashing with behavioral realities, and our beloved becomes a source of puzzlement. 'Why does she act that way?' we ask; 'she isn't really like that.' We may suffer a disillusionment proportionate to the unreality of the projection when we finally realize that what she is really like and what we would like to find in her are two different things. In the course of the total sequence, we are likely to pass through a fairly comprehensive assortment of emotional states.

To be sure, romantic love entails a bit of distorted thinking and perception and creates problems for us. It would be utter folly to repeat the same process every month or every week with a new person. Undoubtedly it is possible to mature and lead a very productive life without going through this experience at all. On the other hand, it is not clear that one should strenuously avoid the experience. The mere fact that it occurs so widely in people who are fairly sound otherwise suggests that it is a rather natural form of expression for certain fundamental human needs. Indeed, the author stands ready to dismiss two common notions of psychologists that run counter to such a conclusion—the notion that romantic love is a form of psychopathology and the notion that it is strictly a culture-bound phenomenon confined to Western societies in recent times. Love seems pathological as long as we employ the independent, objective scientist as the model of maturity and health. The model has been widely espoused by theorists in the Freudian and behaviorist streams of thought, but it is surely a gratuitous model. Nothing in our data compels us to adopt it, and it reflects a rather limited view of natural human propensities.

It is easy to argue that romantic love is culture-bound if we confine our attention to certain forms of literary and formal behavioral expression, but in the literature of the world we can find ample evidence to suggest that the feelings and the idealization that we associate with romantic love have been experienced through the ages by people of all major cultures. Certainly, relationships between the sexes have been subjected to innumerable patterns of regulation in the course of human history. As an inevitable consequence, the form of expression of romantic love is subject to great cultural variation. Furthermore, the experience itself may be either fostered or discouraged in any given setting, and in a given time and place it may well be totally suppressed. We cannot properly conclude, however, that the experience itself is entirely a cultural artifact.

Despite the problems and the agony that romantic love commonly entails, it is easy to find constructive value in the experience. It affords an opportunity for gaining an increased understanding of ourselves and of the people to whom we relate. As a situation in which we explore certain facets of human interaction, it may serve as an essential step toward more constructive forms of relationship. At first, we may choose very inappropriate objects and misperceive grossly. If we learn at all from the experience, however, we will not make quite the same mistake again. Through the most foolish of infatuations, we may gain a clearer picture of the qualities that we really need to find in another person and a greater ability to distinguish an actual approximation to them from sheer illusion.

Some of the abuse that has been heaped upon romantic love in recent years may reflect a contemporary difficulty with love in all its varied forms. During the past few decades, the repression of love has come to replace the repression of sexuality that marked an earlier era, and many people have begun to doubt the existence of love as a phenomenon distinguishable from sex. We have entered a curious age where many people feel free to explore human sexuality in diverse forms but persist in withholding a part of themselves in every encounter because they are afraid of love. Pointing to the impracticality and irrationality of romantic love may serve as a means of warding it off. Yet there is reason to believe that one is likely to be richer for having gone through this experience than for shrewdly avoiding it and confining oneself to heterosexual relationships that are devoid of emotional involvement. To be flexible and open in the realm of interpersonal experience, one must be willing to experience the modes of relatedness involved in romantic love—but of course, not to the exclusion of other modes of relatedness.

As the reader may have noticed, there is considerable overlap between the variables we have discussed thus far in this chapter and those we treated in the preceding chapter. Hence, much of the present argument can be summarized by saying that we need to be flexible with respect to many of the characteristics in which men and women commonly differ. Relating and communicating effectively with members of the opposite sex requires a certain experiential flexibility, since we can understand the feelings of another person only to the extent that they correspond to something in our own experience. Similar reasoning can be applied to understanding and communication across other group lines. Many of the variables we have discussed are those for which we find marked differences between groups that differ in age and status.

Flexibility and the generation gap

The phenomenon currently called the 'generation gap' has been repeatedly described over the centuries. To the extent that it is a continual phenomenon, not just a modern one, it seems unlikely that we can explain much in terms of characteristics peculiar to any single present generation. It seems probable that we can find a broader base for explanation in age changes that commonly occur through life no matter when one happens to be born. As a matter of fact, many changes do ordinarily occur in the personality between youth and later years, yet these changes on the whole are not a sufficient cause for a communication barrier between older and younger people. Such a barrier would not exist if members of each generation had sufficient flexibility or openness to grasp the core of the other's experience.

Each of us tends to regard the members of his own group—those people like us with whom we can best communicate—as being more aware than people outside the group. Thus, it is not surprising to find that the youth and the older person both view each other as unaware. Each perceives the difficulty in communication as a consequence of the unawareness of the other. Yet this mutual perception stems from the fact that both are to some extent unaware and closed to experiences that would provide the needed awareness. The older person is in a better position to understand because he has been where the youth now is, but many people grow more rigid and conservative with age. They become intolerant of diverse activities in which they once freely engaged, and they forget the visions they once saw at an earlier age. Because they forget, they cease to grow, for the experiential base on which growth could take place becomes narrower rather than broader. It is a common mistake of youth, of course, to assume that this dismal picture fits everyone beyond a certain age. Perhaps a greater number of us break even—our gains in growth roughly equal our losses. A very few live to fulfil at an advanced age the promises made possible by a lifetime of accumulated experience. Nonetheless, the generation gap is still half the handiwork of the older generation, since whatever most of us gain with advancing age, we do lose touch with many of the modes of feeling and sensing that we displayed in our earlier years. Accordingly, youthful behavior makes decreasing sense to us, and we wonder about the sanity of the new generation.

The adolescent and young adult, in contrast, have reached a stage in life in which their total range of experience has undergone tremendous expansion. They are confronted with a vast assortment of ideas and feelings that are relatively new to them. Since they were not ready for these ideas and feelings at an earlier age and could not have learned much about them from their elders, they

too readily assume that they are the bold pioneers of this planet
who have finally discovered these things for the first time. They
invent a new jargon to describe their discoveries, since they did not
pay much attention to the jargon that used to be employed. If one
generation speaks of independence and self-directedness, the
next one speaks of the importance of 'doing your own thing.' One
of their most important discoveries is that it is very important to
find some meaning in the world and particularly in their own lives,
as indeed it is, and seeing how chaotic the world is, they reason
that the generation of their parents has really made a gigantic
mess of things because it failed to realize the need for providing
this meaning.

These feelings of the younger generation are hardly new, but
there are many progressive changes in our society that ensure the
specific context of these feelings will vary a bit from one generation
to the next. The contemporary context is one of rapid change in
many forms. To the extent that younger people are more receptive
to varied and intense experiences, they adapt more readily to some
of these changes. To this extent, the age-old communication
problem may be getting more intense. Of course, there are many
contemporary changes that defy satisfactory adaptation. Accompanying the great strides of science and technology are looming
perils that lend to the youthful search for meaning a sense of
urgency that it has never had before. Young people find themselves
in a world whose dominant species continues to increase its own
population at an alarming rate, while polluting the atmosphere,
oceans, and rivers, systematically destroying various other forms
of life, and threatening to upset the whole balance of nature. To
make matters worse, the human species seems to have a unique
proclivity for destroying its own kind. The most powerful nations,
through senseless reciprocation, assemble stockpiles of nuclear
weapons capable of eradicating all life on the planet. Our youth
have found their own nation waging a war that nearly all competent
social analysts regard as intellectually and morally unjustifiable.
Their government has invested vast sums in the development of
new means of destruction, including the most ghastly forms of
chemical and biological warfare, but it seems essentially uninter-
ested in research that might facilitate international communication
and help to reduce international tension. This strange world is
hardly the deliberate handiwork of any one generation, but the
brightest of our young people rightly see a desperate need for
changes that are not being made, and they ask loudly why social

progress must be so slow when technological progress is so rapid. The fact that so many older people in responsible positions (like the majority of their own generation) do not manifest such intense concern intensifies the impression that communication with their elders is difficult to achieve. Of course, as these young people proceed to explore the available channels for dialog, they often discover that a comparable number of their elders share their most serious concerns and that, while a very difficult communication problem exists, it has little to do with the so-called generation gap.

It is still possible, of course, that the special circumstances of our time—the explosion of scientific knowledge, the rapid development of technology, the emergence of new media of communication, the growing threats to terrestrial life—provide a setting in which unparalleled problems of communication between generations can arise. Many writers have suggested as well that contemporary forms of youthful protest bear witness to the special character of the generation gap of our time, but this is open to question. Collectively the various forms of protest might be characterized as a humanistic revolt. Young people frequently complain of the hypocrisy and immorality of their elders who preach democracy, freedom, and Christian virtues but continue to support institutions that deny these things. They tend to deplore traditional national and international power politics as a game that subordinates the welfare of people to the power and prestige of parties and governments. They decry the impersonality of a computerized, bureaucratic social system that seems to treat them as equivalent, interchangeable units. Throughout, they are saying that the needs of individual human beings are of supreme importance and must not be sacrificed to anything else. The humanistic sentiment is not new. It echoes the words uttered by such men as Marx and Thoreau much earlier in the industrial era, but perhaps the voices of protest are getting more numerous. With respect to the number of young people who are speaking out, we may be witnessing a new phenomenon. Strictly speaking, the current humanistic revolt is not entirely a protest of the young. It is a movement within our society that is required as a necessary counterbalance to trends that run in a contrary direction. We may again suggest that it provides an occasion for problems of understanding between generations to the extent that people are not open. There are older people who do not comprehend the need for protest, and there are youths who resent being de-humanized and insist on being treated as individuals but who themselves indulge in a good deal of stereotyped thinking about the people who make up various segments of the adult 'establishment.'

Age differences are often compounded with status differences that pose problems of their own. A status difference often tends to affect the behavior, attitudes, and perceptions of those on both sides of the dividing line in such a way as to reduce the possibilities of effective communication. The discourse between clinician and patient and, in the academic world, among students, faculty members, and administrators should provide the reader with a few familiar examples of the difficulty. The difficulty is partly one of unrealistic expectations. We expect the other person to have certain ideas, attitudes, and motives different from our own, and therefore, we do not converse freely enough to find the common core of experience that would make more extensive communication possible. A client or patient enters a psychotherapeutic relationship with various expectations based on an image that has been cultivated to some degree by the medical profession. These expectations are nearly always inappropriate, unless the client happens to be confronted by a therapist who really needs to hide behind a traditional medical façade. People in general tend to assume that members of the more learned professions, particularly those with doctorates of some kind, demand a certain respect and will be offended if treated as equals. This assumption is valid in some individual cases, but it nearly always interferes with communication.

Obviously people who work hard to enter the learned professions do so in part because superior status is important to them. Having devoted so much time and effort to the struggle, they usually wish to be regarded as wise. Regardless of their specific fields, professional people are often very cautious to avoid actions that would make them look foolish. A physician may accomplish this by resorting to dogmatic assertion when he has the least basis for being certain about his diagnoses and prescriptions. A professor can most easily disguise his intellectual limitations by confining his activities and words to that narrow realm of subject matter in which he happens to be an authority. A university administrator, to ensure the impression that he is really wise enough to remain in his high post, may resort to tactics that interfere still more seriously with free communication. He may avoid direct discussion altogether with most faculty and students and handle everything through a chain of assistants. Unfortunately, in avoiding even superficial communication outside of well defined ceremonies, he

initiates a cycle that can become rather difficult to escape. He
grows increasingly out of touch with students, and he then grows
more fearful of contact because he does not understand what is
going on and is not sure he can cope with it.

Through aloofness, the professor and the administrator do more
for their self-esteem than for their image in the eyes of students.
Students too readily recognize the masks worn by their elders as
masks, even if they do not know exactly what lies behind them.
For their own part, of course, students often resent the relatively
inferior status in which they find themselves, and to bolster their
own self-esteem, they may inadvertently misconstrue many of the
actions and attitudes of faculty members. In the last few years,
breakdown of some of the traditional status barriers has begun to
occur, and in the course of the transition, we have seen considerable unrest on college and university campuses, with struggles
waged most often between students and administrators. We are
slowly moving toward an era in which there will probably be
much freer interchange across the lines that now serve as barriers
to communication, but we have a long way to go. At one time,
while mulling over some of the frustrations he encountered in
trying to 'get through' to the people assembled before him in the
classroom, the author was prompted to write the following bit of
verse. The reader, depending on his own age and status, may feel
it should have been entitled either 'Maudlin Musings of a Juvenile
Academic' or 'The Bizarre Babbling of an Aging Professor.' The
author would prefer to call it simply:

Lecture Notes
You perch before me like a flock
   of owls with eyes all beaming wise
   and heaving sighs until the clock
   decrees again that you may rise.

You see me as a somber clod
   who knows no love, despair, or pain,
   a self-appointed demigod,
   a trifle odd, a bit insane.

Yet I once sat where you sit now
   and heard some other clods orate;
   all wise, I laughed when I saw how
   they scraped their wands upon the slate.

H*

I too have known the midnight light,
   the hour of truth, the drunken spree,
   the joy of love, the lonely night,
   the pain that some of you now flee.

With knowing smiles you glance around,
   amused because you think I take
   my every word as thought profound—
   but don't you make the same mistake?

The need for unification

We have argued that if an individual is to grow he must be flexible.
He must be willing to step outside his characteristic modes of
feeling, acting, and thinking and try different modes. Only by
exploring the avenues that lead to new forms of behavior and
experience can one proceed toward fulfilment of a wider range of
his human potentials. We have also seen, however, that the number
of available avenues is quite large, perhaps so large that no one
individual is likely to explore them all thoroughly. If each of us
really attempted to explore them all, it is unlikely that any two of
us would end up in the same place. We would probably become
more distinctly individual.

Another factor that ensures individuality of development, of
course, is the fact that, by virtue of constitution and early experience, we all have somewhat different patterns of disposition,
tolerance, and capacity. What is understimulation for one person
may be overstimulation for another. Thus, it may be natural for
one person to engage in a bit more exploration in the realm of
social interaction, for another to engage in more exploration in the
fantasy realm, etc. By virtue of a superior capacity, it may even be
highly productive for a given person to pursue a course that is
quite one-sided in some respects. An artist may thoroughly
exploit all the potentialities of a medium that involves only a
single sense, while thoroughly exploring its possibilities for
expressing all forms of human emotion. Fixation in one realm of
functioning may sometimes facilitate unfolding in another realm.

From the standpoint of the position stated in the first section of
this chapter, of course, exploration into new realms is only one
side of the growth process, a side we spoke of in terms of openness
and differentiation. It is possible to overemphasize this side. A
person who seeks unending diversity and change and who is

ceaselessly trying out new modes of thinking, feeling, expressing, and relating can only end up confused. Except for change itself, no ingredient of the total life style is retained long enough to be fully accepted as a characteristic part of the self. As a consequence, the ceaseless polymorphous changer cannot have a very clear concept of his own identity or his interests and values.

In the ideal course of events, each of us discovers through exploration modes of behaving and experiencing that 'work better' for us than modes to which we have previously clung. Having discovered these new modes, we will make repeated use of them. In some cases, we discover the value of alternating between different modes, which we then view as desirable complements to each other. In any case, as we move from old organization, we move to new or revised organization. While we end up with a concept of ourselves and a pattern of living somewhat different from what we had in the past, these still fit together into an essentially unified system. Within such a system, we can act not only on the impulse of this instant, we can also weigh decisions in terms of what we will want and need at various points in the future. We will be able to plan ahead and undertake projects that will extend over various periods of time. Our most serious decisions will reflect meanings and purposes which we regard as central to our life as a whole.

The life that retains a reasonable degree of organization provides a sound base from which to launch meaningful exploration. Having a fair idea of who we are and what we have achieved up to this point in our development, we should have some idea of the kinds of exploration we most need in order to develop further. The ceaseless changer is destined to continue trying just anything for the sake of doing something different, and unfortunately there are some important things he will never be able to try. There are some experiences to which only a person who is relatively well organized has access—experiences that presuppose systematic thought and activity, well ordered values and preferences, and clear self-understanding.

Neither ceaseless change nor rigidly fixed order provides a suitable matrix for constructive growth. Each seems to represent a defensive departure from a natural balance. Either experiential profusion or ordered control may be sought with compulsive insistence. It is a cardinal thesis of the present chapter, however, that flexible exploration and organization are both essential for growth, and each can be best appreciated when considered in relation to the other. There are a number of recent developments in our society and in psychology which bear on this thesis and which may be fruitfully considered in the light of it. In recent years, so-called mind-expanding or psychedelic drugs have become quite fashionable in the United States, and a small segment of our society has adopted these as a way of life. A variety of social protest movements, such as the hippies, have been interwoven with the drug subculture. The hippies decried the hypocrisy of the American power structure, which as they saw it, preached peace and individual liberty while waging war and enforcing unreasonable conformity. In their defiance of mass morality, the hippies not only consumed drugs in large quantities, but departed in many ways from established patterns of social behavior, speech, and dress. The hippies might be regarded as the extreme fringe of a contemporary movement that presses for a departure from convention and exploration of new, individually styled modes. Though this broader movement is a hard thing to define, various new trends in clothing, art, music, and literature may be viewed as an outgrowth of it. The hippies themselves probably fostered a good deal of creative activity on the part of people who were not strictly a part of their movement.

For those at the extreme, unfortunately, the experience is not always a very constructive one. Divesting oneself of conventional ways of doing things sets the stage for discovery and invention. It gives the individual an opportunity for finding better ways and new meanings. Perhaps for some, this happens. For many who took part in the hippie movement, convention was merely discarded for a way of life that consisted of an endless search for new sensations, and drugs were a principal source of these. (No sweeping generalization about hippies is intended here. The word *hippie* has been applied to a rather varied assortment of people.) One well known champion of psychedelic drugs once recommended taking LSD weekly and maintaining some of its effects through the intervening days by smoking marijuana. The effects of marijuana by itself are comparatively mild; it is the LSD that was seen as the key to salvation. Little is known about the physiological action of this drug, but it releases a kind of experiential flood. One is subjected to a deluge of highly varied perceptual effects, images, and feelings. The specific effects vary from one person to another and from one occasion to another. Whatever a person's usual mode of thinking and experiencing may be, the drug is guaranteed to dislodge him and bring in new impressions. The new effect may be inspiring or terrifying. In either case, this chemical cataclysm jars one loose from all customary ruts and thus provides an opportunity for a person to discover many new things about himself and his world. One problem is that it produces a little too much material for easy digestion. The drug state itself lasts only a few hours, but a sensitive individual who takes a strong dose of LSD can spend a few weeks, if not months, sorting out the effects that were produced in the drug state and trying to understand their meaning in the total context of his life. If he takes repeated doses with little spacing in between, he remains in a kind of ambulatory dream state. In this state, he may perceive many things that other people do not, but he cannot make effective use of his new insights, because he is unable to address himself to the reality experienced by those who are not in the state. If he is lucky, he may salvage a cupful of the torrent that flows over him when he finally succeeds in swimming back to the surface. The specific virtues and dangers of LSD are not the concern of the present book. It is undoubtedly true that an occasional experiential upheaval of the sort induced by this drug can be very beneficial. It can lead to personal growth of many kinds. Persistent immersion in the sort of state that LSD induces, however, can only result in chaos.

Psychedelic drugs have been regarded by some as a rapid route to the kind of enlightenment afforded by certain Eastern disciplines. At the same time, many serious students of Oriental philosophy have decried the use of these drugs as a reckless and shabby substitute for gradual and orderly personal growth. In recent years, there has been an upsurge of interest in Eastern thought, and many people in our society have begun to practice forms of meditation that have their origin in either Zen or Yoga. These people see in the practice of meditation and in the Eastern outlook a counterbalance for many excesses of Western living.

Where the West overemphasizes deliberate production and future-orientated striving, they seek to regain the capacity for fully experiencing the present moment and feeling and acting in a more natural or spontaneous fashion. Where the West emphasizes abstract knowledge and understanding through analysis into artificial segments, they seek a more direct, intuitive, or mystical understanding. In many respects, this search might be said to point toward a more feminine mode of experience, since the outlook that assumes exaggerated importance in the West is also one that is identified in the West with masculinity.

By and large, those who have turned to Zen and to the practice of meditation have not displayed the wholesale rejection of Western culture seen in many hippies and drug cultists. They tend to be people of substantial education who have incorporated much of the Western value system in their pattern of living and who have been relatively successful by Western production-orientated standards. But they are people who find themselves on a treadmill that is failing to meet all their needs. They are well organized people, often professional people, who are sufficiently aware to realize that organization is not enough. For such people, Eastern philosophy and meditation can undoubtedly be of great value, for they offer a sorely needed balance. The relaxation of deliberate control that these disciplines foster facilitates not only the emergence of new modes of experience, complementary to those that we selectively overemphasize in most of our conscious functioning, but the achievement of a subsequent more balanced unity as well. Eastern practices, however, are not a panacea for all of Western society. They have relatively little to offer those whose greatest need is for a more organized pattern of living and thinking.

Perhaps Eastern thought and practices will eventually be found to have most to offer to people in their later years of life. On the whole, Western culture has not been very successful in meeting the needs that develop in the later years. According to Hindu tradition, the production orientation fostered in the West is most appropriate in the early and middle adult years when a man must meet the needs of a family, while more solitary and spiritual pursuits are called for in the later stages of life. Even in India, of course, there are few people whose lives conform closely to the ideal stages, but the traditional scheme serves to remind us that our own culture is in many respects a youth-centred one. We attach greater value to the attainments that are possible in youth than to those possible for a person of advanced age, and the East may hold some of the keys we need to find if our personal development through the adult years is to involve continuing growth rather than progressive stagnation. To be sure, we will still have a host of problems that cannot be solved by borrowing the thought and practices of another culture. Similar comments might be made with regard to a variety of therapeutic techniques that have emerged in the last few years through the efforts of humanistic psychologists. There are dozens of these techniques, but their common aim is to increase the awareness and spontaneous expressiveness of the individual. On the whole, they have been viewed as a means of increasing the zest and enhancing the growth of people who are a little too well organized, and many of those who have sought them are already productive members of the business and professional community.

There are some who fear that all the recent developments we have described—the use of psychedelic drugs, an interest in Zen, the practice of meditation, the use of therapeutic techniques that stress sensory awareness and interpersonal encounter—herald the advent of an era in which rational thought will be replaced by an unreflective gnosticism and sensualism in various forms will run rampant. Those who express greatest alarm at such a prospect tend to be fairly restrained people who attach great importance to achieving control through abstract, analytical understanding. For them, the way of Western science holds the solution to our problems. It may well be that going from the present extreme to the state of affairs that these critics depict would not be an improvement. We can find good cause for alarm in some forms of excess, such as we see in the growing body of teenagers who make promiscuous use of all kinds of drugs—psychedelics, narcotics, amphetamines—seeking thrills and escape but without the structure provided either by the hippie form of protest or by a serious quest for inner enlightenment.

If we accept the idea that the optimal mode of living combines organized functioning with some flexibility and openness to new unstructured experience, however, it is evident that a large segment of Western society needs to move in a direction that is more gnostic or mystical in some ways and more sensualistic in others. When it is too closely tied to the world-view that is dominant in the West, science can provide only a limited kind of understanding, and it too readily becomes a tool of a social system that overvalues material, technological progress, whether this results in increased convenience or increased terror. Can anyone seriously doubt that the people of the Western world need to explore new avenues to understanding and seek a broader perspective?

A summary of present theses

In this chapter, we have briefly reviewed the findings of the research reported in this volume and weighed their most immediate implications for theory, and then stepped beyond them to some broader theoretical issues. What we regard as optimal is in some measure a question of value rather than of fact. Therefore, neither the data reported in this book nor the data yielded by earlier studies can provide a final answer to the question of what is optimal. The present findings combine with other considerations, however, to highlight a few basic principles, such as the importance of flexibility. The main conclusions set forth in this chapter are these:

1. There is no general dimension of ideal *v.* non-ideal characteristics. Hence, we cannot meaningfully order people along a single continuum of self-actualization or positive mental health.

2. Some desiderata tend to preclude others. We may think of life styles generally as favoring either (a) an open attitude or (b) an ordering, controlling, or integrative attitude. An individual may be open with respect to some areas of functioning, however, and ordered with respect to others.

3. If people are to achieve maximal realization of their potentials, one clear requisite is the flexible utilization of various modes of experiencing and acting. In a sense, flexibility is an expression of the open attitude, but there is an obvious need for a flexible use of both open and ordering attitudes.

4. Though a static pattern of living is undesirable at any point in life, some stable organization is necessary if all kinds of potentials are to be realized.

References

ADAMS-WEBBER, J. (1963) 'Perceived locus of control of moral sanctions,' unpublished master's thesis, Ohio State University.

ALLPORT, G. W. (1937) *Personality, A Psychological Interpretation*, New York, Henry Holt.

ALLPORT, G. W. (1955) *Becoming: Basic Considerations for a Psychology of Personality*, New Haven: Yale University Press.

ÅS, A., O'HARA, J. W., and MUNGER, M. P. (1962) 'The measurement of subjective experiences presumably related to hypnotic susceptibility,' *Scandinavian Journal of Psychology*, 3, pp. 47–64.

BARRON, F. X. (1953a) 'Complexity-simplicity as a personality dimension,' *Journal of Abnormal and Social Psychology*, 48, pp. 163–72.

BARRON, F. X. (1953b) 'An ego-strength scale which predicts response to psychotherapy,' *Journal of Consulting Psychology*, 17, pp. 327–33.

BARRON, F. X. (1963) *Creativity and Psychological Health*, Princeton, Van Nostrand.

BATTLE, E. S., and ROTTER, J. B. (1963) 'Children's feelings of personal control as related to social class and ethnic group,' *Journal of Personality*, 31, pp. 482–90.

BEISSER, A. R. (1971) 'Identity formation within groups,' *Journal of Humanistic Psychology*, 11, pp. 133–45.

BIALER, I. (1961) 'Conceptualization of success and failure in mentally retarded and normal children,' *Journal of Personality*, 29, pp. 303–20.

BLANKENSHIP, D. G. (1969) 'The experience of control and its effect on behavior in situations of varying degrees of control,' unpublished doctoral dissertation, University of Arizona.

BURKHOLDER, R. B. (1963) 'Personality integration in children,' unpublished master's thesis, University of Arizona.

BURT, C. (1941) *The Factors of the Mind*, New York, Macmillan.

BURT, C. (1949) 'The structure of the mind: a review of the results of factor analysis,' *British Journal of Educational Psychology*, 19, pp. 100–11, pp. 176–99.

CARDI, M. (1962) 'An examination of internal versus external control in relation to academic failures,' unpublished master's thesis, Ohio State University.

CARMICHAEL, L. (1926) 'The development of behavior in vertebrates experimentally removed from influence of external stimulation,' *Psychological Review*, 33, pp. 51–8.

CARMICHAEL, L. (1927) 'A further study of the development of vertebrates experimentally removed from influence of external stimulation,' *Psychological Review*, 34, pp. 34–47.

CATTELL, R. B. (1957) *Personality and Motivation Structure and Measurement*, New York, World Books.

CATTELL, R. B. (1965) *The Scientific Analysis of Personality*, Baltimore, Penguin Books.

CATTELL, R. B. and COAN, R. W. (1959) 'Objective-test assessment of the primary personality dimensions in middle childhood,' *British Journal of Psychology*, 50, pp. 245–52.

CATTELL, R. B., SAUNDERS, D. R., and STICE, G. (1957) *Handbook for the Sixteen Personality Factor Questionnaire*, Champaign, Illinois, Institute for Personality and Ability Testing.

CATTELL, R. B., and WARBURTON, F. W. (1967) *Objective Personality and Motivation Tests, a Theoretical Introduction and Practical Compendium*, Urbana, University of Illinois Press.

COAN, R. W. (1959) 'Perceptual aspects of attributed movement,' *Genetic Psychology Monographs*, 59, pp. 45–100.

COAN, R. W. (1961) 'Basic forms of covariation and concomitance designs,' *Psychological Bulletin*, 58, pp. 317–24.

COAN, R. W. (1964a) 'Facts, factors, andartifacts: the quest for psychological meaning,' *Psychological Review*, 71, pp. 123–40.

COAN, R. W. (1964b) 'Theoretical concepts in psychology,' *British Journal of Statistical Psychology*, 17, pp. 161–76.

COAN, R. W. (1966) 'Child personality and development psychology.' In Cattell, R. B. ed., *Handbook of Multivariate Experimental Psychology*, Chicago, Rand McNally, pp. 732–52.

COAN, R. W. (1968) 'Dimensions of psychological theory,' *American Psychologist*, 23, pp. 715–22.

COAN, R. W. (1972) 'Measurable components of openness to experience,' *Journal of Consulting and Clinical Psychology*, 39, p. 346.

COAN, R. W. (1973) 'Personality variables associated with cigarette smoking,' *Journal of Personality and Social Psychology*, 26, pp. 86–104.

COAN, R. W., FAIRCHILD, M. T., and DOBYNS, Z. P. (1973) 'Dimensions of experienced control,' *Journal of Social Psychology*, 91, pp. 53–60.

COAN, R. W., HANSON, R. W., and DOBYNS, Z. P. (1972) 'The development of some factored scales of general beliefs,' *Journal of Social Psychology*, 86, pp. 161–2.

CRANDALL, V. J., KATKOVSKY, W., and PRESTON, A. (1962) 'Motivational and ability determinants of young children's intellectual achievement behaviors,' *Child Development*, 33, pp. 643–61.

CRUTCHFIELD, R. S. (1955) 'Conformity and character,' *American Psychologist*, 10, pp. 191–8.

DOBYNS, Z. P. (1969) 'A comparison of hippies and college students with respect to beliefs, attitudes, and personality,' unpublished doctoral dissertation, University of Arizona.

ESON, M. E. (1951) 'An analysis of time perspectives at five age levels,' unpublished doctoral dissertation, University of Chicago.

FEHR, R. E. (1963) 'Stimulus determinants of color harmony,' unpublished master's thesis, University of Arizona.

FITZGERALD, E. T. (1966a) 'Measurement of openness to experience: a study of regression in the service of the ego,' *Journal of Personality and Social Psychology*, 4, pp. 655–63.

FITZGERALD, E. T. (1966b) 'The measurement of openness to experience: a study of regression in the service of the ego,' unpublished doctoral dissertation, University of California.

GESELL, A. (1945) *The Embryology of Behavior*, New York, Harper & Row.

GUILFORD, J. P. (1959) *Personality*, New York, McGraw-Hill.

HANSON, R. W. (1970) 'General beliefs scales: toward the assessment of the *Weltanschauung*,' unpublished master's thesis, University of Arizona.

HARVEY, O. J., HUNT, D. E., and SCHRODER, H. M. (1961) *Conceptual Systems and Personality Organization*, New York, Wiley.

HEATH, D. H. (1965) *Explorations of Maturity: Studies of Mature and Immature College Men*, New York, Appleton-Century-Crofts.

JAHODA, M. (1958) *Current Concepts of Positive Mental Health*, New York, Basic Books.

JAMES, W. (1907) *Pragmatism*, London, Longmans, Green.

JAMES, W. H. (1957) 'Internal versus external control of reinforcement as a basic variable in learning theory,' unpublished doctoral dissertation, Ohio State University.

JUNG, C. G. (1933) *Psychological Types*, New York, Harcourt.

JUNG, C. G. (1940) *The Integration of the Personality*, London, Routledge & Kegan Paul.

JUNG, C. G. (1954) *Collected Works. Vol. 17. The Development of the Personality*, London, Routledge & Kegan Paul.

KOCH, S. (1971) 'The image of man implicit in encounter group theory,' *Journal of Humanistic Psychology*, 11, pp. 109–27.

KRIS, E. (1952) *Psychoanalytic Explorations in Art*, New York, International Universities Press.

KUHN, M. H., and MCPARTLAND, T. S. (1954) 'An empirical investigation of self-attitudes,' *American Sociological Review*, 19, pp. 68–75.

LECKY, P. (1945) *Self-consistency, a Theory of Personality*, New York, Island Press.

LEFCOURT, H. M. (1966) 'Internal versus external control of reinforcement: a review,' *Psychological Bulletin*, 65, pp. 206–20.

MCQUITTY, L. L. (1952) 'Another method of measuring personality integration,' *Educational and Psychological Measurement*, 12, pp. 720–9.

MCQUITTY, L. L. (1953) 'A statistical method for studying personality integration,' in Mowrer, O. H. ed., *Psychotherapy, Theory and Research*, New York, Ronald Press, pp. 414–62.

MCQUITTY, L. L. (1954) 'Theories and methods in some objective assessments of psychological well-being,' *Psychological Monographs*, vol. 68, no. 14.

MASLOW, A. H. (1970) *Motivation and Personality*, New York, Harper & Row.

MASON, R. E. (1961) *Internal Perception and Bodily Functioning*, New York, International Universities Press.

PHARES, E. J. (1957) 'Expectancy changes in skill and chance situations,' *Journal of Abnormal and Social Psychology*, 54, pp. 339–42.

REHFISCH, J. M. (1958) 'A scale for personality rigidity,' *Journal of Consulting Psychology*, 22, pp. 11–15.

ROGERS, C. R. (1961) *On Becoming a Person*, Boston, Houghton Mifflin.

ROKEACH, M. (1960) *The Open and Closed Mind: Investigations into the Nature of Belief Systems and Personality Systems*, New York, Basic Books.

ROTTER, J. B. (1966) 'Generalized expectancies for internal versus external control of reinforcement,' *Psychological Monographs*, 80, no. 1 (whole no. 609).

ROTTER, J. B., SEEMAN, M., and LIVERANT, S. (1962) 'Internal versus external control of reinforcements: a major variable in behavior theory,' in Washburne, N. F. ed., *Decisions, Values, and Groups, Vol. 2*, London, Pergamon Press, pp. 473–516.

SPENCER, H. (1897) *The Principles of Psychology*, New York, Appleton-Century-Crofts.

STOLLER, R. J. (1968) *Sex and Gender*, New York, Science House.

STONE, P. C. (1969) 'Experience of control and level of aspiration,' unpublished master's thesis, University of Arizona.

TAYLOR, J. A. (1953) 'A personality scale for manifest anxiety,' *Journal of Abnormal and Social Psychology*, 48, pp. 285–90.

THOMAS, W. E. (1955) 'Perceptual structurization as a function of ego strength: an experimental application of the Rorschach technique,' unpublished doctoral dissertation, Michigan State University.

THURSTONE, L. L., and JEFFREY, T. E. (1965) *Closure Flexibility (Concealed Figures) Test Administration Manual*, Chicago, Industrial Relations Center.

WALLACE, M. (1956) 'Future time perspective in schizophrenia,' *Journal of Abnormal and Social Psychology*, 52, pp. 240–5.

WELSH, G. S. (1959) *Preliminary Manual, Welsh Figure Preference Test*, Palo Alto, California, Consulting Psychologists Press.

WERNER, H. (1948) *Comparative Psychology of Mental Development*, Chicago, Follet.

WITKIN, H. A., DYK, R. B., FATERSON, H. F., GOODENOUGH, D. R., and KARP, S. A. (1962) *Psychological Differentiation: Studies of Development*, New York, Wiley.

WITKIN, H. A., LEWIS, H. B., HERTZMAN, M., MACHOVER, K., MEISSNER, P. B., and WAPNER, S. (1954) *Personality Through Perception*, New York, Harper & Row.

WYRICK, L. C. (1969) 'Correlates of openness to experience,' unpublished master's thesis, University of Arizona.

Index